NIGHT+DAY
ATHENS

Joyce-Ann Gatsoulis

PULSE GUIDES

Distributed in the United States and Canada by National Book Network (NBN).
First Edition. Printed in the United States.
Copyright © 2006 ASDavis Media Group, Inc. All rights reserved.
ISBN10:0-9766013-0-3; ISBN-13:978-0-9766013-0-2

Credits

Executive Editor	Alan S. Davis
Editor	Anita Chabria
Contributing Editor	Marlene Goldman
Author	Joyce-Ann Gatsoulis
Contributing Writer	Diana Porter
Copy Editors	Gail Nelson Bonebrake; Kelly Borgeson, Elizabeth Stroud
Maps	Chris Gillis
Production	Jo Farrell, Samia Afra
Cover Design	Wil Klass, Clara Teufel

Photo Credits: (Front: l to r) Les Byerley, Ochre and Brown Hotel, Central Market-Mary Lou D'Auray; (Back: l to r) 48 The Restaurant, Agora-Mary Lou D'Auray, Bouzouki-George Argyropoulos, Roof Garden Bar-Hotel Grande Bretagne.

Special Sales

For information about bulk purchases of Pulse Guides (ten copies or more), email us at bookorders@pulseguides.com. Special bulk rates are available for charities, corporations, institutions, and online and mail-order catalogs, and our books can be customized to suit your company's needs.

NIGHT+DAY
The *Cool Cities* Series from **PULSE**GUIDES

P.O. Box 590780, San Francisco, CA 94159
pulseguides.com

Pulse Guides is an imprint of ASDavis Media Group, Inc.

The Night+Day Difference

Pulse of the City

Our job is to point you to all of the city's peak experiences: amazing museums, unique spas, and spectacular views. But the complete *urbanista* experience is more than just impressions—it is grown-up fun, the kind that thrives by night as well as by day. Urban fun is a hip nightclub or a trendy restaurant. It is people-watching and people-meeting. Lonely planet? We don't think so. Night+Day celebrates our lively planet.

The Right Place. The Right Time. It Matters.

A Night+Day city must have exemplary restaurants, a vibrant nightlife scene, and enough attractions to keep a visitor busy for six days without having to do the same thing twice. In selecting restaurants, food is important, but so is the scene. Our hotels, most of which are 4- and 5-star properties, are rated for the quality of the concierge staff (can they get you into a hot restaurant?) as well as the rooms. You won't find kids with fake IDs at our nightlife choices. And the attractions must be truly worthy of your time. But experienced travelers know that timing is almost everything. Going to a restaurant in Athens at 9pm can be a very different experience (and probably less fun) than at 11pm; a seaside view might be ordinary in the morning but spectacular at sunset. We believe providing the reader with this level of detail makes the difference between a good experience and a great one.

The Bottom Line

Your time is precious. Our guide must be easy to use and dead-on accurate. That is why our executive editor, editors, and writers (locals who are in touch with what is great—and what is not) spend hundreds of hours researching, writing, and debating selections for each guide. The results are presented in four unique ways: The *99 Best* with our top three choices in 33 categories that highlight what is great about the city; the *Experience* chapters, in which our selections are organized by distinct themes or personalities (Classic, Hip & Cool, Downtown, and By-the-Water); a *Perfect Plan* (3 Days and Nights) for each theme, showing how to get the most out of the city in a short period of time; and the *Athens Black Book*, listing all the hotels, restaurants, nightlife, and attractions, with key details, contact information, and page references.

Our bottom line is this: If you find our guide easy to use and enjoyable to read, and with our help you have an extraordinary time, we have succeeded. We review and value all feedback from our readers, so please contact us at **feedback@pulseguides.com**.

From the Publisher

I've had the travel bug ever since my first summer job during college—escorting tour groups around Europe to evaluate them for my parents' travel company. When I retired from the paper business ten years ago, I set out on a journey to find the 100 most fun places to be in the world at the right time. The challenge of unearthing the world's greatest events—from the Opera Ball in Vienna to the Calgary Stampede—led me to write a guidebook.

The success of *The Fun Also Rises*, named after Ernest Hemingway's *The Sun Also Rises*, which helped popularize what has become perhaps the most thrilling party on earth (Pamplona's Fiesta de San Fermín, also known as the Running of the Bulls), convinced me that there were others who shared my interest in a different approach to travel. Guidebooks were neither informative nor exciting enough to capture peak experiences—whether for world-class events or just a night on the town.

My goal is to publish *extraordinary guides for extraordinary travelers*. **Night+Day**, the first series from Pulse Guides, is for Gen-Xers to Zoomers (Boomers with a zest for life), who know that if one wants to truly experience a city, the night is as important as the day. **Night+Day** guides present the best that a city has to offer—hotels, restaurants, nightlife, and attractions that are exciting without being stuffy—in a totally new format.

Pulse Guides has one guiding principle: Never settle for the ordinary. We hope that a willingness to try new approaches to guidebooks, combined with meticulous research, gives you unique and significant experiences.

Before I met my good Greek friend Soto on a tennis court in London, I had "done" the tourist trip to Athens. It was only when I went to visit him in his hometown that I realized how much I had missed. And that, more than twenty-five years ago, was before the extraordinary blossoming of this Olympic city. I now make a bouzoukia pilgrimage every year and know that our guide will show you the complete, nonstop Athens that has made it one of my favorite cities.

Wishing you extraordinary times,

Alan S. Davis, Publisher and Executive Editor
Pulse Guides

P.S. To contact me, or for updated information on all of our **Night+Day** guides, please visit our website at **pulseguides.com**.

TOC

This book is dedicated to the memory of my
dearest friend Sotiris Krevvatas, whom everyone knew
affectionately as "Soto." His generous spirit and
infectious love of Greece have found no equal.

– Alan S. Davis

Acknowledgments

A special thanks to those who have shown me the Athens that few
Americans have seen: Marianna, Karina, and Dimitri Krevvatas, Liana and
Yiannis Nicolaou, Robert and Marie Schmon, and Costas Zagkos. I also
want to thank Tony Diamantidis and Maggie O'Donnell, Stelios Halvatzis,
Takis Karpoutzoglou and Steve Pantazopoulos (*Insider* magazine), Renee
Pappas, Apostolos Papyiannakis, Anna Vissi, and Michael Voudouris.

Alan S. Davis, Executive Editor

About the Authors

Joyce-Ann Gatsoulis is a journalist focused on travel and business who has
written extensively about central Europe and the Balkans. She currently
lives in Athens, Greece.

Diana Porter is a travel and arts writer who has hitchhiked and sailed her
away around southern Europe and the Aegean, pursuing her interest in
archaeology by day and her interest in clubbing by night.

Introduction

Athens: What It Was

Welcome to Athens, a city that's endured many incarnations since it first cradled Western civilization 2,500 years ago. Today, it's still home to the marble temples where Socrates strolled, the amphitheater where Sophocles introduced the Oedipus complex, and the rock from which St. Paul preached to the men of Athens. It's also a chaotic, cement-sprawled capital, a cocktail of European, Balkan, and Middle Eastern influences, a haven for art and cuisine, and Europe's late-night party capital.

Part of what makes Athens fascinating is its endless layers and juxtapositions. You can spend a day checking out 5th-century BC carvings of pagan gods, light a candle in a Byzantine chapel set among Cycladic-island style houses, have an ouzo-drenched lunch in a bougainvillaea-shaded courtyard, and discover burgeoning painters in the city's edgy and industrial arts district. At night, you can follow the crowds to a chic bar-restaurant for a midnight Mediterranean-Asian fusion dinner, head out to the coast to a seaside nightclub, and listen to Turkish-tinged rembetika blues in the Central Market at dawn, tripping over the ruins of a 480 BC Themistoclean wall on your way out.

How did these layers come to co-exist? Athens has been a focus of myth, legend, and real-life history for more than 5,000 years. During that time, the heart of the city has been the huge, gold rock that looms at its center, the Acropolis. Athens' first recorded structures were Neolithic settlements around the Acropolis in 3000 BC. By the 15th century BC, the settlement had a name, a patron goddess, and a founding myth: As the city grew to greatness, it caught the attention of Athena, goddess of wisdom, and Poseidon, god of the sea. Both wanted to be patron to the city and met on top of the Acropolis to battle it out. Each offered a gift. Poseidon hurled his trident into the rock, and out gushed his offering of saltwater; Athena offered an olive tree. The goddess' gift was wiser, as it provided food, oil, and shelter, and she won the devotion of the city that still bears her name. The gods' battle was immortalized in marble on the Parthenon, the 5th-century BC temple on the Acropolis.

> Cleisthenes consulted the Oracle at Delphi and created the first system of government where the demos (people) were allowed to vote—well, the free, native, male people could vote—and democracy was born.

But the Parthenon is just one of the structures that rose and fell on the Acropolis over the millennia, during which time the city has suffered bitter infighting, chaos, and poverty. It wasn't until around 750 BC that a period of peace allowed Athens to emerge as a culturally and politically important city. By the 7th and 6th centuries BC, Athens had an orderly government with a parliament that would pave the way for democracy. During this time, art and architecture flourished—with Homer penning the *Iliad* and *Odyssey*.

A sign that change was in the wind came in 510 BC, when the statesman Cleisthenes consulted the Oracle at Delphi and created the first system of government where the demos (people) were allowed to vote—well, the free, native, male people could vote—and democracy was born.

Key Dates

510 BC	Statesman Cleisthenes starts democratic government
490 BC	Battle of Marathon
470 BC	Golden Age of Athens begins
323 AD	Constantine moves the capitol from Rome to Byzantium
1453	Ottomans take the empire
1821	Greek War of Independence
1834	Athens named capitol of the modern Greek state
1967	Government taken over by a military junta
1973	Student protests mark the start of the end of the junta
1981	Greece enters European Community
2004	Summer Olympics in Athens

But just as this first democracy was putting down its roots, it met with a threat that could have destroyed it and changed the course of Western civilization. In 490 BC, the Persian emperor Darius sent 30,000 troops to conquer Athens, which could only muster 10,000 troops in its defense. The outnumbered army met the invaders on the plain of Marathon, located—you guessed it—26.2 miles outside the city. In one of world history's most stunning military victories, the Athenians defeated the Persians, sustaining a mere 192 casualties to the invaders' 6,000-plus. According to legend, the messenger Pheidippides ran back to Athens to announce the victorious outcome, then died of exhaustion. His route is today a built-up boulevard, but it still hosts the original marathon race every year.

With the city safe from the Persians, Athens entered an era of peace, prosperity, and progress. This period—from about 470 to 430 BC—is known as the Classical period or the Golden Age of Athens. Athens blossomed politically, culturally, artistically, and philosophically. General-statesman

Pericles launched an ambitious program of construction on the Acropolis, funding the temples that grace the rock today, including the Parthenon. This period also saw stunning achievements in sculpture and painting, culminating in the awesome icons of gods and monsters that graced the Parthenon. Below the Acropolis in the Agora, Socrates inspired the youth of Athens, including his most famous pupil, Plato. The creation of theater and drama led to annual festivals that premiered the works of Aeschylus, Euripides, and Sophocles.

The Golden Age of Athens was a time unparalleled in history, producing masterpieces in architecture, drama, philosophy, and politics. Alas, it was all too brief, and Athens' fortunes went from bad to worse.

But no golden moment can last forever, and Pericles' death was followed by the Peloponnesian Wars, which wracked Athens and Sparta for nearly 30 years. By the late 4th century BC, Athens declined in importance compared with the northern kingdom of Macedonia, led by the military might of Alexander the Great.

In 323 AD, the Roman emperor Constantine moved the empire's capital from Rome to the Greek city of Byzantium, and so began the great Byzantine Empire, during which Athens was little more than a backwater.

Things grew worse for Athens after the empire fell to the Ottomans in 1453. For nearly 400 years, the Greeks lived in occupied poverty, paying taxes to Turkish masters and mostly denied autonomy, education, or any kind of cultural advancement. The Ottomans took over the Acropolis, using the Parthenon as a mosque and the Erectheion, which housed temples to Athena and Poseidon, as a harem.

This went on until the Greek War of Independence in 1821, which won sympathy and funding from European intellectuals, who romanticized the return of Classical Athens. In 1834, once the Turks had been routed, Athens was named capital of the newly formed modern Greek state. Europe's great powers envisioned a city that combined the glories of the Golden Age with the advancements of northern Europe. Accordingly, they gave Greece a Bavarian king, Otto, who was tied to the ancient European royal lines—but spoke not a word of Greek. Otto imported German and Danish architects to build up the city according to this neoclassical ideal.

The Greek people eventually deposed Otto, though, and the next century saw a back-and-forth struggle as the citizens of this new country tried to

Night+Day's Athens Urbie

Night+Day cities are chosen because they have a vibrant nightlife scene, standard-setting and innovative restaurants, cutting edge hotels, and enough attractions to keep you busy for six days without doing the same thing twice. In short, they are fun. They represent the quintessential *urbanista* experience. This wouldn't exist but for the creativity and talents of many people and organizations. In honor of all who have played a role in making Athens one of the world's coolest cities, Pulse Guides is pleased to give special recognition, and our Urbie Award, to two individuals whose contributions are exemplary.

THE URBIE AWARD: Petros Kostopoulos and Dakis Ioannou

Petros Kostopoulos has risen from magazine editor and radio commentator to cultural innovator over the last decade, putting his own indelible mark on the aesthetics of the capital along the way. Through *Klik*, a groundbreaking magazine he edited, and later through *Nitro* and *Downtown*, titles published by his own Imako publishing group, he introduced Greeks to lifestyle concepts that helped reshape Athens from a London wannabe into a vibrant city with its own edgy personality. "We are trendsetters, almost pathologically giving birth to and searching for new ideas," he has said of his cadre of provocateurs. Okay, so Greek excess has taken lifestyle fads to a ridiculous extreme, giving outsiders the impression that Greek society, once politically aware, is now starstruck and preoccupied with celebrity gossip. But the fact that innovative chefs like Lefteris Lazarou came back to open Michelin-starred restaurants like Varoulko is largely the result of Kostopoulos' ability to create a market for haute cuisine and trendy bars. Kostopoulos even served as Donald Trump on Greece's version of the reality show, casting out hopeful apprentices with "Efiges," slang for "You're out."

Dakis Ioannou, an art collector of international renown with a sharp eye for the avant-garde, proved his acumen as a connoisseur and businessman by endowing the city with landmark establishments like the Semiramis Hotel in Kefalari—a place that has taken concept design to new levels with striking results. His DESTE Foundation for Contemporary Art introduced intellectually starved young Greeks to Jeff Koons and proved that art, style, and leisure can happily coexist under the same roof—in this case the oh-so-cool Cosmos bar-restaurant—without being starchy.

find their own identity and build a fitting capital. Still, Athens remained stable enough to host the first modern Olympics in 1896.

Athens: What It Is

The 20th century brought upheaval to Athens. The city was occupied by Nazis during World War II. From 1944 to 1949, the country was torn by civil war, and famine hit Athens, which saw its citizens starving and dying in the streets. A brief period in the late '50s and early '60s brought some peace and prosperity, fostering the production of films like *Zorba the Greek* and *Never on Sunday*. Unfortunately, it also marked the start of the urban sprawl that today is the city's biggest aesthetic blight. But aesthetics were the last thing anyone was worrying about by 1967, when the government was taken over by a CIA-supported military junta. The next seven years were dark ones, as the colonels ran a right-wing regime based on censorship, torture, and imprisonment. November 17, 1973 was the beginning of the end of the junta and the most important date in modern Greek history. Hundreds of students protested outside the Athens Polytechnic and the colonels responded with tanks that killed dozens. The protest led to the junta's downfall a year later and the formation of the stable parliament-and-prime-minister government in place today. Athens began moving into the modern world, entering the European Community in 1981 and being named Europe's first capital of culture in 1985.

Athens assumed it would make a grand showing when it bid to host the 1996 Olympics, the 100-year anniversary of the modern games. But it was soundly rejected because of the city's then-terrible infrastructure and lack of essential transport facilities, including a subway. The snub gave the Greeks a kick in the pants. During the '90s, Greece improved its economy enough to qualify to adopt the euro currency, improved air quality in Athens, and boosted its infrastructure with better roads, a new beltway, and a metro. It all paid off. Greece was named host city of the 2004 Olympic Games and frantically went about preparing by renovating museums and public spaces, cleaning up parks and waterfronts, building more new roads and railways, and importing foreign architects like Santiago Calatrava (who added modernist masterpieces to the Barcelona games) to build landmarks that organizers hoped would be as identified with modern Greece as the Acropolis was with the ancient city.

The renovation frenzy spread throughout the city, filling it with an edgy new energy. The once-abandoned industrial wasteland of Gazi is being reborn as factories and warehouses are converted into art galleries, huge dance clubs, avant-garde theaters, and funky, late-night restaurants. The city's once-sleepy contemporary arts scene is surging, and top culinary talents with experience abroad are returning home and opening fabulous new Med-fusion restaurants that are winning raves from international food critics.

Which is not to say that old-time tavernas and table-dancing bouzoukia clubs are in any danger of disappearing. The quintessential modern Greek experience will always be about staying up until sunrise, swaying to the strains of a big-haired diva singing about love and loss, tossing flowers, ordering up still more bottles of wine and whiskey, and throwing off all care of tomorrow—even if work starts in three hours. After centuries of war, famine, occupation, and depression, the Greeks have a fatalistic Balkan attitude that death and destruction may well come with the dawn, so it's best to live it up to dizzying heights tonight—an attitude rooted in distrustful darkness, but which results in one of the most extravagantly celebratory late-night cities around.

> **The quintessential modern Greek experience will always be about staying up until sunrise, swaying to the strains of a big-haired diva singing about love and loss, tossing flowers, ordering up still more bottles of wine and whiskey, and throwing off all care of tomorrow.**

Welcome to fabulous Athens ...

THE 99 BEST of ATHENS

Who needs another "Best" list? You do—if it comes with details and insider tips that make the difference between a good experience and a great one. We've pinpointed the 33 categories that make Athens exciting, magnetic, and unforgettable, and picked the absolute three best places to go for each. Check out the next few pages of our favorite ways to play in Athens— the glamorous lounges, happening beach scenes, romantic ancient sites, don't-miss museums, tastiest tavernas, and liveliest places to see and be seen.

Archaeological Sites

#1–3: Even Athenians wax lyrical about the city's ancient ruins, although their last visit was probably on a 6th-grade field trip. Originally painted bright colors and lavishly trimmed in gold, the temples today stand stark and white in the hard Attica sunlight, having withstood weather and wars since the 5th century BC.

Acropolis

Plaka, 210-321-0219 • Classic

The Draw: The Parthenon is the ultimate symbol of Western culture.

The Scene: Backpackers and business executives bang elbows on the steep climb to the Propylaia, an imposing portal into the heart of classical Athens. Clamber over marble blocks to the Erechtheion, a small Ionic temple with caryatids (human-form columns), where Athena planted the olive tree that won her the title of patron of the city. *June-Aug. 8am-7pm (rest of the year about 8am-5pm, but call to confirm as hours change seasonally). Ticket valid up to three days; includes admission to Ancient Agora, Theatre of Dionysus, Keramikos Cemetery, Temple of Zeus, and Roman Agora. €*

Hot Tip: Make this the first stop of the day—lines are long by mid-morning.

Ancient Agora

Thisio, 210-321-0185 • Classic

The Draw: Athenian democracy was born on the Acropolis, but its heart beats in the Ancient Agora.

The Scene: The lively atmosphere on Odos Adrianou suggests not much has changed since the days of Pericles, when Athenians came here to trade, shop, debate politics, and gossip. Stroll the site from the Hephaisteion to the Stoa of Attalos to get a feel for the ancient city, right down to its sewage drains. *Daily 8am-5:45pm, but call to confirm as hours change seasonally.*

Hot Tip: Look for the Bema, or tribune—a small marble platform and the world's oldest soapbox, where Athenian orators made speeches.

Roman Agora

Aiolou & Diogenous, Plaka, 210-324-5220 • Classic

The Draw: The octagonal marble Tower of the Winds was built by 1st-century BC astronomer Andronicus to house his water clock. Look for Boreas, the north wind, and other figures on the outside panels.

The Scene: Smaller and less spectacular than the Ancient Agora, the Roman marketplace lies within a quadrangle entered through the Gate of Athena Archegetis, a triple portico with separate entries for chariots and pedestrians. *Daily 8am-5:45pm, but call to confirm as hours change seasonally.*

Hot Tip: Enjoy the agora—and a view of the Acropolis—over an ouzo and some meze at one of the tavernas on the site's periphery.

Art Spaces

#4–6: For centuries, Athens' ancient wonders seemed to stifle fresh creativity. But over the last five years, a series of alternative gallery spaces have opened up, delivering inspiration and aspiration to young Greek artists.

Athinais Multipurpose Cultural Center

Kastorias 34-36, Votanikos, 210-348-0000 • Hip & Cool

The Draw: Cutting-edge everything in a converted 1920s silk factory.

The Scene: With a cinema, a theater, a music hall, the Museum of Ancient Cypriot Art (with a great shop), and several exhibition spaces, it's possible to combine a film, a show, and ethnic cuisine all in one go, in the company of the city's hipsters. *Daily 8am-3:30am, museum 9am-11pm.* €

Hot Tip: No need to culture-crawl on an empty stomach. The complex includes the gourmet restaurant Red, the informal brasserie Botanikos, and the Boiler Bar, with open-air tables in the courtyard through summer.

DESTE Foundation of Contemporary Art

Omirou 8, Neo Psihiko, 210-672-9460 • Hip & Cool

The Draw: Top gallery for both international and Greek artists housed in an old paper warehouse redesigned by New York architect Christian Hubert.

The Scene: Combining painting, sculpture, photography, and installations with shopping, eating, and drinking, it draws a diverse mix. The second-floor gallery hosts contemporary exhibitions loved by artsy types, while the top-floor gift shop stocks a selection of offbeat, arty posters and postcards, ceramics, and T-shirts that lures the collegiate crowd. *Mon-Fri 10am-6pm, Sat noon-4pm. Closes for two to three weeks in Aug.* €

Hot Tip: Cosmos, a chic bar-restaurant done up with minimalist furniture, modern paintings, and industrial-style lighting, is on the ground floor.

Technopolis

Pireos 100, Gazi, 210-346-7322 • Downtown

The Draw: The original. When it opened in 1999, Technopolis (Art City) initiated the revitalization of Gazi. Since then, this once run-down industrial district has become a hive of trendy bars, restaurants, and alternative clubs.

The Scene: The crowd is as stark and cool as the buildings of this former gasworks, which have been cleverly refurbished into a complex for art exhibitions, concerts, happenings, and performances. *Daily 10am-9pm.*

Hot Tip: It's not just Basquiat. This is where UK bands like Faithless, the Tindersticks, and Tricky like to play.

Best

Bar-Restaurants

#7–9: Bar-restaurants (which Greeks call "fun restaurants") are a superb way to have a good time. Most mix funky (but often beautiful) design, top DJs, trendy lounge areas, and excellent chefs. Like some nightclubs, these spots often relocate to the beach in summer.

Central
Plateia Kolonaki 14, Kolonaki, 210-724-5938 • Hip & Cool

The Draw: Central has been "in" for so long, Athens' scenesters are forever declaring that it must be on its way out. But it never seems to get there. Peek through the smoked windows at any hour and you'll see beautiful people sipping champagne cocktails, nibbling sushi, and checking each other out.

The Scene: Creamy white sofas, designer suits and cigars, sushi, and Greek starlets of both sexes grooving to a lush lounge soundtrack. *Daily 10:30am-2am. Moves to Island club mid-May-Sept.* €€€ ⓉⒻ≣

Hot Tip: The best scenes—and your biggest chance of spotting Greek film and pop stars—are at the after-work parties, starting at 6pm on weekdays.

Interni
Ermou 152, Thisio, 210-346-8900 • Downtown

The Draw: This is by far the favorite hangout for models in Athens. Maybe it's the decadent vibe on the edge of Gazi? The rotation of celeb DJs from London and Paris? Or maybe it's the outstanding Mediterranean fusion cuisine, because you know how those models love to eat.

The Scene: Leather beanbag chairs, huge Japanese lanterns, wine-red swags swooping from the ceiling—and a pretty, pretty clientele. *Sept.-June daily 8:30pm-4am. Moves to Mykonos for summer.* €€€ ⓉⒷ≣

Hot Tip: Wednesday is the hottest night, when there's a hip-hop, soul, and R&B party, aptly named "Booty Call."

Septem
Vasileos Georgiou, Glyfada, 210-894-1620 • Hip & Cool

The Draw: This summertime-only seaside spot is an exclusive world unto itself with a chic, white-linen-draped lounge on a private beach.

The Scene: By day, olive-skinned beauties lounge on the sand. By night, the same flock shows up again, this time in sparkly halter tops and capris, to pick at perfect Mediterranean-style seafood at Septem before hitting adjoining Balux's poolside dance floor. *May-Oct. 9am-1 or 2am.* €€€ ⓉⒻ≣

Hot Tip: This place isn't just for dinner—it buzzes all day long, with trendy Glyfada types gossiping over cocktails and sushi, and moneyed beachgoers taking advantage of the on-call masseuses and Pilates instructors.

Best

Beaches

#10–12: It's party central along the clear waters of the Saronic Gulf in summer. Private beaches abound, where for an admission fee, you're guaranteed clean sand and water, chaise lounges, beach bars and volleyball courts, and extras like seaside massages, towel-side cocktail service, and waves of half-clad bathers.

Asteria Seaside Beach
Balux Club, Glyfada, 210-894-5676 • Hip & Cool

The Draw: Close to Athens, and the summer broadcasting base of both the pop radio station Rhythmos and Mad TV (the Greek MTV), Asteria guarantees plenty of beach parties, open-air concerts, and bikini fashion shows.

The Scene: Half the beach is a party with a water park, volleyball, and contests run by scantily clad DJs. The other half, run by club Balux, has a seaside pool, fruity cocktails, white linen chaises, and Astrud Gilberto's cool voice breezing from the speakers. *Daily 8am-7 to 9pm, depending on sunset time.* €

Hot Tip: Call in advance for schedules of concerts, so you can hit or miss them as you choose since special events can change the vibe.

Grand Beach Lagonissi
Athens-Sounio Rd., Lagonissi, 229-107-6000 • By-the-Water

The Draw: By far the most fashionable (and spendy) place to get wet on the Attica coast. Seaside shiatsu massage, fusion finger-food delivered directly to your chaise, water skiing, private bungalows, and clear, turquoise waters.

The Scene: No cut-offs, flip-flops, or faded Speedos. It's a fashion show here, where perfect bodies complement stunning scenery. *Summer 10am-9pm.* €€

Hot Tip: Stay through early evening for cocktails at the floating bar, gorgeously aglow from underwater lighting, and garnished with plenty of beautiful young things on the deck.

Patroklos
Vouliagmeni & Sounio, Vouliagmeni, 229-103-7326 • By-the-Water

The Draw: Though this speck of an island is just a ten-minute water-taxi ride from the crowded Attica coast, it's easy to find a spot on its tranquil beaches where you'll feel like the only lounger on earth.

The Scene: Golden sand, blue waters, and not a soul in sight. Three-hundred meters past the 60km mark on Leoforos Sounio, turn right at Kasidiara, where the water taxi to Patroklos leaves every ten minutes. Call Nikos the boatman at 229-103-7326 or 697-469-3323. *Ferry runs 10am-8pm.* €

Hot Tip: There is one development on the island, but it lacks phone or electricity. Still, Patroklos' fish taverna is a favorite of some of Greece's top chefs.

Bouzoukia in Summer

#13–15: Bouzoukia are a kind of long-necked lute used in traditional Greek music. Although they've only been common in Greece since the 1920's, Bouzoukia clubs have transformed into the old-school of Greek nightlife, beloved by all ages. Step inside one of these rambunctious dens and you'll find it packed with Athenians in a frenzy of drinking, dancing, and flower-tossing.

Posidonio
Posidonos 18, Elliniko, 210-894-1033 • By-the-Water

The Draw: A pleasure dome with booming sound, dazzling lights, and lots of space to shake your thing. The headquarters of one of the country's favorite singers (Nick Vertis), it draws crowds until the wee hours of the morning.

The Scene: Bronzed men sporting soft beige and white and slinky women clad in tight tops and itsy-bitsy skirts flock to this mammoth club, where it's all about dancing, drinking, and fun. *May-Sept. Wed-Sun 11pm-5am.* C ≣

Hot Tip: Avoid the weekend over-crush and mingle at Thursday night's party.

Romeo
Ellinikou 1, Glyfada, 210-894-5345 • By-the-Water

The Draw: The hottest joint in town. A bustling magnet for the young and the young at heart right at the hub of Athens' nightlife.

The Scene: After downing drinks at summer hot spot Glyfada, hipsters take to this vibrant dance floor with its upbeat Greek and Asian tunes. *Mid-May-mid-Sept. Wed-Sun 11pm-about 5:30am.* C ≣

Hot Tip: Guys are expected to shower their gals with flowers. Location subject to change; check local listings.

Thalassa
Posidonos 58, Asteras Glyfadas, 210-898-2979 • By-the-Water

The Draw: Fun, youthful, and just a little bit trashy. Located right next to the beach in Glyfada, it's a perennial seaside bouzoukia favorite. On Friday and Saturday nights in the summer, the place buzzes with hundreds of 20-something bouzouksous hell-bent on letting loose.

The Scene: When the floor is packed, the only place to go is up. By 2am, much of the crowd is dancing on tables and flinging flowers in adoration of whichever singer is performing onstage. There's not much pretension or attitude here, though everyone is decked out. *Tue-Sat, 9:30pm-about 6am.* C B ≣

Hot Tip: The style of this bouzoukia borders on what Greeks call "skiladiko" (doghouses), indicating a slightly downmarket, young, shameless, pop orientation that has a certain beloved kitsch value for Greeks.

Best

Bouzoukia in Winter

#16–18: The winter scene in Athens is hot, with dozens of nightclubs featuring live Greek music and flashy choreography bursting at the seams with swarms of merrymakers singing and dancing atop tables. Be prepared! Clubbing in Athens begins in the wee hours, so don't expect the firmes (main acts) to take the stage before 1am.

Diogenis Studio

Syngrou 259, Nea Smyrni, 210-942-5754 • Hip & Cool

The Draw: When midnight hits, Diogenis comes alive with sexy dancers, shifting stages, strobe lights, and the piercing sounds of popular Greek performers.

The Scene: The velvet-covered stairs of this mecca of entertainment lead to a lavish hall packed with late-night crawlers, from hipsters to serious music lovers. The best artists in town perform aching ballads, robust zeibeikika, and electro-pop. *Oct.-Apr. Thu-Sun, then moves to Thalassa in Glyfada for summer. Shows usually at 10:30pm, though times may vary.* Ⓒ≡

Hot Tip: If you're no night owl, catch the Sunday show at 9:30pm, and be ready for close company since tightly packed tables barely leave breathing room.

Rex

Panepistimiou 48, Omonia, 210-381-4592 • Classic

The Draw: A busy theater in a former life, Rex had become a relic until it underwent a total facelift, and transformed into one of the hottest spots in town. Now it draws top singers to its stage.

The Scene: Middle-aged gentlemen escorting 20-something ladies decked out in the hottest and shortest. *Oct.-May Thu-Sun from 10:30pm.* Ⓒ≡

Hot Tip: Book ahead, or tip your way to the front table. Once there, be ready to dish out at least 200 euros per couple, excluding the carnations (or the more posh gardenias) you see being elegantly tossed around.

Romeo

Winter location changes yearly. Check local listings or hotel concierge for location • Classic

The Draw: The talented bunch on this bill make it worth the bucks. This is art, not just clubbing.

The Scene: Preppy college students, well-off teens in tight tops, and want-to-impress-my-date 30-somethings flock to this bustling night spot where mainstream Greek and Asian hits lure patrons to the dance floor or atop tables. *Oct.-May Wed-Sun from 10pm.* Ⓒ≡

Hot Tip: If seeing the performers is important, reserve a table or get there early (by 10pm). If it's only fun you're after, come late.

Best

Byzantine Sights

#19–21: When the Roman Empire was divided between East and West in AD 395, Greece went East, subsequently becoming part of the Byzantine Empire. With the rise of the Christian faith, pagan-minded philosophy schools were closed and many temples were rebuilt as Byzantine churches.

Byzantine Museum

Vassilissis Sofias 22, Kolonaki, 210-723-1570, 210-723-2178 • Classic

The Draw: The richest Byzantine collection in the world now has more space, much of which was completed for the 2004 Olympics.

The Scene: An arched entrance framed by two palms leads to an internal court-yard overlooked by a 19th-century Tuscan-style porticoed villa that was built by an eccentric French aristocrat who helped fund the Greek War of Independence. *Tue-Sun 8:30am-3pm.* €

Hot Tip: This vast collection can be overwhelming, so focus on the star exhibits, including the gold necklace from the Mytilene treasure.

Kapnikarea

Intersection of Ermou & Kapnikareas, Monastiraki • Classic

The Draw: An 11th-century Byzantine church set against a bizarre backdrop of 21st-century shopping culture.

The Scene: This gem creates a sacred space for a moment of solitary reflection. The exterior displays typical Byzantine raised brickwork, while the interior is enhanced by a dome supported by four Roman columns. *Mon, Wed, Sat 8am-2pm; Tue, Thu, Fri 8am-12:30pm and 5-7:30pm; Sun 8:30am-11:30am.*

Hot Tip: Do like the Greeks do and light an amber beeswax candle for someone you love, and leave a few coins for the church collection.

Kessariani

8km (6mi) east of city center, Kessariani, 210-723-6619 • Classic

The Draw: Built on the site of an ancient Sanctuary of Aphrodite, this beauti-ful 11th-century Byzantine monastery is set in a walled garden planted with Cypress trees halfway up Mount Hymettos.

The Scene: Nestled amid pine forests, this complex was once the retreat of Orthodox monks who earned their keep with wine making and honey pro-duction. Today only the romantic ruins remain, but the crumbling terracotta brickwork and warm hues of gray, fawn, and pink local stone keep perfect har-mony with the lush nature of the site. *Tue-Sun 8:30am-3:30pm.*

Hot Tip: Bring a picnic and lunch on the stone benches close to a ruined basil-ica, just a ten-minute walk from the monastery, for stunning views over Athens, Piraeus, and the sea and islands.

Best

Cafes

#22–24: Drinking coffee is a daily ritual in Athens, preferably accompanied by an endless supply of cigarettes. Young Athenians go for iced frappe (made from Nescafe), while their grandparents remain devotees of the strong, gritty kafe elliniko (Greek coffee). But Athens' cafes aren't just for caffeine. They are also a great place for a casual cocktail.

Aiolis

Aiolou 23 & Agias Irinis, Monastiraki, 210-331-2839 • Hip & Cool

The Draw: Sophisticated but friendly, this trend-setting cafe is just off the busy shopping street Ermou. It's a great place to rest weary feet and have a caffeine fix when the perfume and slinky underwear stores get to be too much.

The Scene: The marble-topped bar and mahogany shelves and cupboards in this space, originally a wool shop, have been adapted to create a warm, old-fashioned atmosphere that draws a posh crowd. At night, the lights are dimmed to set a party mood. *Daily 10am-2am. €* ☒☒☰

Hot Tip: More than just a coffee shop, it has delicious Mediterranean eats.

Kidathineon

Farmaki 1 & Plateia Filomousou, Plaka, 210-323-4281 • Classic

The Draw: All that a cafe should be: elegant, peaceful, and welcoming but not intrusive. One of the best places for morning coffee or an evening aperitif in Plaka, overlooking a leafy, flagstone-paved square.

The Scene: Tourists and Athenians mingle in this old-school spot occupying a neoclassical house with a marble-clad facade, stone floors, and wooden furniture. *Daily 8am-1am. €* ☒☒☰

Hot Tip: In summer, pick an indoor table where locals enjoy a cool respite from both the sun and the tourists baking outside in it.

Stavlos

Irakleidon 10, Thisio, 210-345-2502 • Downtown

The Draw: On a pedestrian street lined with bars just off the Archaeological Promenade, this cafe includes a terrace out front, a bar area, a paved courtyard with open-air seating, a small dance floor with a DJ, and an upstairs gallery exhibiting works by contemporary Greek artists.

The Scene: Originally constructed as the royal stables of King Otto in 1880, today the vibe is chill-out ambient music and vodka-based cocktails for the younger, chic set, plus backgammon and chess boards for their dads. *Daily 9am-3am. €€* ☒☒☰

Hot Tip: Among the not-a-care-in-the-world clientele, watch for touring musicians, who sometimes drop by after playing a concert.

Best

Candlelit Bars

#25–27: Greeks love late nights, especially in the company of their parea (an extensive circle of friends). While communal may be fun, it's not ideal if you want a more one-on-one experience. When the mood for intimacy strikes, Athenians head to local hideouts where dark corners and small tables make the perfect end to the party.

Don Quixote's

Vasileos Pavlou 68, Kastella, Piraeus, 210-413-7016 • By-the-Water

The Draw: An alluring hide away for a late-night drink, on a hill above Mikrolimano with unforgettable views of the fishing harbor below.

The Scene: Creaky wooden stairs lead up to a stunning candlelit rooftop terrace. The lower-level bar hosts low-key drinking to rock, soul, and classic Greek hits. *Tue-Sun 9pm-3am.* =

Hot Tip: The bouncer may seem intimidating, but fear not—the scene is peaceful and romantic once inside.

Melina

Lissiou 22 & Aerides, Plaka, 210-324-6501 • Classic

The Draw: The favorite cafe of its namesake, the stunning 1960s Greek actress Melina Mercouri, best known for her role as a gold-hearted hooker with a strict 6-day work week in *Never on Sunday*. Although Mercouri was originally from Piraeus, she lived in the apartment above this bar for three years and became a regular customer.

The Scene: Located in the heart of Plaka, this cozy spot is decorated with mottled orange walls, marble-top tables, and photos of Melina herself. It serves coffee, cocktails, and light meals to a local crowd. *Daily 10am-2am.* –

Hot Tip: Through summer, tables with blue canvas chairs and glowing gas lamps spill out onto a small terrace area. This is the place to be.

Peacock Lounge

Hera Hotel, Falirou 9, Makrigianni, 210-923-6682, 210-923-5618 • Classic

The Draw: It has an unobstructed view of the Acropolis. After sunset, candles flicker on the tables of this intimate rooftop hotel bar-cafe-restaurant.

The Scene: An elegant but unpretentious bistro where guests of the stately Hera Hotel and a few Greeks out on discreet dates drink and dine in quiet awe of the city panorama, while Norah Jones and Frank Sinatra songs set the mood. *Tue-Sat 5:30pm-1:30am.* F–

Hot Tip: Reserve in advance and request a table near the window in winter—these are the most coveted spots.

Classic Dining

#28–30: Blessed with a Mediterranean climate, Greece is a land of olive oil, fresh fruits and vegetables, and aromatic herbs like oregano, thyme, and mint. Add to that the Dionysian pleasures of an endless supply of fine wine, and it's no wonder that Greeks are people who know what good food is all about.

Archeon Gefsis

Kodratou 22, Plateia Karaiskaki, Metaxourgio, 210-523-9661 • Classic

The Draw: Archestratos wrote the world's first cookbook in 330 BC. Savor his forgotten dishes, like pork with plums, or wild boar cutlets with grilled mushrooms and marrow.

The Scene: In the unlikely district of Metaxourgio (best known for its brothels), this unique restaurant covers three simple dining rooms plus outdoor tables in a large paved courtyard with palms, burning torches, and occasional live performances by flute and string musicians. Loved by foodies, locals, and tourists alike. *Mon-Sat 1-4pm, 8pm-1am.* €€ ≣

Hot Tip: In warm weather, reserve an outdoor table. And if you're brave, try the roasted piglet.

Daphne's

Lisikratous 4, Plaka, 210-322-7971 • Classic

The Draw: Those in the know, from politicians to visiting celebs, flock here for classic but sophisticated meals.

The Scene: A townhouse on a sidestreet in Plaka, with painted frescoes in muted hues set against terracotta floors and wooden furniture. Tables spill outside into a delightful walled courtyard filled with both locals and visitors. *Daily 7:30pm-1am.* €€€ ≣

Hot Tip: The menu features unusual seasonal and regional fare, but the year-round desserts of yogurt with quince or rose petal cordial are irresistible.

Vlassis

Paster 8, Plateia Mavili, Ambelokipi, 210-646-3060 • Classic

The Draw: Decades of consistently delicious paradisiako (traditional) cooking.

The Scene: Informal and relaxed—regular customers range from aging ambassadors to up-and-coming young artists, all feasting on goodies like lahanodolmades (cabbage rolls stuffed with rice and ground meat), pastitsio (oven-baked pasta in a meat sauce) and shockingly yummy galaktobouriko (custard in filo pastry). *Mon-Sat 1-5pm, 9pm-1am, Sun 1-5pm. Closed end of July and all of Aug.* €€ ≣

Hot Tip: This is a rare spot with a real non-smoking section. Smokers get upstairs tables, while cigarette-shunners sit downstairs.

Dance Clubs

#31–33: Visiting the multitude of clubs in Athens is a nightlife adventure, especially given the late starting hours. To keep the heat up, most of these spots relocate to the seaside in summer so revelers can enjoy a beachfront beat. These are winter locations; check local listings for hot-months addresses.

Danza

Aristophanous 11, Psirri, 210-331-7105 • Downtown

> The Draw: The hottest club in Psirri houses its biggest dance floor as well, in an industrial space offset with hot-pink stained glass. Management keeps things fresh with rotating DJs and special events like fashion shows.
>
> The Scene: Slinky dance teams give this club a sexy appeal unrivaled elsewhere in Psirri—or Athens. Twenty-somethings, media types, and fashionistas frequent Danza, located in the same building as gay club Playback, which makes for a lively cross-fertilization. *Wed-Sun from midnight.* C≡
>
> Hot Tip: On Sunday the action starts earlier, about 10:30pm, thanks to their weekly R&B parties.

Mao

Ayion Anaryiorn & Agatharou 3, Psirri, 210-331-7639 • Downtown

> The Draw: Club culture at its best, with edgy decor inspired by the far east and a pulsating beat accented by a Kodo drummer lowered onto a platform to whip dancers into a frenzy.
>
> The Scene: Techno, trance, and house music from rotating DJs draw a fun-loving crowd that ranges in age from late teens into the 30s. *Sept.-May Thu-Sun 11pm-5am.* C≡
>
> Hot Tip: The elevated stage in the back is a great place to watch over the scene.

Venue

Agias Eleousis 3, Psirri, 210-331-7801 • Downtown
Summer location: Athens-Sounio Coastal Hwy., Varkiza, 210-897-1163

> The Draw: Dripping with urban chic, this tri-level elite-meet has personality.
>
> The Scene: With one of the finest DJs in town and set in the funkiest part of the city, this playground of the uptown 30- to 40-something crowd is decorated in lustful reds, with cushy sofas, lounge chairs, leopard prints, and a metal scorpion. *Sept.-May Wed-Sun 11pm-about 5am, then moves to Varkiza.* C B ≡
>
> Hot Tip: Fashion Fridays are a must. Come for dinner and try sushi at the house restaurant, Yohji (opens at 11pm).

Best Dance Clubs by the Sea

#34–36: Each May, the city's hottest clubs migrate to the beaches of the Attica coast, transforming into open-air fantasies. De rigeur are dance floors built right up to the sea, lush designs, and top European DJs. Most change names, locations, and décor from year to year, but a few endure as perennial favorites.

Akrotiri Lounge

Vasileos Georgiou 11, Agios Kosmas, 210-985-9147 • Hip & Cool

The Draw: This luxurious white-and-silver lounge, arranged in outdoor levels for cocktails, dinner, dancing, and poolside posing, has sunset sea views, DJs on summer break from Paris' Buddha Bar, and a mile-long wait out front.

The Scene: It's tough to tell the models, wannabes, and waitstaff apart here. Sit back in your wrinkled whites, pretend to be louche, and let them come to you. *Club 10:30pm-4:30am, restaurant 9pm-2am.* C B ≡

Hot Tip: Strike your best pose and set yourself up by the DJ console smack in the middle of the room. It's the place to be.

Island

Limanakia Vouliagmenis, Varkiza, 210-965-3563 • By-the-Water

The Draw: Just walking in makes you feel like you're on, well, an island: palm trees, purple bougainvillaea, and a Saronic Gulf view, accompanied by sushi, cool bamboo décor, and mellow house music.

The Scene: Laid-back and full of class. You'll still need reservations, connections, or several stunning companions to get in on a Saturday night, but once inside, you're guaranteed a friendly, relaxed, and elegant good time. *May-Oct., club 11pm-about 3:30am, restaurant 9:30pm-2am.* C B ≡

Hot Tip: Call ahead to make sure there's no private party. If you're reserving a dinner table, ask for one at the edge of the terrace overlooking the sea.

Passa

Karamanli 14, Voula, 210-895-9645 • By-the-Water

The Draw: Party in a mansion that opens right out to the beach. The beautiful mosaic floors don't seem any the worse for wear from generations of club kids dancing on them nightly.

The Scene: Sure bets for its latest incarnation are a full-on glam look in the club's trademark hot-pink color scheme and a crowd of rich, sun-kissed types dolled up in glittery tube tops and Manolos. *May-Sept., club 10:30pm-about 5:30am, restaurant 10pm-2am, cafe 11am-2:30am.* C F ≡

Hot Tip: Nab a sofa by the crystal-bauble curtain—a great place to catch your breath and keep an eye on who's coming through the door.

Best Gay and Lesbian Bars

#37–39: Flying solo? Hoping to find Ms. Right (or Mr. Right Now)? Well, Athens has a spot for every desire. Lesbians have far fewer options, but a scene is sprouting up, mostly in the Gazi/Thisio neighborhoods.

Eyeland
Ikarion 24, Gazi, 694-615-0196 • Hip & Cool

The Draw: Athenian lesbians not being as open as gay Athenian men, there isn't much Sappho-inspired nightlife in the capital. Brand-new Eyeland is trying to change that, with a hip club-lounge in the middle of gay Athens' favorite neighborhood, Gazi.

The Scene: In an industrial space, red-red walls reverberate international beats while a crowd ranging from lipstick to pierced to butch dances late-night surrounded by arty wall projections, or lounges around on the upstairs sofas overlooking the scene below. *Tue-Sun 10pm-about 4am.* C≡

Hot Tip: Call in advance for the club's program: It sometimes hosts gay-themed film screenings and other special events.

Lamda
Lembessi 15, Makrigianni, 210-922-4202 • Downtown

The Draw: Pounding house and beat-based Greek hits, an underground aesthetic, and plenty of eye candy at the hottest dance den in town.

The Scene: Dark rooms, strip shows, and close encounters draw a colorful mix of working-class builders, middle-class models, and upper-class businessmen, who all share the motto "dance (and romance) 'til you drop." *Daily 11pm-about 5am.* C≡

Hot Tip: This is not a spot for wallflowers. This is a spot to meet locals, especially on the dance floor.

Playback
Aristophanous 11, Psirri, 210-331-7105 • Downtown

The Draw: In the hottest part of town, this dig comes from the owners of the most illustrious bar of its kind, the history-making Mykonos-based Pierro's.

The Scene: It's all a big party in this kinky joint with spirited, preppy-style 20-somethings and drop-dead charmers sporting the latest in haute couture, all nonchalantly eyeing each other over a long drink. *Thu-Sun 11pm-about 5am.* C F ≡

Hot Tip: This is another club that moves to the beach at summer. It's also a fashion scene, and has one of the most packed dance floors in town.

Best

Glamorous Clubs

#40–42: Looking for good infrastructure, reliable utilities, and responsible politicians? Greece is not your go-to country. For decadent nightlife, however, you've come to the right place. Athens' best nightclubs are ephemeral, splashing out in new (or newly designed) locations each season—so double-check the location for even the longest-running ones.

Bedlam

Zappeion, in the National Gardens, Syntagma, 210-336-9340 • Hip & Cool

The Draw: Fairy lights suspended in trees, views straight into the starry night, and beds for cozy canoodling give this open-air lounge a romantic atmosphere.

The Scene: Trendy types sporting carefully distressed denim and sequin-encrusted Gucci bags picking at finger food, and fresh-faced models dancing the night away (with ever-hopeful sugar daddies plying them with champagne). *Mon-Thu 8pm-3am, Fri-Sat 8pm-4am.* C≡

Hot Tip: When you need a break, have a seat on the wood deck—it's where the club circuit's glitterati hangs out.

Dragoste

Patriarchou Loakim 37, Kolonaki, 210-722-1558 • Hip & Cool

The Draw: This decadent den opens only during the winter months, when crowds line up outside its discreet and unyielding entrance and beg to be allowed to peer through the miasma of smoke at the celebrities within, boogie to the funky fusion beats, and shell out a fortune for a mini-Moët with a straw.

The Scene: Powerbrokers and their surgically enhanced companions, up-and-coming celebrities, and trendy 20-somethings dressed to kill in designer tops, butt-hugging jeans, and Choos, lounging on cushions while smoking hookah pipes, snatching kisses on the crimson settees, and swaying to ethnic beats on the dance floor. *Oct.-Apr. Tue-Sun 10pm-4am.* C F ≡

Hot Tip: Unless you have Naomi Campbell in tow or are on a first-name basis with the doormen, book a table to gain admittance.

Privilege

Location changes seasonally • Hip & Cool / By-the-Water

The Draw: For several years, Privilege has reigned as Athens' most, well, privileged place to name-drop, model-watch, pose, and perhaps even dance.

The Scene: The design changes every year. Recent incarnations included a red-velvet 1930s cabaret look and a decadent Asian-cushion motif. The crowd is always Prada, Versace, semi-famous, and beautiful. *Daily mid-May–mid-June and Thu-Sun during winter, about midnight-6am.* C F ≡

Hot Tip: Look out for the décor's centerpiece—a small stage with canopy bed, a post-modern boudoir—and stake out a place there.

Best

Hotel Rooms

#43–45: When Athens was chosen to host the 2004 Olympics, many of the city's hotels were, um, in need of a boost, shall we say. A flurry of investment and renovation has ensued however, so today you can find accommodation in the style to which you've become accustomed—or would like to be.

Hotel Grande Bretagne

Syntagma Square, Syntagma, 210-333-0000 • Classic

The Draw: Athens' oldest and most prestigious hotel—built as a private mansion, it was converted for lodging in 1872 and has a guest book that reads like a who's who. It's better than ever after a multimillion-dollar renovation.

The Scene: Fitting for a former stately home, the 327 rooms with classic furniture, cream walls, and aristocratic yellow-and-burgundy bedcovers draw international businessmen, politicians, and celebrities. €€€€

Hot Tip: Indulge in a massage and aromatherapy session in the luxurious GB Spa and health club, which includes an indoor pool, a thermal suite, and a gym. Or, if you're a sun worshipper, swim and tan at the rooftop pool.

Ochre & Brown

Leokoriou 7, Psirri, 210 331 2950 • Hip & Cool

The Draw: A location in the heart of the city's hippest district—and just steps away from Plaka and the Parthenon—make this the perfect choice for mixing nightlife with ancient sites.

The Scene: Totally modern, totally cool. The name sets the tone for the decor—gleaming hardwood floors, sleek surfaces, rich fabrics, discreet lighting, and extras like in-room massage and private catering. €€

Hot Tip: If your feet have done all their walking for the day, one of the city's hottest bars is right in the lobby—the Ochre & Brown Lounge.

Semiramis Hotel

Harilaou Trikoupi 48, Kifissia, 210-628-4400 • Hip & Cool

The Draw: It's outrageous. Semiramis' London/New-York-based architect-designer Karim Rashid created a hyper-modern "concept hotel" in a white palette accented with hot pink, lime green, electric orange, and vibrant yellow. An amoeba-shaped pool, gigantic fiber-optic light fixtures, LCD screens running messages in the entryway of each guest room, and submarine-inspired pool bungalows are all part of his rejection of tradition in hotel design.

The Scene: Design fanatics, contemporary art aficionados, business travelers, and residents of posh Kifissia intermingle in the hotel's restaurant, cafe, and pool lounge. €€€€

Hot Tip: Be sure to admire the art adorning the walls—the owner of the hotel has one of the most renowned contemporary collections in Greece.

Best Late-Late-Night Eats

#46–48: In a city where places serving three-course meals at 3am abound, late-night eating takes on a whole new meaning. It's less about "what's open?" and more about "what do I want?" So when you stumble out of that club, get creative.

Estiatorio 24
Syngrou 44, Makrigianni, 210-922-1159 • Hip & Cool

The Draw: A vast menu of Greek home cooking—stews, casseroles, grilled lamb, plus more familiar fare, from omelets to club sandwiches—served in a sleek space so stylish and buzzy it could be mistaken for an after-hours bar.

The Scene: After 4am on weekends, this place fills to capacity with crowds heading home from the nearby posh bouzoukia, trendy dance clubs, and seedy strip shows. Among the usual crowd of glittery night owls, you'll likely spot one of Greece's singing divas chowing down with her entourage, plus the occasional transvestite streetwalker. *24/7. Closed Easter Sunday.* € ▤

Hot Tip: If for some reason you weren't going to order fries, think again.

Kavouras
Themistokleous 64, Exarchia, 210-383-7981 • Downtown

The Draw: This much-loved souvlaki joint is perfectly located when you emerge from any one of Exarchia's jazz, rock, and rembetika clubs.

The Scene: Students, anarchists, leftists, music fans, and many a rock and rembetika star have joined the early morning line here, standing around in the friendly fluorescent glow, shoveling in fat, sauce-soaked gyros while clutching an ice-cold beer or Coke. *Daily 10am-5am.* € ▤

Hot Tip: It's just around the corner from a hotel that's become popular with fresh young things in town on photo shoots.

Papandreou's Taverna
Aristogeitonos 1, Central Market, 210-321-4970 • Downtown

The Draw: For more than 100 years, Athens has headed to the butcher-paper-covered tables, blood-spattered floors, and old-style home-cooked offerings of the city's Central Market after-hours.

The Scene: Old-timers, club kids, designer-suited moguls with arm candy, taxi drivers, prostitutes, and all other late-nighters are equal here, picking at the hearty food and washing it down with carafes of dark barrel red. *24/7.* € ▤

Hot Tip: For the most authentic experience, do as the Greeks do and order up a steaming bowl of patsas, an oily stew made primarily of pig intestines, which Greeks swear prevents hangovers like nothing else can.

Live Music Venues

#49–51: Concert-going in Athens is not just about bouzoukia or rembetika. From buzzing avant-garde and grinding blues to vibrant ethnic and classical, Athens' live music scene is all about range, choice, and quality.

Half Note

Trivonianou 17, Pangrati, 210-921-3310 • Downtown

The Draw: If jazz is your thing, this venue has your stuff. It might be a tad small, but it compensates with a lineup of the biggest names.

The Scene: The only club in town booking international jazz, blues, Latin fusion, and world music acts, as well as local talent. Great sound and a cool atmosphere draw middle-aged yuppies and seasoned listeners alike. *Doors open at 9pm, showtimes vary.* C≡

Hot Tip: Shows usually start at 11pm but get there early to ensure you get in and stake out a good vantage point, as almost all gigs sell out here.

Megaro Mousikis (Athens Concert Hall)

Vassilissis Sofias, Ambelokipi, 210-728-2333 • Classic

The Draw: Athens' pride and joy. If there's one spot to see and be seen, then Europe's biggest concert hall, boasting the best sound in the city, is it.

The Scene: High ceilings, chandeliers, galleries, three halls, one of Europe's biggest church organs, and lots of marble. Top-name national and international artists and orchestras strut their stuff on these stages. *Open year round. No concerts June-Sept. Showtimes vary.* €€

Hot Tip: The hall displays pieces from the Greek Museum of Contemporary Art, now under construction. Most concerts start at 8:30pm, so be there by 8pm to roam around and get a taste of haute culture.

Stavros tou Notou

Frantzi & Tharipou 37, Neos Kosmos, 210-922-6975• Downtown

The Draw: This indie club hosts everything from established groups to up-and-coming bands on three stages, including a club for new artists and Apenanti for Greek music.

The Scene: From the T-shirt-and-torn-jeans crowd to leather-jacketed bikers, hip and cool rules over chic or trendy. *Doors open around 8 or 9pm. Showtimes vary.* C F ≡

Hot Tip: Shun the bigname bands on the main stage and opt for the cozier club where there's more interaction between audience and performers.

Museums

#52–54: With a cultural heritage dating back millennia, Greece is one place where museums really do have some relevance to their surroundings. Like the city's hotels, they underwent massive renovation programs in preparation for the 2004 Olympics.

Benaki Museum
Koumbari 1 & Vassilissis Sofias, Kolonaki, 210-367-1000 • Hip & Cool

The Draw: A first-rate introduction to Greek culture, this museum traces the country's artistic development from the Stone Age up to the 20th century.

The Scene: Antonis Benakis, a very wealthy Greek from Alexandria, Egypt, donated this private collection to the state in 1931. More than 20,000 objects are displayed in chronological order, so a walk from the ground floor to the top is a journey through Hellas, from prehistory to the birth of the modern Greek state. *Mon, Wed, Fri, Sat 9am-5pm, Thu 9am-midnight, Sun 9am-3pm.* €

Hot Tip: The rooftop cafe is a great place to stop for lunch, with a splendid terrace overlooking the National Gardens. The museum shop is a convenient place to pick up tasteful gifts and souvenirs.

Goulandris Museum of Cycladic Art
Neofytou Douka 4 & Irodotou, Kolonaki, 210-722-8321 • Hip & Cool

The Draw: Twentieth-century artists such as Modigliani and Picasso were inspired by the minimalist white marble figures (mainly female nudes with folded arms) created by this prehistoric civilization, which flourished on the Cyclades from 3200-2000 BC.

The Scene: The main collection is displayed in a purpose-built modern museum, while temporary exhibitions are staged in a yellow-and-white neo-classical house next door. *Mon, Wed-Fri 10am-4pm, Sat 10am-3pm.* €

Hot Tip: Stop at the cool and airy atrium cafe for a light lunch, then check out the gift shop and its beautiful replicas of Cycladic marble figurines.

National Archaeological Museum
Patission 44, Exarchia, 210-821-7717 • Classic

The Draw: Undoubtedly the most important museum in Greece, the collection spans ancient civilization from Neolithic times up to the Roman conquest.

The Scene: Overpoweringly vast. Greek-ophiles beware: You'll need more than one visit to see it all. *Oct.-May Tue-Sun 8:30am-3pm, Mon 10:30am-5pm; June-Sept. Tue-Sun 8:30am-5pm, Mon 11:30am-7pm, but call to confirm as hours change seasonally.* €

Hot Tip: Look for the unusual 1st-century BC device that's thought to be the world's first computer.

Best Nouveau Greek Dining

#55–57: Until recently, "Greek food" meant the simple grub of tavernas, while high-end restaurants stuck to French and Italian. But talented Greek chefs who've studied abroad are returning, bringing sophistication and creativity to native tastes. Foodies worldwide now consider Athens a serious destination.

Aristera-Dexia
Pireos 140 & Andronikou 3, Rouf, 210-342-2606 • Downtown

The Draw: This trend-setting favorite not only pioneered Greek fusion cooking, it also was among the first to open in industrial Gazi—now Athens' epicenter of cool. Having the best wine cellar in town doesn't hurt either.

The Scene: A doorman guides you into one of the two entrances, where culinary cognoscenti linger over dishes like pheasant sausage in Madeira sauce. *Mon-Sat 8:30pm-1:30am.* €€€ ▭

Hot Tip: In summer, the hip indoor space closes, tables move outside, the menu is simplfied, and prices drop, making it more of a postmodern taverna.

Milos Restaurant
Athens Hilton, Vassilissis Sofias 46, Ilisia, 210-724-4400 • Hip & Cool

The Draw: The most famous Greek restaurant in the world, with possibly the best fish in Athens, was started in Montreal by an émigré. But while the provenance of Athens' Milos may be Canada, its heart is firmly Greek. Athenians were wary, but one try and even skeptics were humbled.

The Scene: In Athens' glam, sophisticated Hilton hotel, a mature crowd of jet-setters dine among Greek deal-makers, politicians, and foodies. In summer the action moves to an outside terrace. *Daily 12:30pm-6pm, 7:30pm-1am. Closed mid-to-end Aug.* €€€ ▭

Hot Tip: Sit near the open kitchen to see chefs grabbing and cooking fresh produce displayed in cartons much like at a laiki (open marketplace).

Red
Kastorias 34-36, Athinais Center, Votanikos, 210-348-0000 • Hip & Cool

The Draw: Set in a silk factory-turned-arts complex, Red draws an arty crowd with its unusual Mediterranean fusion (think pigeon with cocoa pasta).

The Scene: Culture vultures fresh from gallery openings fill the boudoir-like space. In summer, the scene moves outdoors to a red-painted courtyard. *May-July Fri-Sat only 8:30pm-2:30am, Sept.-Apr. Tue-Sat 8pm-2am. Closed late July and all of Aug.* €€€ ▭▭

Hot Tip: Come early to take in a show or to wander Athinais' many galleries; after dinner, hit the adjoining Boiler Bar for cocktails.

Ouzeries

#58–60: Old-fashioned ouzeries (also known as mezedopoleia) offer a great way to sample the best traditional Greek foods. The long lists of savory small dishes (known as mezedes, similar to tapas) were once meant to make your potent glass of ouzo go down easier. But at many of Athens' best ouzeries, the spicy and savory dishes have themselves become an attraction, and there's certainly no rule that you must drink ouzo—any ouzerie worth its salt will also offer its own wine.

Athinaikon

Themistokleous 2, Exarchia, 210-383-8485 • Classic

The Draw: This old-school central Athens institution breathes history and character, with dark wood, marble-topped tables, and a four-page list of mezedes.

The Scene: A favorite meeting spot for Greek journalists, lawyers, and intellectuals, who linger over wine and cigarettes among the framed 1950s memorabilia. *Mon-Sat 11:30am-12:30am. Closed in Aug.* €€

Hot Tip: Try live clams, bekri meze ("drunkard's tidbits"—pork in wine topped with salted cheese), or, for the daring, amelitita—sauteed lamb testicles.

Orea Ellas

Mitropoleos 59 & Pandrossou 36, Plaka, 210-321-3842 • Classic

The Draw: A lovely setting on the second-floor of a historic building with a panoramic view of Plaka's sorbet-colored homes is draw enough. Fortunately, the food—tasty grilled octopus, savory pies, Cretan olives—also holds its own.

The Scene: Set in the middle of Athens' most touristy street, this quaint ouzerie draws a fair share of sunburned, Teva-clad passers by, but a set of older, refined Greek regulars keeps the atmosphere authentic and the food up to par. *Daily 9am-6pm. Closed two weeks in Aug.* €€

Hot Tip: There are good deals on one-of-a-kind treasures to be found in the Center of Hellenic Tradition, in the same building.

Ouzadiko

Karneadou 25-29, Lemos Shopping Center, Kolonaki,
210-729-5484 • Hip & Cool

The Draw: At last count, this local favorite had 868 varieties of ouzo, while the owners claim more than 3,000 recipes for accompanying dishes.

The Scene: Not big on atmosphere at first glance, since it's set inside a deserted shopping mall on a busy pedestrian street. But inside, all is as it should be: polished wood, old-fashioned chairs, and a Greek mama greeting you at the door. *Tue-Sat 12:30-6pm, 8-11:45pm. Closed in Aug.* €€

Hot Tip: Steer clear of Ouzadiko on summer afternoons, when it's dark and stifling. Go when the Greeks do—on autumn and winter evenings.

Plateias

#61–63: The Parthenon was the world's first purpose-built public gathering space, and the idea of open-air socializing has continued throughout the Mediterranean to this day. While people in colder climes meet within four walls, Athenians still prefer daytime encounters out of doors on the plateia (square).

Exarchia

The Draw: In the heart of the student quarter, this raw and gritty triangular piazza is rimmed by inexpensive (though increasingly trendy) cafes with outdoor seating, where the young Greek intelligentsia meet to do what they must.

The Scene: Subversive and of dubious character, according to more conservative Athenians, this is where revolutionary ideas and youthful love stories are born. Expect to see youngsters who look as if they spent too long in London, bespectacled students, aging hippies, and junkies. It keeps buzzing 'til late.

Hot Tip: Lampposts are plastered with peeling layers of anarchists' manifestos and posters advertising alternative rock concerts if you're looking to join in.

Filomousou

The Draw: The quaintest, most lovable square in Athens swarms with tourists in summer, thanks to its location in Plaka at the foot of the Acropolis and its mix of open-air cafes. In winter, it becomes the domain of romantic Athenians.

The Scene: Surrounded by neoclassical buildings from the late 1800s, the center of this paved pedestrian enclave is planted with trees and peopled with everyone from celebrities to roving backpackers, plus the inevitable waiters who try to entice bewildered foreigners into their establishments.

Hot Tip: In one corner, there's a periptero (street kiosk) selling an extensive selection of English-language newspapers and magazines, so you can catch up with the day's news while the caffeine kicks in.

Kolonaki

The Draw: The smartest district in town, where diplomats, jetsetters, and wannabes gather at the cafes around the plateia. Nearby, the streets of Pindarou and Tsalkof are lined with exclusive designer stores, hence the profusion of open-top BMWs, Porsches, and Jaguars parked on the sidewalks.

The Scene: Suited businessmen, armed policeman, and elderly ladies with permed hair and poodles, plus yuppie girls scouting for rich husbands.

Hot Tip: The excellent Benaki and Cycladic museums are close by. Combine highbrow culture and smart shopping with people-spotting by doing a museum first, checking out the stores, then stopping here for coffee at one of the fashionable open-air cafes.

Rembetika Clubs

#64–66: Earthy Eastern rembetika (sometimes called the Balkan blues) is Athens' most authentic music. Like the American blues, rembetika has its roots in a marginalized population (Greek refugees who fled Asia Minor in the 1920s). In recent years, rembetika has surged in popularity, with a new generation of fans flocking to clubs to enjoy music that alternates between movingly sad and dancably lively. A typical rembetika band will include a bouzoukia (a cross between a banjo and lute), a bagpipe-like baglama, a clarinet, and a plaintive singer.

Mnisikleous

Mnisikleous & Lyceiou, Plaka, 210-322-5558 • Classic

The Draw: One of Greece's only year-round rembetika, Mnisikleous is a haven for real Greek music (and real Greeks), in the heart of tourist-saturated Plaka. The respected rembetika master Babis Tsertos leads the excellent house band.

The Scene: Cigarette smoke, empty wine bottles, and dancing middle-aged Greeks. In summer, performances are on the open-air roof garden with glorious Acropolis views. *Thu-Sun 10pm-6am.* C F ≡

Hot Tip: This place does offer dinner, but you'll be better off filling up at nearby O Platanos taverna beforehand and just ordering wine here.

Stoa Ton Athanaton

Sophokleous 19, Central Market, 210-321-4362 • Downtown

The Draw: Athens' premier rembetika, aptly located inside the bustling, old-world confines of the city's Ottoman-era meat market. For generations, its traditional space—all dark, carved wood and folk tapestries—has drawn the genre's greatest musicians.

The Scene: Suits with cigars shower musicians with flowers and dance passionately to songs of addiction, heartbreak, and whores. *Mid-May-mid-Oct. Mon-Sat 3:30-7:30pm and 10:30pm-about 8am.* C F ≡

Hot Tip: You'll find a cozy, rollicking daytime scene here, especially on cold winter afternoons.

Taximi

Harilau Trikoupi & Isavron 29, Exarchia, 210-363-9919 • Downtown

The Draw: An old favorite in bohemian Exarchia. The wood floors are worn down from years of dancing and the walls are lined with signed black-and-white photographs of past rembetika greats.

The Scene: A friendly, unpretentious mix of Exarchia denizens, students, and musicians gather around the little metal cafe tables with flickering red candles. *Mid-Sept.-Apr. Wed-Sun 10pm-3am.* C F ≡

Hot Tip: It's small, so reserve no matter which night of the week you're going.

Best

Romantic Dining

#67–69: Athens abounds in romantic spots to eat—flower-filled cobblestone courtyards and Acropolis views are par for the course in Plaka. But a handful of places transcend the merely scenic to achieve pure idyllic.

Edodi

Veikou 80, Koukaki, 210-921-3013 • Classic

The Draw: This tiny candlelit dining room has no menu—instead, choose from raw ingredients brought to your table then cooked to order. Options change daily, but the heavenly results—succulent lobster with spicy parmesan sauce, Chinese noodles with smoked fish in a saffron-mastic infusion—have made it a perennial favorite.

The Scene: Despite Edodi's renown, arriving here feels like discovering an unknown gem, hidden on the top floor of an old mansion in an out-of-the-way neighborhood. The dining room looks like a wealthy, whimsical fairy godmother's hideaway. *Mon-Sat 8pm-1am. Closed two weeks in Aug.* €€ ▭

Hot Tip: With its cozy dimness and wood-beamed ceilings, Edodi is at its best in winter. Whenever you go, reserve early. It has only eight tables.

Pil-Poul

Apostolou Pavlou 51, Thisio, 210-342-3665 • Hip & Cool

The Draw: The marble rooftop terrace, dripping with bougainvillaea, looks directly over the moon-bathed Acropolis. If you can tear your eyes away from the view (and your date), the flawless French-Med menu is excellent.

The Scene: Wealthy and sophisticated Greeks of all ages gazing into each other's eyes; you have a good chance of witnessing at least one proposal. *Daily 8pm-1am.* €€€€ ▣▭

Hot Tip: For the best views, request a table at the edge of the terrace. When they're in season, don't miss the sautéed wild strawberries with chocolate.

Tou Psarra

Erechtheos 16 & Erotokritou 12, Plaka, 210-321-8733 • Classic

The Draw: Small tables set on whitewashed stairs under blooming mulberry trees. One of the only places in Plaka that serves genuinely tasty Greek country dishes rather than bland tourist fare.

The Scene: Tucked into a quiet corner at the foot of the Acropolis, Tou Psarra attracts mostly Greeks and the occasional luminary. *Daily noon-2am.* €€ ▭

Hot Tip: If you're determined to go to Plaka for seafood, this is the only place to consider. The catch of the day and appetizers such as marinated octopus are always good.

Best Rooms with a View

#70–72: The quintessential Athens view is of its crowning glory, the Acropolis. In many parts of town, you can see it just by lifting your eyes from the congested city streets. But how much better to have a perfect panorama directly from your hotel room? Athens is also one of the few cities where you can wake up to Greece's other immortal view—the brilliant blues of the Aegean.

Astir Palace Resort
Apollonos 40, Vouliagmeni, 210-890-2000 • By-the-Water

> **The Draw:** An infinity of sparkling turquoise coast and a private beach on a peninsula 15 miles from central Athens.
>
> **The Scene:** The complex is made up of three hotels, recently remodeled with luxurious but simple décor. All have magnificent water views, seaside pools, sophisticated restaurants, and activities ranging from jet-skiing to individual Pilates sessions. €€€
>
> **Hot Tip:** At the peninsula's tip, the airy Aphrodite has the most stellar views and feels like an island escape. Foreign dignitaries prefer the Nafsika, an international conference center; the Arion has the best health club.

Divani Palace Acropolis
Parthenonos 19-25, Makrigianni, 210-928-0100 • Classic

> **The Draw:** The closest luxury hotel to the Acropolis. From the windows on the fourth through seventh floors, you could literally throw a stone and hit Western civilization's greatest masterpiece.
>
> **The Scene:** Persian carpets, pink marble, and the wealthy Greeks who love them. In summer, barbecues on the roof garden with even better views. €€
>
> **Hot Tip:** The hotel is built directly over a section of the 5th-century BC Themistoclean wall; it is displayed in situ in the basement.

The St. George Lycabettus
Kleomenous 2, Kolonaki, 210-729-0711 • Hip & Cool

> **The Draw:** Never mind the blah facade—the St. George has what many consider the best views in the whole city, even better than those from the top of nearby Mt. Lycabettus, and in considerably more glamorous environs.
>
> **The Scene:** Since the hotel is a scenester's hot spot, it doesn't feel touristy. Its '70s-inspired rooms and lounges draw Kolonaki's most fashionable and trendy clientele—as well as elegant Greek and international travelers. €€
>
> **Hot Tip:** A sunset dinner or drink—preferably both—at the hotel's top-floor restaurant/cafe, with a whiter-than-white décor, offers sweeping city views.

Seafood Restaurants

Best

#73–75: With 8,500 miles of coast, Greece is a country with an excellent range of seafood, so while in Athens, you'd be foolish not to check out the psaro-tavernes (fish restaurants). Choose the high-end establishments and you'll be guaranteed fresh-caught wild fish.

Jimmy and the Fish

Akti Koumoundourou 46, Mikrolimanos, 210-412-4417 • By-the-Water

The Draw: Unfortunately, most of Mikrolimano's seafood tavernas on Piraeus' charming sailboat harbor serve up little more than generic frozen-and-fried fare. Jimmy and the Fish is the exception, offering caught-that-day picks.

The Scene: Friendly and relaxed, but definitely not a taverna, as evinced by the well-gelled waiters in tight T-shirts and long butchers' aprons. Crisp blue and white décor; the cheerful yells of fishermen; the buzz of seafood-laden motor-bikes. *Daily 12:30pm-1:30am.* €€€ ▤

Hot Tip: Big parties get the best views—most harborside tables are for groups.

Plous Podilato

Akti Koumoundourou 42, Mikrolimanos, 210-413-7910 • By-the-Water

The Draw: Plous Podilato is the name that delivered modern cuisine to Mikrolimano, for decades known only for its rustic, cutesy fish restaurants.

The Scene: The glass, steel, and wood interior was redesigned in early 2004 to bring in a slightly softer, more seafaring image. Outdoor tables overlook the water. *Daily 12:30pm-12:30am.* €€€ ▤

Hot Tip: Look for colorful starters like risotto with sun-dried tomatoes, olives, shrimp, and smoked Gruyère cheese.

Varoulko

80 Pireos, Keramikos, 210-522-8400
Deligeorgi 14, Piraeus, 210-411-2043 • By-the-Water

The Draw: Easily the best seafood restaurant in the capital. Varoulko, under the direction of chef-owner Lefteris Lazarou, earned a Michelin star in 2002.

The Scene: Patronized by devout foodies, this gem now boasts two year-round sites—one on a dubious side street close to the Neo Faliro metro station, and the other in a gorgeous renovated building in the up-and-coming neighborhood of Keramikos. *Mon-Sat 8:30pm-1am.* €€€€▤

Hot Tip: In Keramikos, stop by the adjacent Eridanus boutique hotel for a drink. Varoulko's menu changes daily depending on the offerings at the morning market, but the chef is known for performing magic with monkfish.

Best

See-and-Be-Seen Bars

#76–78: All cosmopolitan cities nurture name-dropping elitist circles, and Athens is no exception. Fortunately, the Greeks' love of glamour, style, and luxury lets them pull it off with panache—glitzy and at times kitschy, they manage to mix beauty and near-vulgarity with success.

Mommy

Delphon 4 (pedestrian side street off Skoufa 62), Kolonaki, 210-361-9682 • Hip & Cool

The Draw: This glamorous bar-restaurant is peopled with young, trendy media and design 30-somethings, plus the passing model.

The Scene: A bar and three lounges are decorated in '70s revival, with sofas, armchairs, and low-level coffee tables. Walls have modern art, and the bar is draped in beautiful people listening to lounge and ambient music. *Mon-Sat noon-3am, Sun 3pm-3am. May close in July and Aug.* C F ≡

Hot Tip: To-die-for Mediterranean cuisine. Favorites include the turkey bites stuffed with dried apricots in a sesame crust.

Passa

Leventi 4, Kolonaki, 210-721-1310 • Hip & Cool

The Draw: Located just off Plateia Kolonaki, this multilevel establishment with an attitude earned instant success when it opened in November 2003.

The Scene: The street level bar-restaurant is always busy with illustrious guests and hangers-on stopping for coffee, cakes, and snacks. There's a cool mezzanine lounge with sofas, plus a basement club (open Fri-Sat midnight-5am) with pink furry cushions and fetish art installations where a mixed, glamorous, hip crowd sips daiquiris to the sounds of mainstream DJs. *Oct.-Apr. 9pm-about 4:30am.* C B ≡

Hot Tip: Check out the stock of cigars in the powder rooms.

Soul

Evripidou 65, Psirri, 210-331-0907 • Downtown

The Draw: Not to be missed. Soul brought the smart Kolonaki and Kifissia crowd down to Psirri in droves—young, fun, and happening.

The Scene: An internal courtyard garden hosts cocktails and conversation, the front bar rocks to the beat of hard core techno, and DJ-controlled dance music keeps the upper floor gyrating well into the early hours. *Daily 9pm-4am. Closed for three weeks in Aug.* B ≡

Hot Tip: Soul is renowned for its cocktail-shaking bartenders—try their mojito, said to be the best in town.

Shows Under the Stars

#79–81: Athens' moonlit amphitheaters—ranging from 2,000-year-old marble edifices to mountaintop venues with sweeping views—draw top performers and guarantee a singular experience. Tickets generally go on sale two weeks before the show.

Dora Stratou Dance Theatre

Arakinthou & Voutie, Thisio, 210-921-4650 • Classic

The Draw: Greece's leading folk dance troupe. "Um, folk dance?" Trust us, this is worth it. The company spends the off-season traveling around Greece learning centuries-old moves and performs them in authentic costumes.

The Scene: An open-air venue set on the pine-studded slopes of Philopappou. *Performances late-May-Sept. Tue-Sat 9:30pm, Sun 8:15pm. Tickets can be purchased at the box office before the show, or call 210-324-4395.* €€

Hot Tip: The troupe also gives Greek-dancing lessons in English—a good skill to have if you plan on drunken revelry at tavernas and rembetika.

Mt. Lycabettus Theater

At the top of Mt. Lycabettus, Kolonaki, 210-928-2900 • Hip & Cool

The Draw: Open-air shows at the summit of Mt. Lycabettus with acts ranging from Philip Glass to Bob Dylan and Massive Attack.

The Scene: Few artists could ask for a better backdrop than the simple rocks of this amphitheater, which opens out to a stunning cityscape. *Performances May-Oct. Showtimes vary.* €€ ▭

Hot Tip: Many taxis won't take you to the top of the mountain—take the funicular from Aristippou and walk the rest. For a pre- or post-show drink or meal with a view, head to Orizondes, an outstanding restaurant near the theater.

Odeon of Herodes Atticus

Dionyssiou Areopagitou, Plaka, 210-323-2771 • Classic

The Draw: If you stay only one night in Athens, spend it seeing a moonlit performance in this breathtaking Roman amphitheater. All the shows are world class, from ancient Greek drama performed by top international companies to delights from the likes of the Bolshoi Ballet and Luciano Pavarotti.

The Scene: The marble theater, built in AD 160, is nestled into the Acropolis hill, so the moon rises over the city through tiers of Roman arches. *Performances: May-Oct. 9pm-midnight. Tickets available at the Hellenic Festival box office, Panepistimiou 39, off Syntagma Square, 210-928-2900.* €€

Hot Tip: Classical plays are performed in both Greek and English—check ahead to make sure you see a show in English.

Souvlaki

#82–84: The collective name for charcoal-grilled meats, souvlaki encompasses gyros (shredded meat, most often pork but sometimes chicken, cooked on a rotating spit) and kalamaki (pork or chicken grilled on a stick), both of which are served either me pita (wrapped in pita bread, with chopped tomato, onion, and tzatziki) as a carry-out, or by the merida (portion), as a sit-down meal on a plate.

0 Kostas
Adrianou 116, Plaka, 210-322-8502 • Classic

The Draw: The quintessential Greek fastfood stand. This hole-in-the-wall kiosk offers just one choice, kalamaki: chunks of pork sprinkled with oregano, served in pita with tomato, onion, and lashings of garlicky tzatziki.

The Scene: Founded in 1950 by Kostas, who passed away in December 2003 at the ripe old age of 82. His grandson has taken over and vows to keep the place the same. Their motto is Ohi Aghos ("No Stress"). *Mon-Fri 8am-3pm.* € ▤

Hot Tip: Drinks are limited to canned beer and Coke, plus tsipouro served in shot glasses—if you haven't tried it yet, this is the moment.

Ta Agrafa
Valtesiou 50-52 & Benaki, Exarchia, 210-380-3144 • Downtown

The Draw: Just a five-minute walk from Plateia Exarchia, on the tree-lined, pedestrian street of Valtetsiou, it pulls in the grungy student-anarchist crowd.

The Scene: Brightly lit, furnished with wooden tables and throw-away tablecloths. It heaves with hungry clientele, who feast on gyros and kalamaki, kotopoulo kilo (whole roast chicken sold by the kilo), and kokoretsi (a Greek delicacy made from offal). *Mon-Sat noon-2:30am.* € ▤

Hot Tip: Look for arni galaktos (suckling lamb) on weekends. If you're staying close by, you can call and they'll deliver.

Thanassis
Mitropoleos 69, Monastiraki, 210-324-4705 • Classic

The Draw: Possibly Athens' most popular souvlaki house.

The Scene: Bustling and chaotic, with pine chairs and tables outside. Moody waiters trade plates laden with bifteki saras (ground-beef kebabs) wrapped in pita bread with tomato and onion, and souvlaki hirino (pork shish kebab) served with fries. *Daily 9am-2:30am.* € ▤

Hot Tip: Although it stays open late, drawing the Psirri party people, the quality of the food and service degenerates through the wee hours. Don't expect niceties after midnight.

Best

Summer Cinemas

#85–87: Summer cinemas are as much a staple of Greek life as afternoon siestas and sun-bronzed cleavage. These places, set in flower-fringed gardens and on Acropolis-view rooftops, offer the additional charms of cold beer, hot souvlaki, and the smell of jasmine (and your neighbor's cigarette). Films are screened in the original language (usually English) with Greek subtitles. Shows usually begin around 9pm.

Aegli Village Cool

Zappeion, in the National Gardens, Syntagma, 210-336-9327 • Classic

The Draw: Romantically set in the lush Zappeion gardens, the elegant Aegli is surrounded by bougainvillaea and palm trees. The park location means the high-end sound system can be played as loud as necessary. The kitchen has everything from nachos to kebabs—or just enjoy a cocktail from the full bar.

The Scene: With its central location and steady menu of Hollywood hits, Aegli draws crowds, especially chic young things and their well-gelled escorts. *Doors open 8pm, first screening 9pm.* C B –

Hot Tip: Buy tickets well before the show, then have a drink in the adjoining outdoor Aegli. Later, head back to this Italian spot for dinner, or to Bedlam, the open-air nightclub in the park.

Cine Psirri

Sarri 40-44, Psirri, 210-321-2476 • Downtown

The Draw: A pretty garden theater in grungily cool Psirri. Movies from the likes of the Marx Brothers, Alfred Hitchcock, and native son John Cassavetes.

The Scene: In the audience, Psirri hipsters smoking French cigarettes; on the balconies of nearby buildings, locals taking in the free show. *May-Sept. Showtimes vary.* C –

Hot Tip: You're smack in the center of Athens' most cutting-edge nightlife— don't even think about going home after the film.

Thission

Apostolou Pavlou 7, Archaeological Promenade, Thisio, 210-342-0864, 210-347-0980 • Classic

The Draw: An extraordinary location right on Athens' gorgeous pedestrian walkway leaves the Acropolis competing with the films screened here for cinemagoers' attention.

The Scene: The opening of the promenade confirmed this circa-1926 spot as Athens' quintessential alfresco cinematic experience—with nearby cocktails. *May-Sept. 8:30pm-2am.* C B –

Hot Tip: In case of rain, there is a roofed area.

Sushi Restaurants

#88–90: The only surprising thing about the sushi trend sweeping through Athens (no fashionable nightclub worth its velvet ropes is now without a menu of maki) is that it didn't happen earlier. After all, on a peninsula where the Aegean is a stone's throw away, what could be more natural?

Freud Oriental

Xenokratous 21, Kolonaki, 210-729-9595 • Hip & Cool

The Draw: A gloriously simple, stylish restaurant, where classically trained sushi chefs from Japan work magic on local fish pulled fresh from the sea.

The Scene: Beautiful people with bulging wallets and small appetites. *Daily 8pm-1am.* €€€ ▱

Hot Tip: All of Athens' prettiest and pose-iest want to say they've eaten here, but there are only six tables—so book early and look good.

Kiku

Dimokritou 12, Kolonaki, 210-364-7033 • Hip & Cool

The Draw: This Kolonaki institution is the original and, most say, still the best sushi restaurant in town. It's also the most expensive. Popular dishes (apart from the impeccable maki and paper-thin nigiri slices) include light and crispy tempura, fried seaweed, dumplings, and a selection of noodle plates.

The Scene: Rolex-flashing, Havana-puffing Athenian powerbrokers and their entourages, usually including a bevy of next season's supermodels armed to the hilt with Gucci, Christian Dior, and Louis Vuitton. Sometimes a handful of slightly bemused-looking Japanese on business trips. *Mon-Sat 7:30pm-1am. Closed in Aug.* €€€€ ▱

Hot Tip: Japanese customers get a different, longer menu. If you've got the language skills, grab one.

Square Sushi

Diligianni 56, Kefalari, Kifissia, 210-808-1512
Deinokratous 65, Kolonaki, 210-725-5236 • Hip & Cool

The Draw: An eclectic selection of traditional and fusion maki and sashimi at reasonable prices, eaten in a relaxed, attractive, minimalist setting.

The Scene: In Kefalari, the place buzzes with trendy young things, but in Kolonaki, especially before 10.30pm on weekdays, you can find yourself dining privately. *Oct.-Apr. 1pm-1am, May-Sept. 8pm-1am.* €€ ▱

Hot Tip: This is possibly the only place in Athens that offers refreshing steamed edamame, sprinkled with rough Aegean sea salt.

Best

Tables with a View

#91–93: Greece's most beloved actress, Melina Mercouri, once said, "In many ways, Athens is like an ugly woman, but like so many ugly women, she has a lot of charm." The sharp contrast between flower-covered mansions and permanent construction sites is part of the city's inexplicable appeal, and, like an uncomely companion of any sex, best enjoyed with a cocktail.

Filistron

Apostolou Pavlou 23, Thisio, 210-346-7554 • Classic

> The Draw: A vista from the Acropolis to Mt. Lycabettus, which towers over modern Athens. Stop by the roof garden for a classic mezedes-and-barrel-wine dinner, or just enjoy a drink during the postcard-perfect sunsets.

> The Scene: Popular with artists and couples looking for a spark. You can see Athens at its best from here: At night, each temple on the Acropolis is lit from below, and the marble sprawl of the Ancient Agora is plucked straight from a classicist's fantasy. *Daily noon-1am; roof garden 6pm-2:30am. Closed one week in Aug.* €€ 🆇🅱️☰

> Hot Tip: On summer nights, rooftop tables are available by reservation only.

Orizondes

Mt. Lycabettus, Kolonaki, 210-721-0701 • Hip & Cool

> The Draw: At the peak of Mt. Lycabettus, the highest point in central Athens (reachable only by cable-car), forget city views—the landscape spreads like a map all the way out to the Saronic Gulf. The inspired Greek, French, and Asian fusion menu lives up to the setting.

> The Scene: The simple, spare lines of the décor take a backseat to the stunning panorama. Most nights the clientele includes everyone from shipping scions and Greek movie stars to top restaurant critics. *Daily noon-2am.* €€€ 🆇🅱️☰

> Hot Tip: Rely on Sotiris Georgiou, the sommelier, for Greek wine choices.

Vive Mar

Karamanli 18, Voula, 210-899-2453 • By-the-Water

> The Draw: Three levels of sleek décor, sea breezes, and high, shady palms, all overlooking the Saronic Gulf islands. The Italian food and DJ tunes are good, but the big blue view is heavenly.

> The Scene: A trendy but laid-back crowd lingers as long as they can over their crayfish linguine and squid-ink risotto, the better to soak up more of the splendid setting. *Sun-Thu 8am-2:30am, Fri-Sat 8am-4am.* €€€ ☰

> Hot Tip: Request a balcony table when booking, and don't show up late or it may be snapped up, leaving you stuck in the indoor dining room.

Best

Tavernas

#94–96: We all love chi chi dining. But while in Greece, be sure to visit a traditional taverna, where you can savor authentic home cooking and local wine served in rustic style, just as it's been done for centuries.

Karavitis
Arktinou 33 & Pavsaniou 4, Pangrati, 210-721-5155 • Classic

The Draw: Like all of Athens' best tavernas, this one has a long history and a totally unassuming image. Located near the Panathenaic Stadium, it opened in 1926 and continues to this day to serve home cooking.

The Scene: A single-story, whitewashed building with outside tables in a walled garden across the road in summer. Popular with foreign visitors and Athenian residents alike. *Daily 8pm-2am. Closed one week in Aug.* € ▤

Hot Tip: Everything on the menu is guaranteed to be good, but longtime favorites include arnaki (roast lamb) and stamnaki (beef baked in a clay pot).

O Platanos
Diogenous 4, Plaka, 210-322-0666 • Classic

The Draw: One of Plaka's oldest tavernas, dating back to 1932, O Platanos lies hidden away in a peaceful corner off the main drag, close to the Roman Agora.

The Scene: No frills here, despite the increasing commercialization of Plaka. In winter, guests eat in a bright, simply furnished dining room; in summer, on an open-air terrace draped with bougainvillaea in the shade of a towering plane tree. *Mon-Sat 12:30-4:30pm and 7:30pm-midnight.* €€ ▤

Hot Tip: Try a delicious casserole, like lamb or veal with spinach or eggplant.

Philippou
Xenokratous 19, Kolonaki, 210-721-6390 • Classic

The Draw: Philippou may look like an ordinary taverna, but its clientele is anything but. It is Kolonaki's only true "neighborhood taverna"—akin to the corner diner in New York or the local curry house in London. And despite its fame among Athenians, it's totally off the tourist radar.

The Scene: The power set—politicians and professionals, with a sprinkling of Kolonaki's ladies who lunch—dine on quintessential Greek fare in a classic taverna setting. It doesn't get more authentic than this. *Mon-Fri 1-5pm and 8pm-midnight, Sat 1-5pm. Closed two weeks in Aug.* € ▤

Hot Tip: If you're lucky, you might spot Greece's former prime minister Kostas Simitis, who's a regular. But don't look for an entourage; in Philippou's understated atmosphere, even the movers and shakers tone down the flash.

Trendy Tables

#97–99: Every other week sees the opening of a fabulously designed new spot that hopes to lure the city's trendsetters, at least for a moment. While most come and go, some have that elusive mix of ingredients that keeps them buzzing after the first blush.

Balthazar
Tsoha 27 & Soutsou, Ambelokipi, 210-644-1215 • Hip & Cool

The Draw: If the thought of dining in a gorgeous, palm-fringed courtyard, filled night after summer night with scantily clad eye candy isn't enough, the food—perfect ceviche, salmon with mango salsa—makes it irresistible.

The Scene: Dinner among soccer stars, models, and celebrities-of-the-moment in an enclave decorated with hand-painted tiles and colored Japanese lanterns. Follow the crowd to the dark, sexy lounge lit by candles and starlight. *Mon-Sat from 9pm; kitchen closes 2am, club closes 3:30am.* €€€€ F ≡

Hot Tip: Balthazar's courtyard fizzes with fun in summer. It's even a great place just to drink, without dinner reservations.

48
Armatolon & Klefton 48, Ambelokipi, 210-641-1082 • Hip & Cool

The Draw: Greek village food elevated to its ideal, served in an art gallery setting that has made this the toughest place in town to get a table.

The Scene: An unlikely mix of cool '80s retro and soul-warming comfort food (crispy-skinned roast piglet with chilled celery mousse; lamb fricassee), enjoyed by foodies, hipsters, and folks from the nearby U.S. Embassy. *Mon-Sat 9pm-2am.* €€€€ YB ≡

Hot Tip: Celeb chefs make regular guest appearances, alongside Greek chef Christoforos Peskias. Sommelier Yiannis Kaimenakis matches perfect wines.

Hytra
Winter: Navarchou Apostoli 7, Psirri, 210-331-6767
Summer: 40th km of the Athens-Sounio Highway, Grand Resort Lagonissi, 229-107-6000 • Downtown

The Draw: Hytra is Psirri's only truly gourmet restaurant. Well-presented traditional recipes are tweaked with modern twists, charming local foodies.

The Scene: In Psirri, the modern bistro-like atmosphere is packed with fashionable, 30- and 40-somethings. In Lagonissi, it's all about elegance and simplicity: tables on a deck overlooking the sea, which glows with delicately-placed underwater lights. *Mon-Sat 8pm-1am.* €€€ ≡

Hot Tip: In summer, for a reasonable fee, non-hotel guests can enjoy the resort's facilities, such as private beaches and lush gardens.

EXPERIENCE ATHENS

Every city has a thousand faces. Which one you see depends on your angle. We've crafted four in-depth itineraries to help you discover some of the best ways to view Athens, and experience it as well. The *Classic* (p.50), *Hip & Cool* (p.74), and *By-the-Water* (p.122) plans are packed with hot restaurants, smart clubs, and fashionable fun—running from Thursday to Saturday (Thursdays are often the best nights for partying with the locals). *Downtown* (p.100), filled with hipster hangouts, cutting-edge nightlife, and a taste for the alternative, is Friday to Sunday (to catch some Sunday-only events). Whichever you choose, it will keep you buzzing for three perfect, high-energy days. Sleep is purely optional—just the way Athenians like it.

Classic Athens

At first glance, it's hard to imagine that this concrete jungle was once the cradle of Western civilization. But look closer, and the evidence is all around, just where it's been for the last 2,500 years. No other city lets you step back in time so easily to world history's most famous and infamous moments. St. Paul, Socrates, Aristotle, Plato—in Athens, you can follow each of their footsteps into the past. By then, by the gods, you've earned a drink. Along with history, Athens is also alive with buzzing cafes and raucous tavernas whose marble-topped tables and flower-filled courtyards have only been around for a mere century or two. At night, you'll find the spirit of Dionysus is also still very much alive in the flower-throwing, table-dancing frenzy of the rembetika clubs and bouzoukia that keep modern Athens, and you, partying till dawn.

Note: Venues in bold in the itinerary are described in detail in the listings that follow. Venues followed by an * asterisk are those we recommend as both a restaurant and a destination bar.

Classic Athens:
The Perfect Plan (3 Days and Nights)

Highlights

Thursday

Morning	Acropolis, Acropolis Museum
Lunch	O Platanos, Orea Ellas
Afternoon	Ancient Agora
Cocktails	Peacock Lounge
Dinner	Symposium, Strofi
Nighttime	Melina, Mnisikleous

Friday

Breakfast	Grande Bretagne
Morning	Roman Agora
Lunch	Byzantino, Athinaikon
Afternoon	Nat'l. Archaeological Museum
Cocktails	To Parko*
Evening	Aegli Village, Megaro Mousikis
Dinner	Archeon Gefsis
Nighttime	Terina
Late-Night	Romeo

Saturday

Morning	Byzantine Museum, Shopping
Lunch	Maritsa's, Philippou*
Afternoon	Kessariani, Panathenaic Stadium
Cocktails	Aegli Cafe
Evening	GB Spa, Dora Stratou
Dinner	Daphne's
Nighttime	Rex

Hotel: Hotel Grande Bretagne

Thursday

9am Rise early, and climb to the pinnacle of Greece's Golden Age, the **Acropolis**, with the most famous temple of all, the Parthenon. Allow at least two hours to roam. You'll also need time to see the **Acropolis Museum**, a nine-room treasure house packed with statues that once adorned the temples. Don't delay, late mornings here are filled with heat and sweaty tourists.

1pm Lunch Relax over a leisurely lunch in Plaka, at **O Platanos**, which has served up traditional roast lamb and its own barrel wine since 1935. For small, piquant mezedes, head to the 150-year-old **Orea Ellas**, where you can also browse through paintings and ceramics created by top Greek artisans.

3pm Wander back a few thousand years with a stroll through the **Ancient Agora**, where Socrates and St. Paul held forth, and where the councils of the first democracy were held. Be sure to stop in the terrific **Agora Museum**. Afterwards, spend some time in Plaka's charming tangle of old-fashioned streets. Start in what may be

Athens' most quirkily beautiful corner, **Anafiotika**, a cluster of whitewashed island-style houses with bowers of brightly colored bougainvillaea. If you meander through Plaka's byways, you will eventually come across Plateia Mitropoleos, overlooked by **Megali Mitropoli** ("Great Mitropolis") the imposing 19th-century national cathedral, and its infinitely more appealing neighbor, the 12th-century Byzantine Mikri Mitropoli ("Little Mitropolis").

6pm Stop by the Hera Hotel's **Peacock Lounge** for an unbeatable Acropolis view and a big cocktail to ease the pain of all that walking. Catch one of the city's chicest scenes while you're at it. Then head back to the hotel and rest. It's going to be a long night.

9pm Tonight starts at the ancient **Odeon of Herodes Atticus** for a performance of world-class opera, ballet, or classical Greek drama. Its open-air setting is not to be missed.

11:30pm Dinner In Plaka, **Symposium** has long been an insider's favorite, with views of the Acropolis. **Strofi**, a rooftop taverna, is a favorite hangout of Odeon performers. In winter, try to get a reservation at the tiny **Edodi**, where you pick ingredients brought to your table.

2am Wind down the evening with a nightcap at candlelit **Melina**,

once the favorite haunt of Melina Mercouri, Greece's most famous movie star. Or head to **Mnisikleous** for rembetika, and greet the dawn with dancing.

Friday

9am Start the day in style with breakfast amid palms and crystal chandeliers in the Grande Bretagne's marble atrium.

10am Step back into ancient Athens again—or cycle back by renting wheels at **Pame Volta**—to its incarnation under the Romans, at the **Roman Agora**. This marketplace evolved as the city center after the original Agora declined. Duck into the nearby tiny-but-worthy **Museum of Greek Popular Instruments** to hear unique pieces such as the bagpipe-like baglama and a bouzoukia inlaid with mother-of-pearl. Then pop up the street to the **Museum of Greek Folk Art**. While the dimly lit government-run building won't win any design prizes, the displays of filigreed jewelry, tapestries, and fascinating stone and wood carvings make this one of Athens' secret treasures.

1pm Lunch Return the bikes, but if you've fallen for Plaka, lunch on the Plateia Filomousou at **Byzantino**, one of its best-known tavernas. Or, choose from a few venerable institutions: **Thanassis** for Eastern-style souvlaki or **Ideal**, in Omonia, for traditional Greek cuisine. You can also head toward your next stop, the National Museum, and dine along the way on mezedes and ouzo at the local favorite **Athinaikon**.

3pm Devote a few hours to exploring the treasures of the **National Archaeological Museum**. Then ramble along the cobblestoned shopping street of Ermou. Pause to peek inside the exquisite Byzantine church of **Kapnikarea**, which pops up in the middle of all the boutiques.

7pm Start the evening with a drink and a nibble at **To Parko***, a favorite of dealmakers and diplomats from the embassies in the area.

8:30pm Bask in the summer night with the uniquely Greek experience of catching a film under the stars. Check what's showing at **Aegli Village Cool**, or at Thisio's self-titled **Thission** cinema, or at Plaka's **Cine Paris**, on a rooftop with a sublime view of the old city. For something grander, arrange for tickets to the **Megaro Mousikis** (Athens Concert Hall), for a classical concert or ballet.

11:30pm Dinner It doesn't get more traditional than the torchlit garden of **Archeon Gefsis** ("Ancient Flavors"). For a more modern feel, go back just a century to the

barrel-lined walls and rustic garden of the much-loved taverna **Karavitis**. If you're coming from a show at the Megaro, try nearby **Vlassis**, lauded for its classic Greek home cooking.

2am After dinner, if you're feeling mellow, return to Plaka for a nightcap at **Terina**, where tables overlook the fallen pillars of the Ancient Agora. Or head to **Romeo** for one of the best bouzoukia in all of Athens.

 Saturday

10am Ease into the day with a room service breakfast, then devote the morning to a bit of shopping. But first, grab a coffee and wander to the landmark Syntagma Square, which houses Parliament, 15 minutes before the hour to catch the hourly changing of the guards, called evzones. Once these handsome fellows have done their show, duck into nearby **Ikotehnia** for handicrafts, or the 110-year-old **Zolotas Jewelers**, which has helped make a name for Greece in quality jewelry. If you want to try a curious Greek trend, head to **Mastiha Shop**, and check out products with mastiha (mastic), a tree gum. Afterward, stroll in the **National Gardens**, an exotic-plant-filled oasis in the city center. A walk through the gardens leads you to the entrance of the colossal **Temple of Olympian Zeus**, the largest temple on mainland Greece. Or make your way to the newly revamped **Byzantine Museum**, home to a vast and rich collection of illuminated manuscripts, gold, and jewels from the 1,000-year empire.

1pm Lunch Back to Kolonaki for calamari salad at **Maritsa's**, the Greek take on coq au vin at bistro-like **To Kafeneio**, or the neighborhood taverna, **Philippou***, a favorite of the power set.

3pm Hop in a taxi and drive about 15 minutes to **Kessariani** Monastery for a relaxing idle among the ruins. It's a great place to have an impromptu dessert-picnic.

6pm Back in town, another lovely walk through Kolonaki brings you to Athens' greatest Olympic treasure, the **Panathenaic Stadium**, which houses the Olympic flame every four years, and where the first modern Olympics was held in 1896. Return to Syntagma Square through the National Gardens, stopping at **Aegli Cafe** for an Acropolis-view drink.

7pm Treat yourself to a massage at the **Hotel Grande Bretagne Spa** if you're in the mood for a bit of very elegant pampering, or hit the health club to get your blood pumping for a night out. But in summer, head to Philopappou Hill for an open-air folk dance performance from the **Dora Stratou Dance Theatre**.

11pm Dinner For a perfect last-night meal, adjourn to **Daphne's** for lovingly prepared Greek classics. Or reserve a table at the roof garden of **Filistron***, and enjoy the sweeping panorama of the moonlit Acropolis and Agora. Don't leave town without sampling the haute Med-French cuisine at **Spondi**, with its reputation for unique and delicious desserts.

1am In warm weather, work off dinner and work in one last Acropolis view with a moonlit stroll along the **Archaeological Promenade** between Plaka and Thisio, ending up with a nightcap at **Athinaion Politeia**. In winter, plan on staying up till the wee hours with a late-night booking at the classic bouzoukia club **Rex**.

Classic Athens:
The Key Neighborhoods

Kolonaki is all about glamour and money. Here is where you will find the city's most fabulous set, and also dozens of chic cafes, sophisticated and exclusive shops, and even a museum or two.

Makrigianni is a middle-class residential enclave that is being infused with boutiques and a sprinkling of trendy restaurants and bars thanks to the metro and the new Archaeological Promenade.

Plaka is Athens' oldest neighborhood, with charmingly windy pedestrian streets weaving under the shadow of the Acropolis. While tourists flock here, it's also loved by locals.

Syntagma Square is home to Greece's parliament (and the evzone guards, who are chosen in part for their good looks). A bustling and vibrant area near the National Gardens, it has played host to some of the most important events of modern Greek history.

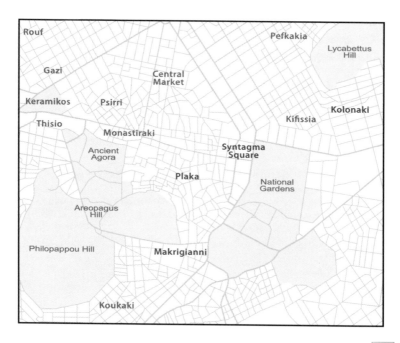

Classic Athens:
The Shopping Blocks

Plaka

We won't tell you it's not touristy, because Plaka can't hide its busloads of Midwesterners. But tucked between T-Shirts-4-Less and Trinket World, there's more than one worthy boutique.

The Bead Shop Ward off bad spirits with handfuls of evil-eye beads, from pinhead-size to a half inch in diameter. Pal. Benizelou 6, 210-322-1004

Center of Hellenic Tradition Quality crafts from metalwork to weaving from genuine Greek artists. (p.70) Entrances at Mitropoleous 59 & Pandrossou 36, 210-321-3023

Greek Women's Institution Offers copies of some of the needlework on display at the Benaki Museum, made by island women. 3 Kolokotroni, 210-325-0524

The Poet Handmade sandals by a nationally known poet. (p.72) Aghias Theklas 2, 210-321-9247

Syntagma

You'll still find the tourist fare so common in Plaka in this bustling nearby area, but with a greater mix of upscale and interesting boutiques offering everything from custom-made clothing to cakes.

Aristokratikon Classic chocolaterie once patronized by Grace Kelly and Jackie Kennedy. Karageorgis Servias 6, 210-322-0546

Christakis Savile Row has its suit makers and Athens has Christakis, which has custom-tailored shirts and more for Greek and global magnates since the days of Onassis. Kriezotou 5, 210-361-3030

Diplous Pelekys Inexpensive, authentic, and original souvenirs, mostly from Crete, that you won't find in the average tourist shop. Voulis 7 & Kolokotroni 3, 210- 322-3783

Ikotehnia Handmade, well, handicrafts. The real stuff. (p.70) Filellinon 14, 210-325-0240

Lalaounis Acclaimed jeweler (with a shop on New York's Madison Ave.) whose designs have graced the figures of Jackie O., among others. (p.70) Panepistimiou 6, 210-362-4354

Mastiha Shop Products made from mastic, a tree gum and a Greek obsession. (p.71) Panepistimiou 6, 210-363-2750

Zolatas Jewelers Old Greek jeweler inspired by ancient designs. (p. 73) Panepistimiou 10, 210-360-1272

Classic Athens:
The Hotels

Divani Palace Acropolis • Makrigianni • Modern (250 rooms)

Best Rooms with a View When Themistocles built the Great Wall at the foot of the Acropolis in the 5th century BC, he hardly could have imagined that 2,000 years later a section of it would be integrated into the design of a seven-story concrete and glass hotel. Located on a narrow street leading up to Dionissiou Areopagitou, part of the Archaeological Promenade, just a five-minute walk from Plaka, the Divani Palace Acropolis is a great find if location is your priority. Renovated in 2003, its rooms have classical furniture and misty pink fabrics. All have a private balcony, most looking onto the Acropolis (make sure to request this view when you book). Downstairs is an indoor pool, while the Socrates Roof Garden restaurant serves candlelit dinners, accompanied by live music and views of the floodlit Acropolis. One note: Guests are an ever-changing mix of tour groups, conference-goers, and individual travelers who value service and location, but don't place a premium on ambience (except for those views!). €€ Parthenonos 19-25, 210-928-0100, divaniacropolis.gr

Electra Palace • Plaka • Timeless (150 rooms)

Who would believe that this smart five-story hotel with a yellow-and-white neo-classical facade, complete with cornice details and wrought-iron balconies, was built in 2003? The spacious marble lobby exudes elegance, and rooms, with dark wood furnishings, wooden floors, and Persian carpets, continue the motif. All rooms have marble baths, and each suite boasts a Jacuzzi and shower. There's a luxury spa, fitness center, and an indoor pool in the basement, and a rooftop pool and restaurant in the shadow of the Acropolis. Ask for a front "superior" room, which boasts Acropolis-view balconies. Electra also has three non-smoking floors. €€ Nikomidou 18, 210-337-0000, electrahotels.gr

Hera Hotel • Makrigianni • Timeless (38 rooms)

Athens hotels tend to fall in two categories: classic or modern. The Hera is nei-ther. Breaking the mold, this recently opened hotel near the Acropolis is designed in '20s Art Nouveau style, from the wrought-iron canopy ushering guests inside, to the dark-wood paneling, and the delicate fabrics and graceful curves of the furniture in the rooms. The effect is something of a gentlemen's club of another era. In winter, the hotel caters to a discerning, largely Greek clientele who appreciate Hera's personal touch. In summer, the crowd gets younger (mostly 30s) and the atmosphere more relaxed. Sixth-floor rooms with verandas reward with Acropolis views, and don't miss the hotel's romantic Peacock Lounge bar-cafe, almost at eye-level with the Acropolis. €€ Falirou 9, 210-923-6682 / 210-923-5618, herahotel.gr

Herodion • Makrigianni • Timeless (90 rooms)

Management at the Herodion claims that no other hotel in Athens has a roof terrace in such close proximity to the Acropolis. From up on high, you could almost throw a coin into the Odeon of Herodes Atticus, the ancient Roman open-air theater where the Hellenic Festival takes place each summer. The hotel entrance lies on a peaceful residential street, a five-minute walk from the new Acropolis metro station. Tastefully refurbished in early 2003, all of the rooms in this five-story 1970s building are decorated in misty green and cream and have gray ensuite marble bathrooms. Ask for a back room with an Acropolis view (the front ones look onto the less-than-exciting street below). The hotel restaurant incorporates 21st-century designer chic: Whitewashed concrete walls are played against a gray marble food counter with an open-plan kitchen behind so diners can watch the cooks at work. € Rovertou Galli 4, 210-923-6832, herodion.gr

Hotel Grande Bretagne • Syntagma Square • Timeless (327 rooms)

Best Hotel Rooms Originally built in 1842 as a private mansion opposite King Otto's royal pile (now the Parliament), this eight-story hunk of a house was converted into a hotel in 1872. Since then, anyone who is anyone visiting Athens (Winston Churchill, Jackie Kennedy, Yasser Arafat, and Jean-Paul Gaultier among them) has had the porter lug their bags into the marble lobby adorned with Persian carpets, neo-Baroque furniture, and potted palms. Reopened after a full makeover in 2003, the GB now boasts an open-air pool and bar-restaurant on the rooftop (where you can watch the sun set behind the Acropolis) and an herb-scented spa, offering treatments like reflexology foot baths and an "Ancient Greek Ritual." Rooms have marble bathrooms and complimentary minibars. While many look out onto Syntagma Square's lively parade of people, asking for a deluxe king with an Acropolis view is our pick. For breakfast head to the hotel's Winter Garden, an atrium space with a stained-glass ceiling, two enormous Oriental vases, and a grand piano. €€€€ Syntagma Square, 210-333-0000, grandebretagne.gr

Classic Athens:
The Restaurants

Archeon Gefsis • Metaxourgio • Greek • Contemporary (G)
Best Classic Dining Ever fantasized about lying down to eat propped up on one elbow, ancient-style? Here's your chance. You'll be waited on hand and foot by nymph-like waitresses in togas, and the table will have a spoon and knife but no fork (just like Dionysus did it). Hedonism works its way into the menu too, with dishes like cuttlefish in ink with pine nuts. And in case you were wondering, Archeon Gefsis means "Ancient Flavors"—the recipes here come straight from the long-forgotten cuisine recorded by Archestratos, a poet who lived around 330 BC. A theme restaurant? Yes, but when in Athens ... *Mon-Sat 1-4pm and 8pm-1am.* €€ ⊠ Kodratou 22, Plateia Karaiskaki, 210-523-9661

Athinaikon • Exarchia • Greek • Meze
Best Ouzeries Lawyers, journalists, and politicos in suits and ties flock to this down-to-earth eatery in the afternoon. Located on a pedestrian street between the busy thoroughfares of Akademias and Panepistimou, the interior matches the clientele, with classic no-nonsense wood furniture and marble-top tables. Try the gigantes (haricot beans in tomato and olive oil), prawn croquettes, and swordfish souvlaki. *Mon-Sat 11:30am-12:30am Closed in Aug.* €€ ⊠ Themistokleous 2, 210-383-8485

Byzantino • Plaka • Greek • Traditional
Serving traditional Greek dishes and excellent fresh fish, with tables outside overlooking Plateia Filomousou, this is one of Plaka's best-known tavernas. Choose from daily specials like cuttlefish with spinach or lamb fricassée or opt for mezedes and barbecued meat from the fixed menu. The interior is simple, with a marble floor and exposed-brick and whitewashed walls, while outdoors old-fashioned tables and chairs are arranged on the paved piazza. Busy, chaotic, and typically Greek. *Daily 9am-1am.* €€ ⊠ Kidathineon 18, 210-322-7368

Daphne's • Plaka • Greek • Modern (G)
Best Classic Dining Hidden in upper Plaka, opposite the Temple of Olympian Zeus, Daphne's is set in a restored 19th-century neoclassical townhouse. The dining room is decorated with warm ochre, rusty red, and muted-green Pompeii-style frescoes, and out back there's a pretty courtyard garden that's heated through winter. A favorite of visiting celebrities, Daphne's serves classic Greek dishes, such as spicy pork in wine and coriander, and rabbit in sweet wine sauce, to a very cosmopolitan set that is upscale but casual. *Daily 7:30pm-1am.* €€€ ⊠ Lisikratous 4, 210-322-7971

Eden • Plaka • Vegetarian
With all that skewered meat roasting over charcoal, Athens is a vegetarian's horror show. But salvation is at hand at Eden, which was instantly successful when it opened as Greece's first vegetarian restaurant in 1982. A far cry from your usual hippie haunt, this is a cheerful place where everything on the menu is organic, from the lentils to the carrot cake. The wines are organic too. *Wed-Mon noon-midnight.* €€ ⊠ Lissiou 12, 210-324-8858, edenvegetarian.gr

Edodi • Koukaki • Contemporary (G)

Best Romantic Dining This unusual but excellent restaurant is set in a mansion just a ten-minute walk south of Plaka, and is still largely undiscovered by tourists but loved by locals, especially those with a sense of romance. The dining room walls are hung with large puppets, there are only eight tables, and the food and service are outstanding. There's an emphasis on seasonal ingredients (brought to your table raw so you can choose), which are used to create sublime dishes like pheasant stuffed with figs or lamb stuffed with fresh herbs and raki. Reserve well in advance. *Mon-Sat 8pm-1am. Closed two weeks in Aug.* €€ ▬ Veikou 80, 210-921-3013

Filistron • Thisio • Meze

Best Tables with a View With large windows overlooking the Archaeological Promenade and a roof terrace with magical Acropolis views, this place is a true find. The menu offers a variety of mezedes—including krithokouloura (homemade rye bread with cherry tomatoes, feta cheese, and olives). The interior is warm and cozy, but for a truly memorable dinner, reserve a rooftop table and enjoy Athens' ancient sites by moonlight. This is the kind of place where sophisticated locals take a table for a few hours, with friends coming and going as often as the drinks. *Daily noon-1am; Roof garden: 6pm-2:30am. Closed one week in Aug.* €€ TB ▬ Apostolou Pavlou 23, 210-346-7554

Ideal • Omonia • Modern

Ideal may look like somewhere your grandma would go for tea, but this respected institution serves up some of the city's best classic Greek cuisine to a crowd that is older, but still stylish. It opened its doors in 1922, but a 1990 remodel created a neo-Art Deco setting, complete with stained-glass ceilings, tiled floors, and dainty vases on the tables. Order a steamy portion of Smyrni-style meatballs with ouzo and cumin, finish off with quince and whipped cream, and admit you can't always judge by appearances. *Mon-Fri noon-midnight.* €€ ▬ Panepistimiou 46, 210-330-3000

Karavitis • Pangrati • Taverna

Best Tavernas Near the Panathenaic Stadium, this terracotta-roofed taverna has been busy since 1926. The dining room is basic—stone floor, wooden-beamed ceilings, and an entire wall stacked with wine barrels. Through summer there are tables outside in a walled garden across the road where you can eat in the shade of a towering palm tree. The menu focuses on grilled meats. Try the gigantes fournou (oven-baked beans), and bekri meze (beef cooked in red wine) and round off with yiaourti meli (yogurt with honey). *Daily 8pm-2am. Closed in Aug.* € ▬ Arktinou 33 & Pavsaniou 4, 210-721-5155

Maritsa's • Kolonaki • Modern

Take a table at Maritsa's, on the steps leading through Kolonaki, and you'll have a view of the Parthenon rising up above the concrete jungle that is Athens. Leaf through the menu's creative Greek dishes and choose a bottle of chilled white wine. If it's winter, you'll be in the dining room, decorated in orangey-pink and cream, with large, modern canvases on the walls and a selection of fine cigars at the bar. This is a favorite of yuppie broker types from the nearby stock market. *Mon-Sat noon-12:30am.* €€ ▬ Voukourestiou 47, 210-363-0132

O Kostas • Plaka • Souvlaki
Best Souvlaki Despite its location in touristy Plaka, O Kostas is an institution among locals. Founded in 1950 by Kostas, who passed away late 2003, this tiny joint is now run by his grandson. O Kostas exclusively serves kalamaki, pork slices stuffed in pita and topped with tomato, onion, and tzatziki. With space for two on stools outside, much of the experience is rubbing elbows with locals while being engulfed by the smells of grilled meat. *Mon-Fri 8am-3pm.* € ▤ Adrianou 116, 210-322-8502

O Platanos • Plaka • Souvlaki
Best Tavernas Serving home cooking since 1932, this is one of Plaka's oldest tavernas. The interior is simple, with wooden furniture and green-and-white tablecloths, but the big draw is the outdoor seating, on a terrace in the shade of a giant plane tree (from which the establishment takes its name). While the food is solidly good, the lure here is that everybody knows this place and locals love it as much as tourists. Order the lamb with okra, just like Mom makes, with a side of roast potatoes and a carafe of barrel retsina. *Mon-Sat 12:30-4:30pm and 7:30pm-midnight.* €€ ▤ Diogenous 4, 210-322-0666

Orea Ellas • Plaka • Meze
Best Ouzeries Hidden away in an arcade on the mezzanine level of the Center of Hellenic Tradition, this is a gem of an eatery for a light lunch. The atmosphere is timeless and relaxed, and you'll feel comfortable even if you come here alone: It's a perfect place to write those postcards you've been carrying around for days, and sit mulling over the meaning of life. Choose from a selection of mezedes such as cheese filled filo-pastries, octopus salad, and grilled peppers. Round things off with a short, sweet, syrupy Greek coffee, and check out the stalls selling traditional arts and crafts. *Daily 9am-6pm. Closed two weeks in mid-Aug.* € ▤ Mitropoleos 59 & Pandrossou 36, 210-321-3842

Philippou* • Kolonaki • Traditional
Best Tavernas One of Athens' most authentic neighborhood tavernas, Philippou, which has been around since 1923, caters more to locals, politicians, and deal-makers than the tourist crowd. Set in a quiet corner of Kolonaki, Philippou serves traditional taverna fare such as briam (roasted vegetables), and moussaka, as well as local wine. Though the menu is typical, the quality and level of service are above and beyond. In summer tables spill out into the sidewalk. *Mon-Fri 1-5pm and 8pm-midnight, Sat 1-5pm. Closed two weeks in Aug.* € ▤ Xenokratous 19, 210-721-6390

Rozalia • Exarchia • Traditional
Local students, left-wing professors, and tourists in-the-know frequent this laid-back taverna, located on a tree-lined pedestrian street in Exarchia. Outdoor tables are set in a walled garden (covered with a temporary roof and heated in winter), while the dining room and kitchen are across the street. A waiter will bring a tray laden with colorful cold appetizers. Main dishes include kebabs of pork filet, bacon, and green peppers, and fried cod with skorthalia (garlic sauce). *Daily noon-4pm and 8pm-1am.* € ▤ Valtetsiou 58, 210-330-2933

Spondi • Pangrati • International (G)
Awarded a Michelin star in 2003, Spondi has a French chef renowned for refined fusion cuisine. Watch for fillet of sea bass in fennel, olive oil, and

vanilla sauce, and partridge with chestnuts. Finish off with Italian grappa and cigars in the three small dining rooms decorated with exposed brickwork and large modern canvases that are popular with Athenians looking to impress or digest the best. In summer, the prime tables are in a bougainvillaea-covered courtyard. *Daily 8pm-12:30am.* €€€ ▤ Pirronos 5, 210-756-4021, spondi.gr

Strofi • Makrigianni • Traditional
Ideal post-theater, thanks to its location just a few blocks from the Odeon of Herodes Atticus. Many actors, musicians, and ballerinas think so too, as evidenced from the autographed photos on the walls. It might not look like much from the outside, but the Acropolis views from the roof terrace and the satisfying taverna menu, including fava (puree of yellow split beans), taramosalata (smoked roe pâté), and rabbit stifado (stew) make Stofi stand out. *Daily 7:30pm-1am.* €€ ▤ Rovertou Galli 25, 210-921-4130

Symposium • Makrigianni • Modern (G)
A truly romantic choice, with tables in a courtyard that's converted into a glass conservatory in winter. Most of the produce is organic and from the owners' farms in Epirus and Zagori (the son of shepherds, the chef is known to forage his own mushrooms), right down to the stone-milled flour used in the bread and the freshly pressed olive oil. This is not a spot for scenesters, but rather for sophisticates looking for forward-thinking modern Greek fare. Look for snails in Roquefort sauce and wild boar with leeks. The wine list matches the quality of the food. *Mon-Sat 8pm-1am.* €€€ ▤ Erechtheiou 46, 210-922-5321

Thanassis • Monastiraki • Souvlaki
Best Souvlaki This mythical souvlaki joint has seating both inside and out, with throw-away tablecloths and rickety wooden chairs arranged along the sidewalk, just a stone's throw from Monastiraki metro station. Popular with locals—and hectic on weekends—it serves up the complete repertoire of charcoal-grilled kebabs along with salad, pita bread, and chips. *Daily 9am-2:30am.* € ▤ Mitropoleos 69, 210-324-4705

To Kafeneio • Kolonaki • Meze
The ambience is French bistro, the clientele pure Kolonaki plus a smattering of embassy staff. Dark wood-paneled walls and crisp white table linens set the scene in this refined but relaxed lunchtime favorite. Look for Greek classics like stuffed zucchini, which you might follow with braised pork and wild celery in lemon sauce. There are tables on the sidewalk throughout summer and at night, candles add a romantic touch. *Mon-Sat noon-midnight. Closed in Aug.* €€ ▤ Loukianou 26, 210-722-9056

To Parko* • Ambelokipi • International
Located next to Megaro Mousikis concert hall, this legendary, low-key bar/cafe/restaurant is ideal for a pre- or post-theater meal or cocktail. The tree-filled, casually elegant restaurant offers healthy meals, attracting Athens' diplomats and performers from nearby theaters. It's a very hip crowd in search of anything from coffee to dinner. The adjoining outdoor cafe-bar has sofas, music loud enough to enjoy but not too loud for conversation, and an unstuffy bar patronized by a crowd in their late 20s and 30s. *Daily noon-1:30am.* €€ Ⓕ▤ Eleftherias Park, 210-722-3784, toparko.gr

Tou Psarra • Plaka • Traditional

Best Romantic Dining Touting waiters trying to lure customers from the sidewalk can be a nuisance, but for once succumb to their persistent advances and enter the world of Tou Psarra. You'll be in good company—Brigitte Bardot and Laurence Olivier have eaten here, too. The place has been on the go since 1898, with basic wooden tables and chairs arranged on mulberry-shaded, whitewashed steps leading up to the Acropolis. Bouzoukia music fills the air as staff dashes back and forth with plates of olive-oil-soaked appetizers and charcoal-grilled fish, and, of course, bottles of local wine. *Daily noon-2am.* €€ ▣ Erechtheos 16 & Erotokritou 12, 210-321-8733, psaras-taverna.gr

Vlassis • Ambelokipi • Traditional

Best Classic Dining Eating at Vlassis is like going to an old friend's house, which explains why so many local artists and politicians have been coming back since the 1980s. From appearances, it's nothing special—a two-story townhouse packed with wooden furniture and white linens, tucked on a small side street. But good food and good service keep it a favorite. Start with a tray of cold appetizers, and for the main try the pasticada, a Corfu dish of beef cooked in wine and prunes. Finish with Greek coffee and a glass of Metaxa. *Mon-Sat 1-5pm and 9pm-1am, Sun 1-5pm. Closed end of July and all of Aug.* €€ ▣ Paster 8, Plateia Mavili, 210-646-3060

CLASSIC

Classic Athens:
The Nightlife

Aegli Cafe • Syntagma • Bar/Lounge
Green umbrellas and orange trees in terracotta pots frame this open-air terrace, with a view of Mt. Lycabettus to the north and of the Acropolis rising above Plaka to the west, and a crowd that ranges from 20-something clubbers to wedding parties. There's also a porticoed area with pleasant outdoor seating, which leads into the adjacent Aegli Restaurant *(see Hip & Cool Restaurants, p.84)*. Enjoy a drink on the edge of the National Gardens. *Daily 9am-2am.* F⎯ Zappeion, in the National Gardens, 210-336-9363, aeglizappiou.gr/BistroCafe.html

Aegli Village Cool • Syntagma • Cinema
Best Summer Cinemas Set in the scented green gardens of the Zappeion, this open-air summer cinema offers respite from concrete and traffic, despite being smack in the city center. Most of the films are U.S. productions (with Greek subtitles), but be sure to arrive early to get a ticket. There's a small bar within the cinema complex, as well as the neighboring Aegli Cafe (see above), which is run by the same management. *8pm-1am.* C B ⎯ Zappeion, in the National Gardens, 210-336-9327, aeglizappiou.gr/Cinema.html

Athinaion Politeia • Thisio • Bar/Lounge/Nightclub
This remodeled old grocery has grown to cover four levels. The ground floor houses a bar with frescoed walls and large windows hung with red silk curtains, the mezzanine has plasma TVs and board games, the top floor is a restaurant, and the basement has a DJ and space for private functions. In front, on the Archaeological Promenade, chairs are arranged under large umbrellas, with a great view of the Acropolis rising up behind the Ancient Agora. *8am-2am.* F ≡ Akamantos 1 & Ag Pavlou, 210-341-3795, athinaionpoliteia.gr

Cine Paris • Plaka • Cinema
One of Athens' most popular cinemas is in a neoclassical building on the edge of Plateia Filomouosu. In winter, films are shown in the old-fashioned hall, followed by late-night live Greek music (under the name of Zygos on weekends, see p.67). In summer, the scene moves outdoors, and a screen is set up on the roof terrace. *9pm-1am.* C⎯ Kidathineon 22, 210-322-2071

Dora Stratou Dance Theatre • Thisio • Dance
Best Shows Under the Stars Young dancers from all over the country compete each year to join this troupe. Founded in 1953, it aims to preserve and celebrate Greece's vast variety of regional dances, from the rizitiko of Crete and the zeibekiko of Anatolia to the syrto (circle dance) of the mainland. Each evening (May-Sept.), women clad in beautiful gold-embroidered costumes with full skirts and flowing veils dance with their partners to the strains of the lyra (three-stringed fiddle), the gaida (bagpipe), and the klarino (clarinet), at an open-air theater on Philopappou Hill, opposite the Acropolis. Tickets available from the box office before the show or by calling 210-324-4395. C Arakinthou & Voutie, 210-921-4650, grdance.org

Kidathineon • Plaka • Bar/Cafe

Best Cafes Clients include mustachioed history professors, sunburned Dutch tourists with cameras, and the occasional Russian mafioso, complete with mobile phone and Muscovite blonde in tow. The setting is an old-fashioned glass-and-marble-front cafe, with outdoor tables on a leafy flagstone-paved piazza in the heart of Plaka. Come here for morning coffee, a gin-and-tonic aperitif, a glass of red wine and mezedes, an after-dinner whiskey, or an afternoon ice-cream. *Daily 8am-1am.* F▤ Farmaki 1 at Plateia Filomousou, 210-323-4281

Megaro Mousikis (Athens Concert Hall) • Ambelokipi • Concerts/Opera

Best Live Music Venues Opened in 1991, this modern venue hosts classical music, ballet, and opera. You'll hear Greek musicians like the Athens State Orchestra as well as visiting foreign artists like the London Philharmonic Orchestra. The main auditorium seats 2,000. Tickets are available from the concert hall box office, and at Omirou 8 in Kolonaki in the city center. *Most performances begin at 8:30pm; check local listings. No concerts June-Sept.* C▤ Vassilissis Sofias, 210-728-2333, megaron.gr

Melina • Plaka • Bar

Best Candlelit Bars Named after 1960s actress Melina Mercouri (Greece's answer to Brigitte Bardot), the interior of this cozy bar is done up with marble-topped tables, candles, mirrors, and slightly bizarre Baroque-style gilt cherubs. You'll find it in a yellow neoclassical building with blue trim, clad with ivy and vines. It also has a wooden-platformed terrace and several tables outside throughout summer. *Daily 10am-2am.* ▭ Lissiou 22 & Aerides, 210-324-6501

Mnisikleous • Plaka • Rembetika

Best Rembetika Clubs A cleaned-up version of the dark, smoke-filled rembetika dens that started out in Piraeus in the 1920s, where Greek refugees from Anatolia related their sorrows through this captivating and decidedly Eastern form of music. Although it's located in touristy Plaka, Mnisikleous is still popular with Greeks, who group around cramped tables to eat and drink, eventually succumbing to the intoxicating strains of the bouzoukia and dancing in front of the stage. In summer, the performance moves to a roof terrace with the floodlit Acropolis forming the backdrop. Waitresses are armed with plates of carnations, should you wish to throw flowers. Reserve a table in advance. *Thu-Sun 10pm-6am.* C F▤ Mnisikleous & Lyceiou, 210-322-5558, mnisikleous.gr

Odeon of Herodes Atticus • Plaka • Theater/Concerts/Dance

Best Shows Under the Stars This 5,000-seat ancient Roman amphitheater was built in AD 160 by Herodes Atticus in honor of his wife. In summer, the Hellenic Festival happens here, making the most of the first-rate acoustics to host music, dance, and theater. Recent performers include Jethro Tull, French mime artist Marcel Marceau, and the National Dance Company of Ireland. Tickets available from the Hellenic Festival box office, Panepistimiou 39, 210-928-2900. *May-Oct. 9pm-midnight.* C Dionyssiou Areopagitou, 210-323-2771, hellenicfestival.gr

Peacock Lounge • Makrigianni • Bar/Restaurant

Best Candlelit Bars Location, location, location. That's the motto at least for Peacock Lounge, perched in perfect position for direct views of the Acropolis. Night lights from the Acropolis itself add ambience, along with subtle candlelight, making this one of the most amorous spots in Athens for an oversize cocktail or quiet dinner. Though most of the people inside are guests of the Hera Hotel, the grand locale and unpretentious setting make Peacock Lounge appealing for anyone in search of romance. *Tue-Sat 5:30pm-1:30am.* F⊟ Hera Hotel, Falirou 9, 210-923-6682 / 210-923-5618, herahotel.gr

Rex • Omonia • Bouzoukia

Best Bouzoukia in Winter Smack-dab in the center of Athens, Rex is one of the city's first nightclubs. What started out as a theater is now a full-fledged club, with clear stage views and great sound. A tad smaller than its massive counter-parts along Iera Odos or on the coast, this posh spot draws upper-middle-class 40-somethings and platinum blond babes of all ages. Hosting everything from pop icons to troubadours, Rex is all about showcasing your wares. Cash to the man in charge will always get you a better vantage point. *Oct.-May Thu-Sun from 10:30pm.* C≡ Panepistimiou 48, 210-381-4592

Romeo • Glyfada • Bouzoukia

Best Bouzoukia in Winter One of the city's hottest clubs, Romeo may not host the biggest names, but it has a talent for picking the best of the up-and-coming crop of singers. A trendsetter, it was the first to tune in to the upbeat pop/Asian twist in Greek music that attracts the hipper crowds in the small hours and keeps them on their toes until daybreak. Romeo is all about adapting to the changing styles and mixing show and dance in equal doses, and treating its patrons to entertainment on a more personal level. *Oct-May Wed-Sun from 10pm.* C≡ Winter location changes yearly. Check local listings for current location. (Summer location: Ellinikou 1, Glyfada, 210-894-5345, p. 136)

Terina • Plaka • Bar/Cafe

This cafe-restaurant, inspired by French bistros, has Art Deco furniture, comfy sofas, modern stained-glass features, and a soundtrack of ethnic, soul, and disco. The main draw is the lovely summer terrace, set on Plateia Palaias Agoras, a square overlooking the Ancient Agora, which makes it perfect for peo-ple-watching. Stop for a late-night drink, or for a morning coffee, when shop-keepers at the nearby stores will be hanging out traditional kilim rugs with geo-metric designs. *Daily 8am-2am.* F≡ Kapnikareas 35, 210-321-5015, terina.gr

Thission • Thisio • Cinema

Best Summer Cinemas When the going gets hot, Athenians take to the outdoors. Summer cinemas are a true Greek experience and there is no better place to soak up that bit of culture than at Thission, which has been a part of Athens' summer spectacle since 1926. Though a number of the films are imports and screened in their own language, with Greek subtitles, Thission's location along the pedestrian walkway linking the city's archaeological sites lends this place its historic appeal. Films are screened rain or shine, with the use of a roofed sec-tion for those wet nights. *May-Sept. 8:30pm-2am.* C B ⊟ Apostolou Pavlou 7, Archaeological Promenade, 210-342-0864 / 210-347-0980

To Tristato • Plaka • Bar/Cafe

Located on a side street behind Plateia Filomousou, this homey cafe features salmon-pink walls, marble-topped tables, and dark wooden shelves lined with china teapots. It's one of the few places that serves traditional Greek herbal teas such as faskomilo (sage) and menta (mint). To boost your energy, opt for a sweet treat—apple pie, cheesecake, or panna cotta with caramel and chocolate sauce, or try the syrupy homemade rose-petal liquor. *Daily 9am-1am. Closed in Aug.* F≡ Diadalou 34 & Aggelou Geronda, 210-324-4472

Zygos • Plaka • Live Music

Through winter, the old-fashioned hall of Cine Paris hosts late-night live Greek music under the name of Zygos, where national singer-songwriter heroes such as George Dalaras perform to a select audience of serious music lovers. There's a bar upstairs where you can refuel to keep the mood just right well into the early hours. *Mid-Oct.-Easter Fri-Sat from 10pm (with some extended shows Thu-Sun).* C≡ Kidathineon 22, 210-324-1610

CLASSIC

Classic Athens:
The Attractions

Acropolis • Plaka • Archaeological Site
Best Archaeological Sites The big "must do" of any visit to Athens, the Acropolis hill is a rocky mass rising above the modern apartment blocks that make up the city center. Each year, three million visitors pass through its monumental gateway, the Propylaea, supported by soaring Doric and Ionic columns. To the left of the Propylaea stands the Temple of Athena Nike, while the largest and most impressive building is the Parthenon, on the highest point of the site. Built from marble and supported by a multitude of Doric columns, it was intended as a sanctuary and temple for Athena and housed a giant gold-and-ivory statue of her. Originally the building would have been red, blue, and gold, proving that kitsch is not necessarily a contemporary phenomenon. In the 5th century, the Parthenon was used as a church. Under the Ottomans, it was converted into a mosque and used for some time to store gunpowder. It was bombarded by the Venetians in 1687 and stripped of its most valuable sculptures by the still-controversial Lord Elgin (a former British ambassador) in 1799. Close by, the Erechtheion Temple was built on the site of a mythical battle between Athena and Poseidon. The south side features six caryatids (columns carved to represent maidens)—five of the originals are in the Acropolis Museum and one in the British Museum (looted by Elgin), so what you see here are copies. *June-Aug. 8am-7pm (rest of the year 8am-5pm, but call to confirm as hours change seasonally).* € (Ticket covers a number of other archaeological sites, valid seven days). 210-321-0219 culture.gr

Acropolis Museum • Plaka • Museum
Many of the ancient statues and carved stones (including five of the original six caryatids) from the Acropolis can be found here, in the southeast corner of the Acropolis complex. The big story continues to be the much-hoped-for return of the controversial Parthenon Marbles (a.k.a. "Elgin Marbles," a collection of statues and carvings), seized by Lord Elgin in the late 18th century and thereafter kept by the British Museum, whose excuse for not returning them is that Athens could not display them adequately or safely. Which is why Greece is building a New Acropolis Museum—a $100-million all-glass structure designed by architect Bernard Tschumi, constructed over an early-Byzantine Christian settlement that will be visible through the glass floor, while the Parthenon will be on view through a glass ceiling. No one is sure exactly when it will be completed—latest rumors hint at 2007. *Summer: 8am-5:30pm; Winter: Mon-Fri 8am-4:30pm, Sat-Sun 8am-2:30pm, but call to confirm, as hours change seasonally.* € On the Acropolis, 210-323-6665, culture.gr

Agora Museum • Thisio • Museum
For Europeans who think that America invented the shopping mall, take them to the 2nd-century BC Stoa Attalou (Stoa of Attalos) and point out that it was an ancient Greek idea. This two-story marble and limestone structure with a porticoed arcade once contained 42 separate shops selling everything from grapes, roses, and turnips to water clocks. It was restored by the American School of Archaeology during the 1950s, which brought it back to its former glory. Today

it houses the Museo tis Agoras (Agora Museum), displaying items relating to Athenian democracy, plus pottery shards and grave offerings. *Daily 8am-5:45pm, but call to confirm as hours change seasonally.* Admission covered by Acropolis ticket. Adrianou 24, Ancient Agora, 210-321-0185, culture.gr

Anafiotika • Plaka • Neighborhood

A village within a city, Anafiotika is made up of two-story whitewashed cubic cottages with blue wooden window frames and balconies, overgrown with vines and bougainvillaea, reminiscent of the settlements found on the Cycladic islands. Quirky, but there's a simple explanation. It was built by workers from Anafi (one of the Cycladic islands), who were brought to Athens in the mid-19th century to construct King Otto's Royal Palace, following Greece's victorious struggle for independence and the proclamation of Athens as the new capital. Take some time to wander its narrow winding streets, still inhabited by descendants of those early migrant workers. Northeast slope of Acropolis

Ancient Agora • Thisio • Archaeological Site

Best Archaeological Sites If modern Athens focuses on traffic-filled Syntagma Square, ancient Athens centered on this chaotic but photogenic tangle of monuments and ruins dating from the 6th century BC to the 5th century AD. In its heyday, the agora (market) was the place to shop, govern, gossip, and legislate— or simply idle away the hours. Home to law courts, temples, and public offices, anyone who was anyone (including Socrates) could be spotted here. This is where politicians and philosophers gave birth to democracy—the Assembly originally met at the Agora. The site is dominated by Greece's best-preserved ancient temple, the 5th century BC Temple of Haephaistos, a hefty structure with 34 Doric columns, dedicated to its namesake god of fire and metalwork. It was converted into a Christian church during the Byzantine period. *Daily 8am-5:45pm, but call to confirm as hours change seasonally.* Admission covered by Acropolis ticket. Adrianou 24, Ancient Agora, 210-321-0185, culture.gr

Archaeological Promenade • Thisio • Walk

The "Unification of Archaeological Sites," when completed, will be a 4km (2.5mi) traffic-free promenade running from Keramikos Cemetery to the Panathenaic Stadium, linking all the major ancient sites of central Athens. The first phase, a wide cobbled walkway planted with trees and lined with pieces of contemporary sculpture and street lamps, skirts the foot of the Acropolis and passes the Ancient Agora. It's already a favorite promenade of Athenians and tourists alike, not least for the many open-air cafes that line the Apostlou Pavlou stretch, offering Acropolis views. Dionissiou Areopagitou & Apostlou Pavlou

Byzantine Museum • Kolonaki • Museum

Best Byzantine Sights Housed in a late 19th-century villa, this museum traces Byzantine art from the 4th century AD onward, making it one of the top Byzantine showcases in the world. Reopened for the 2004 Olympics following a costly revamp, it is now bigger and better than ever. Previously only a fraction of the 15,000 items were on show, but storerooms have been emptied out and a glittering array of invaluable golden icons, intricately crafted jewelry, gold and silver crosses and candlesticks, mosaics, and ceramics have been spruced and polished and are ready to dazzle. *Tue-Sun 8:30am-3pm.* € Vassilissis Sofias 22, 210-723-1570 / 210-723-2178, culture.gr

Center of Hellenic Tradition • Plaka • Shop

It's easy to miss the unassuming entrance to this rambling three-story historic building, which would be a pity. This place is an island of genuine, high-quality work by Greek artists, in the wasteland of Plaka's plaster Aphrodites and tacky T-shirts. On the second floor are workshops selling handmade ceramics, folk paintings, and metalwork from artists all over Greece. There's also the Orea Ellas ouzerie, and an art gallery with Acropolis views, featuring works from contemporary Greek artists. *May-Sept. 9am-8pm, Oct.-Apr. 9am-6pm.* Entrances at Mitropoleous 59 & Pandrossou 36, 210-321-3023

Hotel Grande Bretagne Spa • Syntagma • Spa

Everything about the Grande Bretagne Spa—the hand-carved sconces, the glittering mosaics that pave its indoor pools, the amethyst grotto, and the customized treatments—breathes luxury. Come for the signature hot stone massage, detoxifying linen wrap, exfoliation, and fountain plunge to feel more pampered than you ever could have imagined. If you want, double your pleasure by booking treatments in the couples suite. Services are by appointment only. *Daily 9am-9pm.* €€€ Syntagma Square, 210-333-0000, grandebretagne.gr

Ikotehnia • Syntagma • Shop

Ikotehnia supports traditional artisans of Greece rather than hawking cheap tourist-targeted knockoffs. It's full of rare handicrafts from rural areas, with an emphasis on weaving. The majority of the items here, from tapestries to rugs and pillows, are made on a loom. Prices depend on quality, which is measured in knots per square meter. *Mon, Tue, Thu, Fri, Sun 8am-8pm, Wed, Sat 8am-2:30pm.* Filellinon 14, 210-325-0240

Kapnikarea • Monastiraki • Church

Best Byzantine Sights In the middle of a busy pedestrian shopping street sits this tiny 12th-century Byzantine church. Ancient carved stones are incorporated into the brickwork, while the central dome is supported by four Roman columns, creating an early Christian architectural gem. A temple to a goddess once stood here, but it's the Virgin Mary who claims the sacred spot's dedication today. *Mon, Wed, Sat 8am-2pm, Tue, Thu, Fri, 8am-12:30pm and 5-7:30pm, Sun 8:30am-11:30pm.* Intersection of Ermou & Kapnikareas, culture.gr

Kessariani • Kessariani • Monastery

Best Byzantine Sights This lovely old monastery was home to an order of monks who kept bees and grew grapes for wine. Today it's only ruins, but makes an excellent spot for a picnic with its forest setting and amazing views over Athens. A chapel for St. Anthony was added in the 16th century, a bell tower in the 19th century, and a church is still housed on the site today—so dress appropriately. *Tue-Sat. 8:30am-3:30pm.* 6 miles east of city center, 210-723-6619

Lalaounis • Syntagma • Shop

You may have been to the swanky branch store on Madison Avenue, but don't miss the chance to see the full collection of this celebrated gold jewelry that has graced the necks of luminaries from Jackie O. and Elizabeth Taylor to Melina Mercouri. *Mon, Wed 9am-3pm, Tue, Thu, Fri 9am-8:45pm, Sat 9am-3:30pm.* Panepistimiou 6, 210-362-4354, lalaounis.com

Mastiha Shop • Syntagma • Shop

Mastiha Shop uses mastic, a tree gum, to flavor its array of products. Shelves spill over with mastic-flavored olives, pastas, and even sweets like chocolate-covered halva. Mastic-based creams, toothpastes, and other body treatments fill one section of the small space, while other items just carry the Mastiha Shop label without the mastic, such as jars of preserves, pears cooked in red wine, anchovies floating in olive oil, and bags of dried fruits. For a sampling, try one of the mastic-flavored chewing gums at the counter. *Mon-Fri 9am-9pm, Sat 9am-5pm.* Panepistimiou 6, 210-363-2750, mastihashop.com

Megali Mitropoli (Great Mitropolis) • Plaka • Church

Religion plays a big role in the lives of most Greeks, many of whom discreetly cross themselves when passing a church. On Plateia Mitropolis stands the Great Mitropolis, Athens' cathedral, a little-loved gargantuan 19th-century structure. But next to it, the tiny 12th-century Little Mitropolis is infinitely more appealing—the outer walls of this Byzantine jewel are carved with reliefs of animals and allegorical figures. *Daily 7am-1pm.* Plateia Mitropoleos, 210-322-1308

Museum of Greek Folk Art • Plaka • Museum

Covering five floors, this vast collection of national folk art dates from 1650 to the present. A strong Middle Eastern influence prevails, from the costumes embroidered with gold and silver to the filigreed jewelry and hand-painted ceramics. The highlight is the Theofilis Room, reconstructed from a house on the island of Lesvos, frescoed by Theofilis Hadjimichael (1868-1934), a self-taught primitive painter inspired by Greek mythology and scenes from early 20th-century life. *Tue-Sun 10am-2pm.* € Kidathineon 17, 210-321-3018, culture.gr

Museum of Greek Popular Instruments • Plaka • Museum

There's more to the Greek's national music than sweet lyrics and easy tunes. Located near the Roman Agora, instruments here range from gypsy flutes to shepherds' goatskin bagpipes, with many samples beautifully inlaid with silver, ivory, and tortoiseshell. Headsets are provided to hear the instruments being played. A small museum shop sells CDs, and occasional open-air performances are staged in the courtyard in summer. *Tue, Thu-Sun 10am-2pm, Wed noon-6pm.* Admission free. Diogenous 1-3, 210-325-0198, culture.gr

National Archaeological Museum • Exarchia • Museum

Best Museums This world-famous museum recently underwent a massive renovation program, undertaken, of course, to coincide with the 2004 Olympics. It's overpoweringly vast; you can't possibly see everything in one go. However, once within the doors, point yourself toward the colorful 17th-century BC Thira Frescoes from Akrotiri on the island of Santorini, which were buried below lava following a catastrophic volcanic explosion, and the Mycenaen collection, featuring hordes of finely crafted gold work dating from the 16th century BC, notably the much-photographed death mask of a bearded king thought to be Agamemnon. *Oct.-May Tue-Sun 8:30am-3pm, Mon 10:30am-5pm; June-Sept. Tue-Sun 8:30am-5pm, Mon 11:30am-7pm, but call to confirm as hours change seasonally.* € Patission 44, 210-821-7717, culture.gr

National Gardens • Syntagma • Park
A green refuge for young lovers, mothers with baby buggies, and old men with political grudges, this jungle of exotic trees and tropical shrubs was laid out during the second half of the 1800s as the royal garden of King Otto and Queen Amelia. At the east end stands the classic Zappeion Hall, built in 1888 and used for major political and cultural events. A series of winding paths lead to a small zoo and a duck pond with lilies—strutting peacocks and stray cats galore. It has been open to the public since 1923, when the wooden benches and the first cafe were added. *Daily dawn to dusk.* East of Vassilissis Amalias

Pame Volta • Plaka • Bike Rental
Just a few years ago, it would have been cruel and inhumane to suggest touring central Athens by bike. But in mid-2004, many of Athens' historical areas become pedestrianized, and one enterprising business renting bicycles is taking advantage of this new, relatively car-free center. Pame Volta (Let's Go For a Ride) rents bikes by the hour or day. It's a unique way to see the best of Athens and a new way to see an old city, even for those who have been before. *Wed-Fri 9am-5pm, Sat-Sun 11am-7pm, Mon-Tue closed.* € Hajihristou 20, Acropolis, 210-922-1578, pamevolta.gr

Panathenaic Stadium • Pangrati • Historical Site
Originally built in 330 BC for the Panathenaic Games, this elegant three-sided stadium was abandoned after the fall of the Romans. Over the centuries, blocks of marble were carried off for use on other buildings, leaving no more than a pile of ruins. Rumor has it that local witches staged secret midnight rituals here. The stadium was restored in white marble (hence its nickname, Kallimarmaro, meaning "beautiful marble") by Ernst Ziller for the first modern Olympics in 1896. Each October, exhausted athletes come staggering in as they cross the finish line of the Athens' marathon, and at the 2004 Olympics, it was chosen to host archery and the marathon finish. It seats 70,000. *Daily dawn to dusk.* Vasileos Konstantinou, 210-752-6386, culture.gr

Parliament • Syntagma • Historical Site
The highlight here is the changing of the evzones guard at the Tomb of the Unknown Soldier in front of the Parliament building (erected in 1838 as King Otto's royal palace). Some women say these fancy fellows are perfection personified: Picked from among Greece's tallest and best-looking recruits, they are trained to remain silent for hours. The guards are dressed in foustanella (kilts) with 400 pleats (one for each year of Ottoman occupation), a red beret, and red shoes with black pom-poms. If you can tear your eyes away from them, check out the Tomb of the Unknown Soldier, which celebrates all the freedom fighters who gave their lives for Greece and which features a bas-relief sculpture of a dying soldier, carved in 1930 but inspired by Ancient Greek sculpture. If you can't get those evzones out of your mind, don't miss the full changing of the guard on Sundays at 11am. Syntagma Square, culture.gr

The Poet • Plaka • Shop
White-haired Stavros Melissinos really is a respected and published poet, but as you'll see from the many magazine clippings peeling in the sun in front of his workshop, he also believes he should work among people every day—in this case, custom-fitting them for handmade leather sandals in dozens of different

designs—to maintain his salt-of-the-earth touch. After more than 50 years, he seems to have morphed into a parody of himself, posing for photos and hawking his books to travel-guide-toting tourists, but no one (including past customers Jackie O. and the Beatles) would deny that his sandals are the best in Athens. *Mon-Sat 10am-6pm, Sun 10am-4pm.* Aghias Theklas 2, 210-321-9247

Roman Agora • Plaka • Archaeological Site
Best Archaeological Sites Dating from the 1st century AD, this pillared courtyard was built under Roman rule to replace the original Greek Agora. Once surrounded by shops selling food, cloth, ceramics, and jewelry, the annual bazaar of wheat, salt, and oil would have been held here as well. Its best feature is the octagonal Tower of the Winds, built in 50 BC. Each of the eight sides represents a wind, including Boreas (north wind), blowing on a conch shell; Apeliotes (east wind), carrying fruit and grain; and Zephyros (west wind), scattering blossoms from his lap. Inside the structure, a water clock was driven by a stream from the Acropolis, while the top of the tower was crowned by a weather vane. At the opposite end of the Agora stands the Fetiye Mosque (Mosque of the Conqueror), built by the Ottomans in 1458 on the site of a Christian church, making it Athens' oldest Islamic monument. On the night of August's full moon, a free classical concert is staged here. *Daily 8am-5:45pm, but call to confirm as hours change seasonally.* Admission covered by Acropolis ticket. Aiolou & Diogenous, 210-324-5220, culture.gr

Temple of Olympian Zeus • East of Plaka • Archaeological Site
Roman Emperor Hadrian thought he was a god, an unfortunate trait suffered even by some of today's world leaders. When he came to power in the 2nd century AD, he found this vast temple, dating back to 515 BC, unfinished. He set an army of builders to work, and in no time at all he had 104 massive Corinthian columns (of which only 15 remain) holding up the largest temple on mainland Greece. He then commissioned two colossal gold-and-ivory statues, one of Zeus and one of himself, to be placed inside. To thank him, the Athenians built a triumphal arch next to the temple, inscribed to define the border between "Athens, the ancient city of Thessius" and modern Athens, "The city of Hadrian." *Oct.-Apr. 8:30am-3pm; May-Sept. 8:30am-5:30pm, but call to confirm as hours change seasonally.* Admission covered by Acropolis ticket. Vassilissis Olgas 1 & Amalias, 210-922-6330, culture.gr

Zolotas Jewelers • Syntagma • Shop
Taking its inspiration from ancient Greece, Zolotas displays sophisticated, classic pieces in minimalist glass cases, letting each one stand out like a minerature work of art. The company has been around since 1890 and continues to help Greece build its reputation for its quality jewelry industry. Some of the work actually bears a Greek motif, such as 18-karat gold earrings with Athena engraved in rose quartz. The shiny room in back displays Zolotas' collection of silver plates, tureens, and the like. *Mon, Wed 9am-4pm, Tue, Thu-Fri 9am-8:30pm, Sat 9am-4pm.* Panepistimiou 10, 210-360-1272, zolotasjewelers.gr

Hip & Cool Athens

Forget understated. Hip and cool in Athens isn't about wearing black and discussing neo-anything. In this view of the city, there's a dash of glitter, a shot of glam, and a dollop of the Greek talent for peering into the abyss of tacky without falling in. Ok, so sometimes they fall. Hard. But it's still cool. After all, where else can you lounge under the stars in a former royal garden in the middle of the city, next to champagne-sipping playboys and models, then dance until dawn while Europe's hottest DJs spin the turntables, ending with one last cocktail on a rooftop overlooking the Acropolis? Here's your guide to the Athens that would have Aesop turning in his grave. Wait, was he Greek or Roman?

*Note: Venues in bold in the itinerary are described in detail in the listings that follow. Venues followed by an * asterisk are those we recommend as both a restaurant and a destination bar.*

Hip & Cool Athens:
The Perfect Plan (3 Days and Nights)

Highlights

Thursday

Breakfast	**St. George Lycabettus**
Morning	**Benaki Museum**
Lunch	**Prytanion, Kiku**
Afternoon	**Shopping in Kolonaki**
Cocktails	**Central, De Capo***
Evening	**Mt. Lycabettus Theater**
Dinner	**Orizondes*, Red***
Nighttime	**Balthazar***
Late-Night	**Diogenis Studio**

Friday

Breakfast	**Poolside Breakfast**
Morning	**DESTE**
Lunch	**Square Sushi**
Afternoon	**Shopping, Ananea Spa**
Cocktails	**Envy Belle Helene*, Frame***
Dinner	**Boschetto, Milos**
Nighttime	**En Delphis, Mommy**
Late-Night	**Dragoste**

Saturday

Morning	**Free time**
Brunch	**Messiah*, Septem**
Afternoon	**Zappeion Gardens**
Dinner	**Aegli*, Big Deals***
Nighttime	**Bedlam, Privilege**

Hotel: **The St. George Lycabettus**

Thursday

9am Enjoy one of the best scenes and best views in Athens by starting your day with a breakfast at the hotel. Take in the Acropolis panorama, as well as the excellent people-watching in this hip local gathering place.

10am Walk down Kolonaki's tree-and-boutique-lined streets to the **Benaki Museum** and its top-notch collection of Greek art. Don't miss the museum's gift shop, one of the only places in the country to buy certified repro-ductions of ancient Greek jewel-ry. Also check out the museum's roof top with a view over the National Gardens.

12:30pm Lunch For serious people-watching, head to **Prytanion**, where you can have a grilled-veggie salad at sidewalk tables with a view of the celebrities and poseurs vying for attention. You could also take advantage of Athens' current love affair with sushi by lunching at **Kiku**. If you're feeling more traditional, try the wild-herb pies and hundreds of ouzos at **Ouzadiko**.

2pm The heart of Kolonaki has the most highly concentrated—and high-end—retail district in the country. The queen of local designers is Sophia Kokosalaki, whose work has been in Vogue; **Bettina** is the only shop that sells her designs. The boutique **Old Athens** sells '60s-starlet kitten heels and hand-stitched crocodile clutches at a sliver of the cost you'd find them for at home. If you're developing a taste for Greece's new wines, stop in at **Cellier** for a few of the best. Finally, **Kem** can be relied on for its finely crafted leather handbags, totes, and luggage. If shopping doesn't interest, try the area's art—some of Greece's most respected galleries are here. **Zoumboulakis** shows big-name artists, while **Astrolavos** could easily be mistaken for a trippy toy store. Also nearby is the **Goulandris Museum of Cycladic Art**, not to be missed for fans of artists like Modigliani and Picasso, who were inspired by the stark female figurines.

6pm By late afternoon, everyone gravitates to Plateia Kolonaki for coffee, gossip, and more people-watching. There's the old guard of politicians, media types, and ladies who lunch at the cramped tables of **Da Capo***. A more mellow school heads for the spacious tables and better service of **Lykovrisi***, while the youngest and most status-conscious of all get by the doorman at **Central***, where there's the option of sushi with an after-work cocktail.

7pm If it's summer, take the funicular up to the top of **Mt. Lycabettus**, Athens' highest hill, and take in a performance at the **Mt. Lycabettus Theater** while you enjoy the stellar view.

11pm Dinner For a post-show dinner, head to mountaintop **Orizondes***, close to the amphitheater and celebrated for its Mediterranean fusion food. In winter, when the amphitheater closes, book a table at romantic **Red***, in Gazi's Athinais arts complex, and wander the galleries. Or try **Freud Oriental**, the chic restaurant with fabulous sushi and a trendy crowd.

1am Taxi over to **Balthazar*** for late-night drinks and dancing with the "in" crowd in a beautiful courtyard. Or nibble and drink to the thumping Latin beats at **Tapas Bar**. Gay travelers will want to check out **Eyeland**, a hot new lounge club for lesbians and their friends.

3am For the flashiest show in town, head to **Diogenis Studio** to catch Greece's most famous divas in the all-night table-dancing spectacle that is a Greek bouzoukia performance. As the sun comes up, follow the designer-clad crowd to **Estiatorio 24**, a bonafide Greek diner.

Friday

10am After a poolside breakfast, take a taxi to the **DESTE Foundation of Contemporary Art**, which showcases the cutting-edge holdings of contemporary art collector Dakis Ioannou. Browse the funky galleries and gift shops before grabbing a taxi to head north to the privileged environs of Kifissia. Kifissia is like the Kolonaki of the north, but with more trees, older and prettier buildings, and an even more glamorous resident profile. Its many cafe-and-boutique-lined streets, outstanding restaurants, and fashionable denizens give it a southern European brand of snob appeal year round.

1pm Lunch Get a table at **Square Sushi** on Plateia Kefalari, with a view to an old church and an assortment of bronzed cleavage and stiletto heels.

3pm Now revive with a coffee in the garden of the going-on-120-years-old **Varsos**. Then stroll the shady streets, admiring Greek boutiques like **Fanourakis**, with its one-of-a-kind "fabric" jewelry or the inimitable Lalaounis, whose sculptural jewelry pieces earned him an invitation to France's Academie Des Beaux Arts. Shoe fiends won't want to miss **Preview** or **Kalogirou**, where they can stock up on European designer footwear at good prices. Non-shoppers should detour to the mansion housing the **Goulandris Museum of Natural History**, a well-presented collection of Greece's flora and fauna, including some knockout wild orchids. Or, if you are in need of pampering, grab a taxi and head to the **Ananea Spa** at the Life Gallery Hotel. It's a ways, but the atmosphere is intimate, the treatments are progressive, and it's a great place to spend a relaxing afternoon.

7pm Time for a cocktail. Go up to verdant **Envy Belle Helene***, where the clientele is almost as beautiful as this stylish outdoor bar-restaurant's namesake, whose face famously launched a thousand ships. To show off your new purchases, go no farther than **Frame***, the St. George Lycabettus' oh-so-hip garden-lounge. You could also check out the stellar views and the scene at the rooftop terrace at the Hilton's slick **Galaxy*** bar. Then head back to the hotel to refresh.

10pm Dinner Try flawless Northern Italian cuisine at the tables under the pines at **Boschetto**. Serious foodies can delight in slightly modernized Greek fish dishes at the Hilton's **Milos Restaurant**, or see if a celeb chef is doing a stint at the neo-Greek classic **48***. If you're in the mood for four-star romance, book a table at the moonlit marble terrace at **Pil-Poul**. Or, try Herve Ponzato's award-winning fusion cuisine at **St'Astra**.

Midnight Start your night with a drink at the street party that is **En Delphis** before heading next door to cozy **Mommy**, where artists and fashion editors mingle in rooms set up like a retro-futurist dream.

2am Now you're ready for pulsing **Dragoste**—a techno take on a French boudoir. You can also try womblike **Passa** with its fluffy pink walls, leather fetish art, and always-posing clientele, or in summer, reserve a table to gain entrance at trendy **Liberty**. For more intense dancing, go up the coast to hopping **Bebek**, where a chic, energetic crowd grooves until the sun rises.

Saturday

10am We're guessing you slept in, but if not, choose an activity from another itinerary. Maybe the Acropolis?

2pm Lunch Have a long brunch at **Messiah***, where late Saturday afternoons draw the biggest scene. There's Eggs Benedict, DJs, and Athens' fashion crowd. Then stroll through Plaka and check out **Frissiras Museum**, which finds new European artists

before they make it big. Alternatively, head down to the coast, stopping the taxi at the club Balux on **Asteria Seaside Beach**. Plan for lunch at **Septem**, coastal Athens' most sophisticated restaurant. For lunch in winter, follow the chic young Greeks to **Milton's**, the exception to Plaka's cookie-cutter tavernas. Or crowd into the cozy jewelbox **Aiolis** for salads and cappuccinos. Then lounge around and take in the views, whether seaside or street-side.

8pm Return to town, and take a walk through the lilac-scented Zappeion Gardens, inside the National Gardens.

10pm Dinner There you'll find **Aegli***, where a memorable dinner awaits. A wintertime option is to cab it up to Kifissia. Food at booming **Big Deals*** is a very big deal, as is the adjoining lounge scene. Foodies will love **Gefsis Me Onomasia Proelefsis**, which gets its ingredients from Greece's most exclusive small farmers.

Midnight To close out your last evening in Athens, reserve a table for the glamorous all-night party that is **Privilege,** or hit **Bedlam**, the summer club of choice in central Athens for its late-late-late-night dance scene. (In winter, Bedlam's chef John-Louis Capsalis cooks inside at the lounge Bedlam Secret View.)

Hip & Cool Athens:
The Key Neighborhoods

Exarchia is only a few blocks from Kolonaki, but miles away mentally. Here you'll find live music from rock to jazz, traditional neighborhood joints, and a healthy dose of collegiate intellectualism, since it's a popular area for students.

Kifissia is a leafy, suburban enclave filled with laid-back lounge bars, located just off the chatter-filled cafes around Kolonaki Square. This is the kind of area where you can eavesdrop on a high-flying deal being brokered by the chic female execs in high heels at the next cafe table.

Kolonaki is the stomping ground of the city's rich and fabulous. Here you'll find the Hermes-clad new money crowd that uses its Porsche Cayennes and Audi TTs to nudge out the less flashy upper middle class.

Monastiraki has a great flea market and is home to the Ancient Agora.

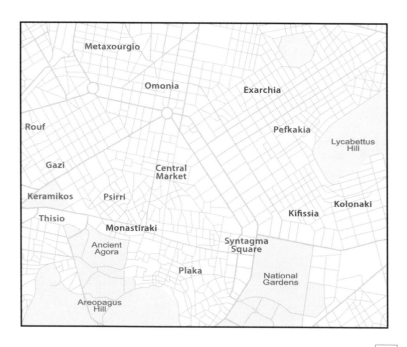

Hip & Cool Athens:
The Shopping Blocks

Kifissia

Money cruises these exclusive streets with the authority of dogs in a junkyard. Well-groomed dogs.

Carla G Items from hot, new Greek designers as well as the shop's own label. Levidou 16, 210-968-1462.

Preview Enough designer shoes to sate even a rabid fashionista. Bring the plastic. (p.99) Panagitsas 6, Kifissia, 210-801-1120; Patriarchou Ioakim 19, Kolonaki, 210-722-4731

Soho Soho Hip young socialites wouldn't dare pack for a weekend without stopping by for some new additions to their wardrobe, whether cocktail dresses or strappy sandals. Kolokotroni 8, 210-623-4707

Zoumboulakis Funky silk screens and artwork adorn this little shop attached to a great gallery. (p.99) Kriezotou 7, 210-363-4454

Kolonaki

Attitude is the only way to get served in Kolonaki's chic boutiques. The neighborhood's home to the cream of international brands like Cartier and Ralph Lauren, most along Voukourestiou. Poke around streets like Tsakalof, Patriarchou Ioakim, and Kanari for local fashion houses, including Old Athens, Thalassa, and Yes.

Afternoon Expensive, avant-garde, and elitist. Just what you're after. (p.95). St. George Lycabettus Hotel, Deinokratous 1, Plateia Dexameni, 210-722-5380

Bettina Top Greek designers in minimalist setting. (p.96) Pindarou 40 & Anagnostopoulou 29, 210-339-2094

Cellier Way beyond retsina. This gem will open your eyes to the possibilities of Greek vino. (p.96) Kriezotou 1 & Papdiamanti 10, 210-361-0040

Deux Hommes Greece's answer to Dolce & Gabbana creates collections with fluid, yet body-conscious lines. Kanari 18, 210-361-4155

Fanourakis Famous Greek jeweler known for its intricate brooches of insects and butterflies. (p.97) Patriarchou Ioakim 23, 210-721-1762

Kem Leather goods from wallets to purses from a beloved Greek brand. (p.98) Patriarchou Ioakim 2, 210-721-9230

Mastic Spa Mastic, a tree gum, is the key ingredient in products here, from olive oil to toothpaste. (p.98) Irakleitou 1 & Solonos, 210-360-3413

Old Athens Miss full skirts and croc handbags from the '50s? Look no further than this vintage and reproduction wonder. (p.98) Kanari 17, 210-361-4762

Hip & Cool Athens:
The Hotels

Athenaeum InterContinental • Syngrou • Modern (543 Rooms)
Athens' largest hotel and one of Greece's biggest convention centers. The
InterCon does a good job of balancing the needs of high-end business travelers
with the desires of chic seekers of fun and sun, starting with its location:
between central Athens' business district (reachable by free hotel shuttle) and
the beaches of the southern suburbs (reachable by taxi or tram). Still, guests
are mostly here for business—whether that's clinching corporate deals or a concert gig (so it's not all pinstripes and briefcases in the lounge). The marble lobby
is spiced up with art from the owners' private collection, like the neon-blue man
at reception. Identical standard rooms aren't quite so funky, but have marble
floors, cool blue furnishings, double-headed showers, sunny sitting areas, and
at least two phones per room. The Club section, on the eighth and ninth floors,
has private check-in, an Acropolis-view lounge, CD and DVD players and
libraries, and complimentary evening cocktails. "Acropolis view" rooms are the
best. €€€€ Syngrou 89-93, 210-920-6000, intercontinental.com

The Athenian Callirhoe • Makrigianni • Trendy (84 Rooms)
The Callirhoe stands out both because it was one of the first hotels in Athens to
pay serious attention to style and design in its pre-Olympics renovation and
because it finished the project in plenty of time—meaning other hotels have
been copying the successful results all over town. But this quietly cool hotel is
still one of the best. Its sleek lobby, which could easily pass for a lounge bar, is
lit by '70s-inspired orange-and-black metal lamps and tree-trunk-thick candles.
The more minimalist rooms have black leather furniture, huge white duvets, and
tasteful dove gray and pale wood accents. Some executive rooms have balconies—but note that Acropolis-view executive rooms are sans balcony. The chic
restaurant is done in purple, green, and silver, and at sunset, the rooftop bar is
filled with pretty people enjoying the Acropolis view. The concierge can arrange
anything from tickets to the Odeon of Herodes Atticus to transport by private
helicopter. €€€€ Kallirois 32 & Petmeza, 210-921-5353, tac.gr

Athens Hilton • Ilisia • Modern (527 Rooms)
When the Athens Hilton re-opened in 2003 after its two-year head-to-toe renovation, some people couldn't believe it was still a Hilton. Its staid atmosphere
was gutted along with the old interiors, and its new, zen-like tranquility sits well
with corporate travelers with yoga mats strapped to their briefcases and a taste
for Canali suits. Gone are the institutional beige rooms, replaced by light-filled
spaces with funky angled walls in sage green and smoked blue glass, wood
floors, brushed-metal details, and marble bathrooms. It's also got a hot pool
scene, where Athens' high society pays huge membership fees to hang by the
city's biggest plunge. In summer, stake out a lounge chair and eavesdrop on the
Greeklish gossiping of high-powered female advertising execs and journalists
swapping insider tips about business deals and bikini waxes, often in the same
sentence. The rooftop Galaxy Bar now needs a doorman to keep order among the
young scions and fashionistas who flock here in the evenings; getting in is

easier in summer, when it opens out to a terrace barbecue with a great party scene and sparkling city views. Downstairs, foodies love Milos, a branch of New York's first haute Greek restaurant. Skip the overrated balcony and mountain-view rooms here. The best location is a mid-to-high floor room overlooking the pool. €€€€ Vassilissis Sofias 46, 210-728-1000, athens.hilton.com

NJV Athens Plaza • Syntagma • Trendy (159 Rooms)

The Plaza is the star city property of the innovative Grecotel chain, which has led the way in bringing a much-needed infusion of style to Greek hotels. This is imme-diately apparent in the lobby, with its stacked bubble lamps topped with spiky lampshades, sleek-lined leather couches, and fashionable clientele. Ask for rooms on the eighth or ninth floors that have an Acropolis view along with the standard designer fabrics, pulsing massage showers, and Bulgari toiletries. Individually styled suites range from subdued earth tones with tasteful antique prints to the zebra-striped "Versace" room, with furniture and fabrics from the outrageous Italian. Downstairs, there's a 24-hour business center; the dark-wood-and-leather Explorers' bar, a popular spot for politicians coming from nearby Parliament; and the Parliament restaurant, which serves organic Mediterranean cuisine. There's no workout area or pool, but the hotel offers access to facilities at nearby gyms. €€€€ Vasileos Georgiou A 2, 210-335-2400, grecotel.com

Ochre & Brown • Psirri • Trendy (11 Rooms)

Best Hotel Rooms One of the city's newest hotels—it opened in early 2006—has picked up on the trend for small, stylish, and highly personalized boutiques that cater to experienced and discerning travelers. Ochre & Brown's eleven rooms are all smartly outfitted with modern furniture, high-tech amenities, and vibrant yet taste-ful bursts of color, such as purple orchids and orange pillows. The best rooms have city views over the neighborhood of Thisio (others face North, with an alley view), but the standout choice is the junior suite, with an Acropolis view from the private and spacious terrace. This fashionable spot is located in hip Psirri, yet it's still with-in walking distance to major sites like the Parthenon. Its lounge and restaurant have become haunts for the locals, and the concierges are experts on the best nightlife. €€ Leokoriou 7, 210-331-2950, ochreandbrown.gr

Periscope • Kolonaki • Trendy (22 Rooms)

The brand-new Periscope is less a hotel than an experience. Visitors—nary a one over 40—step off the quiet, boutique-lined street and enter a ground-floor cafe-bar lobby with top-floor views, thanks to the hotel's very own periscope. Guests, who tend to be arts- and technology-savvy locals and their international counterparts, can fiddle with a remote control wirelessly connected to the powerful periscope and zoom in on part of the Athens landscape while giant wall-mounted screens project the scenes. In the spacious rooms, fine bed linens and fluffy pillows soften the black-and-white color scheme and the furniture's modern, spare design. Ask for a "torpedo" class room with a balcony overlooking Mt. Lycabettus. This hotel suc-cessfully combines design, art, and leisure in a neighborhood concerned with very much the same. €€ Haritos 22, 210-623-6320, periscope.gr

The St. George Lycabettus • Kolonaki • Trendy (154 Rooms)

Best Rooms with a View This jewel pulls off an artful balance between posh and cool. It's got an impeccable address in the heart of chic, boutique-filled Kolonaki, and it's worth booking here for the lobby scene alone: all high heels and high gloss, and sudden gusts of perfumed air-kisses as the city's truly chic and famous pop in for lunch or a massage in Kolonaki's hottest insiders' haunt. Set on the pine-clad slopes of Mt. Lycabettus, it also has forest breezes and lofty Acropolis views (be certain to ask for an "external" view, otherwise you'll be looking at their internal courtyard). The upper-crust dine at Le Grand Balcon, the acclaimed rooftop restaurant, while Athens' youngest and trendiest vie to get into Frame, the ground-floor '70s-style lounge. Fashionistas adore Afternoon, the hotel's late-night boutique, for its cutting-edge selection by up-and-coming Greek designers. And everyone loves the carefully designed rooms (each floor done according to a different theme, from colorful Art Nouveau to soothing neutrals and bamboo) and a dip in the rooftop pool. €€ Kleomenous 2, 210-729-0711, stylcabettus.gr

Semiramis Hotel • Kifissia • Trendy (51 Rooms)

Best Hotel Rooms The Semiramis, owned by renowned art collector Dakis Ioannou and designed by überstylist Karim Rashid, has finally filled the longed-for niche of a New York- or London-quality hip hotel in Athens. Ioannou commissioned Rashid to "create a work of art" in the northern suburb of Kifissia. The result? Attitude, darling. Everyone's here because it's terminally cool, but everyone pretends not to notice. Dedicated fashionistas prop up the bar at cocktail hour, the pool hosts a constant parade of "this old thing?" glamour, and Kefalari socialites flock to the restaurant to pick at salads. Visitors enter through a glowing pink cube and during their stay are surrounded by sheets of curving glass in pink, lime, and orange. Rooms showcase a rotating selection of cutting-edge contemporary art, culled from Ioannou's collection. The best standard rooms overlook Kefalari Park, but for a splurge, book a fourth floor penthouse studio with private rooftop balcony and views out to Piraeus. Take note—while Kifissia's cool breezes and shady streets are blissfully removed from downtown Athens' heat and smog, it's a long haul to get to sights and museums, though you're mere steps away from some of Athens' most exclusive restaurants and boutiques. €€€€ Harilaou Trikoupi 48, 210-628-4400, semiramisathens.com

Hip & Cool Athens:
The Restaurants

Aegli* • Syntagma • International
If the lush National Gardens keep Athens bearable in summer, the graceful, landscaped Zappeion section elevates it to the sublime. The center of Zappeion is a landmark 19th-century hall, surrounded by avenues of flowering trees, murmuring fountains, and marble sculptures of gods and heroes. This is the picture-perfect setting of Aegli, whose menu happily lives up to the surroundings. French-Greek chef Jean-Louis Capsalis makes the most of both branches of his heritage with dishes like a salad of fresh crab and mint drizzled with lemon-infused olive oil, grilled grouper with spinach and sea urchin juice, and cold strawberry soup with tangerine confit. This place is at its best in summer, when the veranda swarms with beautiful couples and European politicians. Also within the gardens are the dance club Bedlam (outdoors in summer), and an under-the-stars cinema, also called Aegli. *Daily 1-4pm and 8pm-midnight.* €€€ ⅏Ⅎ≡ Zappeion, in the National Gardens, 210-336-9363, aeglizappiou.gr

Aiolis • Monastiraki • Meze
Best Cafes A cosmopolitan crowd of foreign correspondents, poets, and painters frequents this beautiful old coffee house. The space pulls off the perfect mix of trendy and traditional. You can grab a seat outside in front of the 19th-century facade with a view of the car-free stone walkway, the Byzantine-style church of Aghia Irini, and the bustling flower market. At night, join the crowd in the gorgeously designed interior with its burgundy walls and seasonal touches like the silvery baubles cascading from the ceiling in winter and potted bamboo in summer. There's always frothy cappuccino and a great menu of salads, snacks, and pastas. *Daily 10am-2am.* € ⅏Ⅎ≡ Aiolou 23 & Agias Irinis, 210-331-2839

Akrotiri Lounge • Agios Kosmas • Mediterranean (G)
This chic seaside spot with chef Christophe Clesienne's exquisite French-Med cuisine is good enough to make foodies brave the club scene, and the advertised "animal spirit" of the place. See *Hip & Cool Nightlife*, p.91 for description. *Daily, restaurant: 9:30pm-2am; Club: 11pm-about 3:30am.* €€€€ ⅏Ⅎ≡ Vasileos Georgiou 11, 210-985-9147, akrotirilounge.gr/en.htm

Balthazar* • Ambelokipi • Mediterranean
Best Trendy Tables After nearly 20 years as the place for fashionable Athenians to see and be seen in summer, Balthazar's star shows no signs of fading. It seems the draw of a 19th-century courtyard oasis paved with hand-painted tiles, canopied by gracious date palms, glimmering with colored lanterns, and filled with scantily clad eye candy, can weather the decades. If anything, this place is getting hotter, with the addition of high-power chef Giorgos Tsaktsiras, whose sublime fusion dishes, from shrimp ceviche to wild grape sorbet, have made this a place to come to for the food. Of course, it would be a pity to leave after dinner, just when the party's getting started. *Mon-Sat from 9pm; kitchen closes 2am, club closes 3:30am.* €€€€ ⅏Ⅎ≡ Tsoha 27 & Soutsou, 210-644-1215, balthazar.gr

Bedlam • Syntagma • Contemporary
> In summer, the food is mediocre. But in winter, rush to make reservations, when it moves into a decadent boudouir-like space in the historic stone building adjacent to the renowned restaurant Aegli. *See Hip & Cool Nightlife, p.91 for description. Mon-Sat 8pm-2:30am.* €€€ ⅺℲ▤ Zappeion, in the National Gardens, 210-336-9340

Big Deals* • Kifissia • International (G)
> It's true what downtowners say about Kifissia: It's packed with botoxed blonds, trust-fund kids, and cigar-chomping social climbers. Which also means it's full of some of Greece's most glitzy restaurants and nightclubs, with shameless names like Privilege, Envy, and, yes, Big Deals. It's fun to sit back and enjoy their over-the-topness—assuming you can get in. But this is one spot where the hauteur of the scene, the eye-boggling sexiness of the waitstaff, and the stratospheric prices are matched by the brilliance of the food itself. Brightly plumed yuppies and their surgically enhanced companions flock here to feast on quince-stuffed monkfish paired with sweet corn mousse and the fantastic pineapple crème brûlée. Afterward, schmooze with Athens' high society in the swanky, mirror-walled lounge. *Mon-Fri from 8pm, Sat-Sun from 1pm; kitchen closes 2am, bar closes 3am.* €€€€ ⅺℬ▤ Harilaou Trikoupi 50, 210-623-0860

Boschetto • Kolonaki • Italian
> Amid fragrant pines and candlelight at this idyllic restaurant, you'll find upscale young lovers and businessmen out to impress, which they inevitably do over the creative nouvelle cuisine at the city's top Italian restaurant. The menu changes seasonally but always includes flawless starters, hearty homemade pastas, and desserts like the heavenly panna cotta, accompanied by a cup of Athens' best espresso. Ask for a table outside or, in cooler weather, by the window. *Mon-Sat 12:30-4pm and 8pm-midnight.* €€€€ ▤ Evangelismos Park, 210-721-0893

Central* • Kolonaki • International
Best-Bar Restaurants For the past few years, this creamy-white lounge, bar, and restaurant has been one of the most popular haunts of Athenian celebs, socialites, and wannabes. From early afternoon onwards, it attracts shoppers laden with bags from the nearby boutiques and moneyed types taking long lunches. Toward evening, cappuccino cups are replaced with champagne flutes and tumblers of whiskey, the music is cranked up a notch, and tarted-up starlets and their suited consorts pile in to nibble sushi, sundried tomato salads, and sinful desserts—the hot chocolate cake with vanilla milkshake is a famous diet-breaker. In summer, Central closes here and re-opens on the coast as dreamy Island. *Daily 10:30am-2am. Moves to Island club mid-May-Sept.* €€€ ⅺℲ▤ Plateia Kolonaki 14, 210-724-5938

Da Capo* • Kolonaki • Cafe
> For generations, this has been the Kolonaki cafe of choice for former prime ministers, fur-swaddled socialites, soap opera starlets, bouzoukia divas, and everyone who wants to be anyone in Athens' high society. This seems strange when you realize it's strictly self-service, with merely adequate snacks and cramped tables. That's the price you pay for the chance to rub shoulders with Greece's elite and to get one of the best people-watching vantage points in town. *Mon-Sat 7am-midnight, Sun 8:30am-midnight.* € ▤ Tsakalof 1, 210-360-2497

Envy Belle Helene* • Politia • International
Beautiful young things unencumbered by the silly need to work hang out at this verdant, luxurious open-air cafe all day long. There are groovy DJs, long, cool cocktails, and a small menu of artfully presented little snacks. *Daily 10am-2am.* €€ ⍰ Constantinou Paliologou 1, Plateia Politia, 210-800-1111

Estiatorio 24 • Makrigianni • Traditional
Best Late-Late-Night Eats Forget what you think you know about 24-hour Greek diners. Despite its 90-year history, Estiatorio 24 buzzes after hours. The Mondrian-esque walls in this bilevel space are covered with arty black-and-white city photos, giving an unusually sleek feel. But the crowd is pure late-night: Designer-clad divas, blissed-out club kids, red-eyed taxi drivers, and greasy strip-show patrons pack this place at 4am, and would surely riot if a single item on the long menu of hearty Greek home cooking was ever changed. *24/7. Closed Easter Sunday.* € ⍰ Syngrou 44, 210-922-1159

48* • Ambelokipi • Contemporary (G)
Best Trendy Tables From bouzoukia diva Anna Vissi to model-perfect poster boy Sakis Rouvas, all of Greece's paparazzi favorites have been spotted at this minimalist temple to modern Greek cuisine. The high-ceilinged, warehouse-like space (formerly an art gallery) is illuminated with sculptural light fixtures that constantly change from warm, orangey hues to icy greens and blues, courtesy of interior designer Arnold Chan. The key question is, does the food live up to the décor? In a word, yes. Chef Christoforos Peskias cooks up inspired dishes using traditional Greek ingredients in modern ways, like curried calamari rings with a tzatziki dip and sauteed rabbit with hilopites (village pasta) from Monemvasia. The wine list has more than 500 labels from restaurant owner Doris Margellos' private vault in Paris. Book early to avoid disappointment. *Mon-Sat 9pm-2am.* €€€€ ⍰ Armatolon & Klefton 48, 210-641-1082, 48therestaurant.com

Frame* • Kolonaki • International
Frame does a retro-'70s thing, with brown-and-orange shag carpets, rainbow walls, and hanging bubble chairs, which seat Athens' trendiest tushes plus a fair share of high-flying internationals (including Madonna, according to the waitstaff). Everyone seems happy to shell out for offbeat comfort food like chicken with Bloody Mary sauce. In summer, the menu turns more Med-fusion, and the dining area moves outside to the less funky but more all-purpose-pretty garden, draped with linen canopies and snow-white tables. *Daily 11am-3am.* €€€€ ⍰ St. George Lycabettus Hotel, Deinokratous 1, Plateia Dexameni, 210-721-4368, sgl-frame.gr

Freud Oriental • Kolonaki • Sushi (G)
Best Sushi Restaurants With its obscure name, small size (just six tables), and subtle large gray door as an entrance, Freud Oriental remains a spot for sushi sophisticates in the know. The Spartan white on white setting serves as a minimalist backdrop for a venue that has the reputation for some of the best sushi and sashimi in town. The sushi chefs hail from Japan and work with the local catch straight from the Aegean. Just beware that the ultra-hip scene in upscale Kolonaki requires advance reservations and ample funds in your wallet. *Daily 8pm-1am.* €€€ ⍰ Xenokratous 21, 210-729-9595

Gefsis Me Onomasia Proelefsis • Kifissia • Contemporary (G)

The name of this place—which means "Flavors of Designated Origin"—may sound like a bad translation from a Slavic language, but it's a siren song to foodies. Every ingredient comes from select regional farmers throughout Greece (the kind who raise lambs on herbs, grow organic vegetables, and personally hand-press their olives). A highlight is the vast array of Greek artisanal cheeses. Favorite dishes include cucumber mousse topped with goat cheese and fresh-water roe and filo pouches filled with veal and tomatoes, topped with spicy yogurt sauce. *Mon-Sat 8pm-12:30am.* €€€€ ≡ Kifissias 317, 210-800-1402

Kiku • Kolonaki • Sushi

Best Sushi Restaurants Sushi joints are suddenly sweeping through Athens, but Greeks are often more interested in trend-following than quality. This place—the only restaurant where you'll find actual Japanese people both in the kitchen and at the sushi bar—is the exception. The selection of local fish, including flawless tuna, sea bass, and squid, is outstanding, while the cooked dishes could go head-to-head with top offerings in Tokyo. Diners are a mix of Rolex-flashing, Havana-puffing Athenian powerbrokers and their posses and quiet Japanese travelers, who get a separate menu in Japanese. *Mon-Sat 7:30pm-1am. Closed in Aug.* €€€€ ≡ Dimokritou 12, 210-364-7033

Lykovrisi* • Kolonaki • Cafe

If you want to bypass the Greek status-seekers lining up for brioche and name-dropping at the tiny tables at Da Capo, cross the plateia for comfy chairs that invite you to sit back and gossip for hours. Enjoy good service, good coffee, and cocktails among a more casual crowd of academics and 20- to 30-somethings. *Daily 8am-2am.* € ≡ Plateia Kolonaki 8, 210-361-6712

Messiah* • Kolonaki • International

This stylish addition to Kolonaki's playground of swanky bar-restaurant-nightclubs draws a crowd of fashion and media types for Italian-influenced dinners in the orange-gold lounge, and dancing downstairs in the club. But the best time to see and be seen here is Saturday afternoon, when it buzzes with the liveliest brunch scene in town. The table-hopping party starts around 2pm, both in the lounge and out in the shady courtyard, and goes on until early evening, fueled by Eggs Benedict, Bloody Marys, and a rotating stable of DJs. Oct.-June Tue-Fri from 9pm, Sat-Sun from 2pm; kitchen closes 1:30am, club closes 6am. €€ B≡ Lemos Shopping Center, Karneadou 25-29, 210-729-4290

Milos Restaurant • Ilisia • Contemporary (G)

Best Nouveau Greek Dining A chain restaurant that started in Canada may sound off-putting, but Milos has allayed skeptics' fears with some of the best seafood in the city. Everyone from high-profile politicos to foodies gravitates here. Located in the lower level of the Athens Hilton, Milos displays an unending variety of fish on ice in the open kitchen, as well as an array of fresh produce. Half the fun is watching chefs transform these ingredients into enticing fare at tables close to the action. Highlights in the past have included almond-based taramosalata, fried shrimp, and monkfish saganaki served with a Greek wine and feta sauce. *Daily 12:30-6pm and 7:30pm-1am. Closed mid-to-end Aug.* €€€ ≡ Athens Hilton, Vassilissis Sofias 46, 210-724-4400, milos.ca/en/athens/index.html

Milton's • Plaka • International
It was a risk opening up this shamelessy chic little spot—all mod minimalist lines and strawberry mojitos—in the middle of quaint Plaka's twee tavernas, but it has paid off. It's at its best in summer, when fashionable locals lounge on the cool, shaded sofas, picking at arugula and chicory salads and rabbit with blackberry sauce—or just sipping cocktails and watching the world go by. *Daily 10am-2am.* €€ F≡ Adrianou 91, 210-324-9129

Ochre & Brown Restaurant • Psirri • Mediterranean
A new entry in the very stylish enclave of Psirri, Ochre & Brown has already drawn a following of local hipsters with its tasty Mediterranean cuisine and sleek design. Clean lines and simple materials (hardwood floors, soft lighting) give it a tranquil feel, but it still turns into a lively cocktail scene on weekends. It's part of a new hotel, a chic boutique that is also making a name for itself as a favorite of sophisticated travelers. *Daily 8pm-2am.* €€ F≡ Leokoriou 7, 210-331-2950, ochreandbrown.com

Orizondes* • Kolonaki • Contemporary
Best Tables with a View The star here is the view, as it should be in a place whose setting is at the peak of a mini-mountain reachable only by cable car. Sitting on the stone terrace at sunset may be one of the most sublime experiences in all of Greece—the Acropolis glitters below, and the rest of Athens unfolds like a map all the way out to the island of Aegina. It would be tough for any chef to compete with such a setting, but Yiannia Metaxas succeeds with French and Asian twists on Mediterranean classics. Standouts include a tart of monkfish foie gras and sour apple, and a gilthead (sea bream) moussaka with eggplant and pinenut puree. *Daily noon-2am.* €€€ ⒕≡ Mt. Lycabettus, 210-721-0701

Ouzadiko • Kolonaki • Meze
Best Ouzeries This ouzerie's location in a deserted shopping mall doesn't inspire confidence, but tell that to the crowds of high-end folks who've kept it booked every weekend for the last three years. What's the draw? More varieties (closing in on 1,000) of high-voltage ouzo than you'll find almost anywhere else, accompanied by a constantly revolving menu of excellent mezedes—crispy pies of wild greens, cumin, and feta; grape leaves stuffed with minced lamb and spices; wonderful tzatziki (yogurt, garlic, and dill dip); and melanzanosalata (smoked eggplant puree)—and a chocolate soufflé that will knock your socks off. *Tue-Sat 12:30-6pm and 8-11:45pm. Closed in Aug.* €€ ≡ Lemos Shopping Center, Karneadou 25-29, 210-729-5484

Pil-Poul • Thisio • French (G)
Best Romantic Dining If you're in love, this movie-set marble terrace swathed in bougainvillaea and overlooking the moon-bathed Acropolis will be everything you could want in a restaurant. Even the mostly French menu is romantic, from lobster with passionfruit and champagne sauce to the grilled wild strawberries and chocolate—which explains why this is the most popular place in town to pop the question. If you're on the hunt (or the rebound), head straight for the new lounge bar for cocktails, fusion snacks, and beautiful people. *Daily 8pm-1am.* €€€€ ⒕⊒ Apostolou Pavlou 51, 210-342-3665, pilpoul.gr

Prytanion • Kolonaki • International

Tiny, stone-paved, car-free Milioni is one of the most expensive slices of real estate in Athens, with its boutiques and fashionable-people-filled sidewalk cafes, all shaded by graceful old trees. Of these, Prytanion is indisputably the best place to be seen lunching on bruschetta and huge grilled-vegetable salads. You'll be surrounded by Athens' high-powered moguls and well-designed wives, but more importantly, you'll have the best view of all the glittery nouveau riche strolling by. *Daily 9am-2am.* €€ ▭ Milioni 7, 210-364-3353, prytaneion.gr

Red* • Votanikos • Mediterranean (G)

Best Nouveau Greek Dining This lounge is the star of Athinais, the popular, trend-setting arts complex built in a converted silk factory. It's not just the proximity to the galleries, theater, and concert hall that draws the arty, upscale crowd, it's also the audacious but delicious take on Mediterranean cuisine. You're guaranteed to try something you won't see on any other menu, whether it's pigeon with cocoa pasta; crab salad with apple, cumin, mango, and lime; or venison with chili and dates. Come early for a show or to wander the galleries; later, try the Boiler Bar. *May-July Fri-Sat only 8:30pm-2:30am; Sept.-Apr. Tue-Sat 8pm-2am. Closed most of July and Aug.* €€€ ▭▭ Athinais Center, Kastorias 34-36, 210-348-0000, athinais.com.gr

Sea Satin • Kolonaki and Alimos • Contemporary

When the fashion crowd gets hungry for a taste of Mykonos in winter, they flock to this trendy-but-traditional seafood taverna for a casual island feel with a dollop of Kolonaki style. After 11pm, the long wood-plank tables are packed with suited scions and pretty babes in one-sleeve tops sharing huge platters of whole grilled fish, piquant taramosalata (fish roe dip), fresh horta (wild greens), and live cockles in their shells, while those who can't get a table gossip over the bouzoukia music at the stylish pale-blue bar. *Kolonaki: Oct.-May Mon-Fri 10am-3pm, Sat-Sun 3pm-3am; Alimos: Tue-Sun 1:30pm-3am.* €€ ▭ Fokilidou 1, Kolonaki, 210-361-9646; Stratigou Sarafi 5, Alimos, 210-981-4319

Septem • Glyfada • Mediterranean

Best Bar Restaurants If your idea of summertime dining in Greece is lounging on white sofas by the sea as the sun sets, picking at fresh sea bream, and being surrounded by fashionable people, this is the place for you. Besides being a restaurant, chic Balux next door is also one of the trendiest and exclusive seaside summer clubs on Athens' coast, which means you should definitely plan to stay on after dinner for the late-night club scene around the pool. *May-Oct. 9pm-1am or 2am.* €€€ ▭▭ Vasileos Georgiou, 210-894-1620, balux-septem.com

Square Sushi • Kifissia and Kolonaki • Sushi

Best Sushi Restaurants Chic décor, an exhaustive selection of quality sushi, and reasonable prices set this stylish Japanese restaurant apart from the numerous sushi bars that started popping up all around Athens when the raw fish craze finally hit Greece. Decorated simply with a black, white, and dark wood color scheme (the central Athens restaurant also has touches of purple and red), Square Sushi offers a tempting range of maki, nigiri, and sashimi. And if you simply can't get out of your hotel bed, this spot delivers until 12:30am. *May-Sept. 8pm-1am; Oct.-Apr. 1pm-1am.* €€ ▭ Diligianni 56, Kefalari, Kifissia, 210-808-1512; Deinokratous 65, Kolonaki, 210-725-5236, squaresushi.gr

St'Astra • Exarchia • Mediterranean (G)

St'Astra (meaning "Towards the Stars") happened when Herve Pronzato, arguably Greece's most celebrated chef, left behind the white-linen dining room of the classically French, Michelin-starred Spondi to start all over again in a funky glass box atop an old hotel right in gritty downtown Athens. It worked because foodies and fashion types followed him devotedly, happy to travel even to lefty-anarchist territory for the promise of Pronzato's foie gras on fig coulis with mavrodaphne (a sweet red wine) sauce, risotto with baby squid, and sea bass with wild fennel sauce. And the once-dowdy Park Hotel was happy to take a chunk out of its multimillion-dollar restoration project to outfit its rooftop space with sleek Italian furniture, a bamboo bar, cowhide rugs, and striped Murano glass chandeliers, to cater to the sensibilities of the glam groupies who now pack the place nightly. *Mon-Sat 7pm-2am.* €€€ ⊞⊟ Park Hotel, Alexandras 10, 210-889-4500, parkhotel.gr/htmlsite/stastra.html

Vardis • Kifissia • French (G)

This is the pull-out-all-the-stops standard for five-star French dining. Expect tables glittering with gold and silver, pink marble, flawless service, showy but unforgettable cuisine—and prices to match. Starters might include pigeon cassoulet with foie gras in fig juice or octopus boiled in milk with hazelnut sauce. Then try the superb cockerel cooked with tarragon and a timbale of taglione with mushrooms or leg of lamb scented with citrus fruit and spring onions. In summer, diners move outside to a poolside garden. *Sept.-July Mon-Sat 8:30pm-12:30am.* €€€€ ⊟ Petelikon Hotel, Deligianni 66, 210-623-0650, hotelpentelikon.gr/english/vardis/vardis-01.htm

Varsos • Kifissia • Cafe

Trendsters in tight jeans and silver-haired suits alike don't consider a trip to Kifissia complete without sitting a spell at this 110-year-old institution. Pick up anything from *Australian Vogue* to *Foreign Affairs* at the international newsstand out front, order a sweet Greek coffee and one of Varsos' famous meringues, and watch the world go by. Or walk through the old-fashioned interior and drool at the traditional treats on your way to the tables in the back garden. *Mon-Fri 7am-1am, Sat 7am-2am, Sun 7am-midnight.* € ⊟ Kassaveti 5, 210-801-2472

Hip & Cool Athens:
The Nightlife

Akrotiri Lounge • Agios Kosmas • Lounge/Nightclub
Best Dance Clubs by the Sea The champagne cocktails and exquisite nouvelle nibbles are stratospherically priced at this silver-and-white seaside scene, but you get what pay for: gorgeous sea views, poolside schmoozing with pretty Europeans, model-perfect waitstaff, late-night dancing to Parisian DJs, and plenty of touches like cigarettes and silver lighters brought to your table on request. *Daily 10:30pm-about 4:30am, restaurant 9pm-2am.* C B ≣ Vasileos Georgiou 11, 210-985-9147, akrotirilounge.gr/en.htm

Balthazar* • Ambelokipi • Bar/Restaurant
Artists, models, and the mundanely beautiful fill the lantern-lit courtyard nightly, creating one of Athens' most elite bar scenes. *See Hip & Cool Restaurants, p.84, for description.* C B ≣ Tsoha 27 & Soutsou, 210-644-1215

Balux • Glyfada • Beach/Nightclub
By day, palm-fringed Balux is a plush seaside escape—an exclusive beach with on-site masseuses, Pilates instructors, and private cabanas with finger food and cocktail service. The same luxury carries over into its nighttime incarnation as a trendy late-night lounge, which fills up with sophisticated yet casual 20- to 30-somethings in halter tops and golden tans. Though the crowd is always stunning and fun, the mood is definitely more mellow than at many other high-attitude beach clubs. *Apr.-Oct. Mon-Sat 11:30pm-about 4:30am.* C B = Vasileos Georgiou, 210-894-1620, balux-septem.com

Bebek • Kalamaki • Nightclub/Restaurant
It's hard to tell indoors from outdoors at this seaside club, since the building, with an exposed rock facade, literally opens up in the summer, giving way to a big terrace. Bebek is an upscale spot with two faces: a gourmet restaurant that warms up around 10pm to the sounds of R&B and lounge music, and a club that gets going around midnight. The club starts with house, moves on to Greek pop around 2am, and finishes off the morning with more house and dance music for the truly tireless. The restaurant attracts an elegant clientele in their mid-30s and 40s. Later on, the 30-something, casual-chic set gets increasingly boisterous, chatting and dancing around the three bars. *Mon-Sat 9:30pm-about 5:30am.* C F ≣ Posidonos 3, 210-981-3950

Bedlam • Syntagma • Nightclub
Best Glamorous Clubs During the sultry summer months, this happening under-the-stars lounge comes alive among the lush flowering trees of the National Gardens. Cushions scattered under long, low canopies are an invitation to sprawl elegantly beneath strings of soft lights decking the surrounding palms. Come for the drinks, the fashionable fusion soundtrack (to which pretty boys and girls delicately shake their booties), and the atmosphere, but give the over-priced fingerfood a pass. In winter, however, when the club moves into an adjacent boudoir-like lodge, it offers a delectable menu of nouvelle concoctions from

acclaimed chef Jean-Louis Capsalis. *Mon-Thu 8pm-3am, Fri-Sat 8pm-4am.* C≡
9 Zappeion, in the National Gardens, 210-336-9340

Diogenis Studio • Nea Smyrni • Bouzoukia
Best Bouzoukia in Winter This relative newcomer to Athens' nightclub scene is
equipped with state-of-the-art lighting and sound. Boasting two clubs in one—
Apollon being its alterego—it offers vantage points for all, plenty of breathing
space, and crystal-clear acoustics. It hosts everything from alternative shows to
groundbreaking music-theater, and attracts seasoned listeners who have cash to
spare. *Oct.-Apr. Thu-Sun, shows 10:30pm, though times may vary. Moves to
Thalassa in Glyfada for summer.* C≡ Syngrou 259, 210-942-5754

Dragoste • Kolonaki • Lounge/Nightclub
Best Glamorous Clubs Unpack your best designer looks and spend extra time
preening before heading here. The name of this jewelbox of a club means "passionate love" in Romanian, and there is no doubt that the decadent décor gives
the Middle Eastern-influenced scene a turn-of-the-century Parisian flair perfect
for inspiring your primitive urges. Upstairs, the jeunesse dorée of Athens lounge
on cushions slurping from bowls of noodles and poking chopsticks at stir-fried
seafood. After dinner they take drags on aromatic hookah pipes, available on
request. The gossip and drinks flow against an eclectic soundtrack that seam-
lessly progresses from Indian and Arabic to white-label trance or top-ten hits.
Oct.-Apr. Tue-Sun 10pm-4am. C F ≡ Patriarchou Ioakim 37, 210-722-1558

En Delphis • Kolonaki • Bar
En Delphis' location, straddling the border between edgy Exarchia and elegant
Kolonaki, is representative of the ambience here. In winter, the tiny bar is
packed to the walls, while in summer it's not so much a bar as a street party.
Action spills out onto the pavement at the junction of two pedestrianized alleys,
leaving plenty of space for hanging out. Located next to Mommy, En Delphis
heats up first, and goes strong from around 9pm to 1am. As the evening wears
on, people head toward Mommy, making it a great one-two punch for an evening
out. The flirty bar attracts a fascinating mix: tank-topped muscle men, trendy
clubbers, 40-something single women, older businessmen, and young couples.
Mon-Sat 2pm-about 4:30am. C≡ Delphon 5, 210-360-8269, endelphis.gr

Eyeland • Gazi • Bar/Nightclub
Best Gay and Lesbian Bars There's no shortage of gay bars in Athens, but the
city's lesbian population is just starting to come into its own. Eyeland recently
opened its industrial space in the heart of ultra-hip Gazi, melding art, music,
and dance with its wall projections and techno, house, and other international
beats. Those taking a break from the dance floor can head upstairs and watch
the action from the comfort of their own sofa. The crowd here runs the gamut
from tough-girl butch to well-coiffed chic. *Tue-Sun 10pm–about 4am.* C≡
Ikarion 24, 694-615-0196 / 694-632-4620

Frame • Kolonaki • Bar/Restaurant

Rumor has it that Madonna once ate here, but no one seems to remember quite when. Still, trendy Athenians flock to this hip bar-restaurant both in winter—when it's set in a shag-carpeted, orange-and-silver lounge—and in summer, when it migrates to a white-canopied garden across the road. *Daily 11am-3am; kitchen opens 12:30pm.* C F ≡ St. George Lycabettus Hotel, Deinokratous 1, Plateia Dexameni, 210-721-4368, sgl-frame.gr

Galaxy* • Ilisia • Bar/Lounge

The fabulous crowd lining up and begging for tables at a bar at the Hilton? Believe it. The hotel's sleek multimillion-dollar renovation transformed the whole place into something worthy of a spread in *Wallpaper*, and the star is this supercool rooftop lounge, with its million-dollar views, '60s-meets-silver-spaceship décor, and fashionistas checking each other out to a groovy French-electronica-lounge soundtrack. It's easier to get in during summer, when it opens out to a rooftop terrace and offers a nightly barbecue. *Mon-Thu, Sun 8pm-3am, Fri-Sat 6pm-4am.* B ≡ Athens Hilton, Vassilissis Sofias 46, 210-728-1000, athens.hilton.com

Liberty • Paleio Faliro • Bar/Nightclub

Liberty re-opens with a fresh new flavor each June. The quirky themes are often decidedly tongue-in-cheek, such as an incarnation involving (seriously) a white picket fence, a rolling green lawn, and lots of wicker (accompanied by a French electronica soundtrack, of course), and, more recently, a circus-y look, with a tented red entry, red and blue silk swags, and funhouse mirrors behind the bar. But it's done with such style that there's been no trouble luring the Manolo-and-Gucci crowd—indeed, this place is gaining a name as the toughest summer club to get into on weekend nights. *May-Oct. Mon-Thu 10pm-3:30am, Fri-Sat 10pm-5am.* C ≡ In the park behind Posidonos 22, 210-982-1200

Mommy • Kolonaki • Bar/Lounge

Best See-and-Be-Seen Bars Young-ish art and media scenesters adore this little pop-art lounge, still laid out like the apartment it once was. There's a living room with leopard-print sofas, kooky coffee tables, oversize lamps, shaggy rugs, and a dining room with a decent menu and a rotating display of in-crowd art. But just like home, everyone seems to gravitate to the kitchen, decked out with black-and-white floors and a shiny bar that keeps the self-consciously casual crowd well supplied with cosmos. The DJ spins a cocktail of house, salsa, hip-hop, and the occasional '80s surprise. *Mon-Sat noon-3am, Sun 3pm-3am. May close in July and Aug.* C F ≡ Delphon 4, 210-361-9682, mommy.gr

Mt. Lycabettus Theater • Kolonaki • Concerts

Best Shows Under the Stars While classical theater troupes orate their way through Oedipal complexes in the Odeon of Herodes Atticus, the likes of Moby, Calexico, and Massive Attack play at this mountaintop theater that is in its own way just as spectacular as the ancient Roman venue. Here you can see all of Athens glittering below through electric-pink sunsets (courtesy of the air pollution). If you're feeling adventurous, follow the folks climbing the rocks above the performance area for an unbelievable free seat. Don't worry about going thirsty. Nimble beer vendors will find you. To get here, take the funicular from Aristippou, then walk ten minutes to the amphitheater. *June-Sept. Showtimes vary.* C ≡ At the top of Mt. Lycabettus, 210-928-2900, culture.gr

HIP & COOL

Ochre & Brown • Psirri • Bar/Restaurant

A sleek and minimalist space that still manages to feel intimate with lots of nooks for drinking and people-watching, this new entry into the Psirri nightlife scene has already earned a loyal following of neighborhood hipsters. *See Hip & Cool restaurants p.88, for details.* C⬛B≡ Leokoriou 7, 210-331-2950, ochreandbrown.com

Passa • Kolonaki • Bar/Nightclub

Best See-and-Be-Seen Bars During the winter, a posing, black-clad crowd packs this Barbarella-inspired den—decked out with fluffy pink walls, dozen of mirrors, and kinky, leather-dressed mannequins behind the bar. The summer seaside incarnation isn't quite so funky—though the requisite white linen chaises are bedecked with hot-pink lights. But the people-watching is even better, as those black one-sleeves are traded for sparkly microminis and Manolos. *Oct.-Apr. 9pm-about 4:30am; May-Sept. 10:30pm-about 5:30am, restaurant 10pm-2am, cafe 11am-2:30am.* C⬛≡ Leventi 4, 210-721-1310 (Summer location: Karamanli 14,Voula, 210-895-9645, p.135)

Privilege • Gazi • Nightclub

Best Glamorous Clubs The reason Privilege has endured as Athens' reigning nightclub may just be that its very name taps into the national desire to be, well, privileged. It re-creates itself every season with a whole new look and location, taking the trend of the moment and whipping it up to its most over-the-top incarnation. Recent themes have included a Cabaret-style cocktail lounge, and an opulent Middle Eastern look. There are plenty of extras, like a private champagne bar and a VIP room with four-poster beds. The crowd is always guaranteed to contain Greek celebs plus a smattering of foreign luminaries—and, naturally, the velvet rope is the toughest in town. Though doors open at midnight, the party doesn't start until after 2am. *Daily mid-May–mid-June and Thu-Sun during winter, usually midnight-6am.* C⬛F≡ Location changes seasonally; check local listings for current whereabouts, 210-801-8304, privilege-athens.com

Tapas Bar • Gazi • Bar/Restaurant

One of the hottest bars in Gazi at the moment, Tapas Bar—true to its name—has a distinctive, dignified Spanish flair. The space—tiny, narrow, and always packed—has a prominent bar surrounded with stools on which dapper men, some in suits, and well-turned-out women in their late 20s perch and nibble on a selection of tiny bites. Evenings here start out with jazz and funk, but later, when the clientele is spilling outside, Latin sounds dominate. *Mon-Fri 1pm-about 4am, Fri-Sat 2pm-about 4am.* C⬛≡ Triptolemou 44, 210-347-1844

Voyage • Kolonaki • Bar/Restaurant

The Athens branch of the legendary Mykonos spot shares much of its beauty. The décor in this three-level mansion is lifted straight off of the island with its clean, whitewashed look that draws mature, sophisticated patrons. The first floor has a grand salon with two distinct areas: the lounge and the bar, which combine antiques with minimalism and feel more suitable for a glass of Nemea's best than a shot of tsipouro. The second floor has an all-white dining room, and the roof garden is best for lounging in white canvas chairs while taking in the Acropolis views. Service is courteous and friendly. *Mon-Sat 8pm-about 3:30am.* C⬛F≡ Kriezotou 11, 210-361-5996

Hip & Cool Athens:
The Attractions

Afternoon • Kolonaki • Shop

Afternoon is one of the most stylish boutiques in Athens—so avant-garde it's only open late in the day. In this dramatic store, which is designed like a theater dressing room with spotlights, black painted walls, and glass-fronted wooden wardrobes, the creative clothing, shoes, hats, and bags are designed by a diverse selection of up-and-coming Greek designers. *Tue-Thu 3-11pm, Fri-Sat 3-9pm Sun 3-7pm.* St. George Lycabettus Hotel, Deinokratous 1, Plateia Dexameni, 210-722-5380, sglycabettus.gr/facilities/afternoon.asp

Ananea Spa • Ekali • Spa

Far from the urban madness of Athens, the Ananea Spa at the Life Gallery Hotel takes 45 minutes to reach from downtown, but is worth the trip if detoxing and de-stressing are on your agenda. Small and personal, the spa offers body treatments you'll almost want to eat, like a lime-and-ginger massage or a coconut scrub. Guests can luxuriate in mud or rose-petal baths; bliss-out in an indoor swimming pool lined with candles; and decompress poolside with a tray of tea and fruit. Of course the usual spa features—fitness center, sauna, and steam room—are also available. €€€ Life Gallery Hotel, 103 Thiseos, 210-626-0456, lux-hotels.com/gr/life-gallery/spa.php

Asteria Seaside Beach • Glyfada • Beach

Best Beaches One of the closest beaches to central Athens, the Asteria has just about everything—except tranquility. This long stretch of fine gold sand and turquoise water has been taken over by private management, so for the price of admission you get beach volleyball, a water park, bars, a manicured garden area, and, often, the biggest all-day party in town. Both the pop radio station Rhythmos and Mad TV (the Greek MTV) regularly broadcast from here in summer, which means plenty of concerts, bikini fashion shows, celebrity walk-ons, and more topless thong-bunnies than you can shake a carrot at. For something more subdued, pay the higher admission fee to use the smaller, more exclusive section of the beach, run by club Balux. Here, you can lounge on white linen chaises around the pool and have mai-tais and Med-fusion finger food brought to your cabana while acid jazz breezes in from the speakers. *Daily 8am-between 7 and 9pm.* € Balux Club, 210-894-5676, balux-septem.com

Astrolavos • Kolonaki • Art Gallery/Shop

Is it a toy store? An art gallery? A silly breathing space in the middle of snootier-than-thou Kolonaki? It doesn't matter—funky little Astrolavos can't help but make you smile. With its focus on fun installations, on-the-verge artists, and special cheap art events, you're bound to find something to love in this new entry to Athens' art scene—one that's also been met with praise from serious critics. *Mon, Wed, Sat 11am-3pm, Tue, Thu-Fri 11am-8:30pm.* Irodotou 11, 210-722-1200, astrolavos.gr

Athinais Multipurpose Cultural Center • Votanikos • Entertainment Complex
Best Art Spaces Athinais is one of the brightest stars of downtown Athens' transformation from industrial wasteland to hyper-hip art district. The former silk factory is now a sophisticated arts complex housing Greece's Museum of Ancient
Cypriot Art, with treasures dating back to the 9th century BC; gallery spaces; a
concert hall; a theater; and an art-house cinema. It also has two excellent
restaurants (the lush Red and the more affordable brasserie Botanikos) and the
sleek Boiler Bar. While some factory-cum-art-spaces make good places to host
raves and display the work of rising artists, Athinais pulled off its rebirth with
style—the art in its galleries, the food in its restaurants, and the symphonies
performed in its theater are of the very highest quality. *Daily 8am-3:30am,
museum 9am-11pm.* € Kastorias 34-36, 210-348-0000, athinais.com.gr

Benaki Museum • Kolonaki • Museum
Best Museums With a collection spanning 2,500 years of Greek art housed in a
luscious wedding-cake-like mansion, the beautiful Benaki Museum is one of
Greece's sparkling jewels and an absolute must-do. Unlike the vast sprawl of the
National Archaeological Museum, it's possible to see the Benaki's hand-picked
collections in one visit—but that doesn't mean that anything on display is less
than first-rate. There's a superb collection of Classical sculpture and pottery,
intricately carved Hellenistic gold jewelry, stunning Byzantine shrines, and the
guaranteed crowd-pleaser: two enormous Ottoman-era sitting rooms. Each ele-
ment was carefully taken apart at the original homes in northern Greece, transported here, and pieced back together, to delightful effect. The Benaki gift shop
is also a destination in itself, offering exquisitely reproduced ceramics and jewelry. *Mon, Wed, Fri-Sat 9am-5pm, Thu 9am-midnight, Sun 9am-3pm.* €
Koumbari 1 & Vassilissis Sofias, 210-367-1000, benaki.gr/index-en.htm

Bettina • Kolonaki • Shop
This bright-white minimalist shop is the only place in Greece where you can buy
Sophia Kokosalaki's luxurious, Ancient Greek-inspired designs. The
Thessaloniki-born designer, who has become a key figure on the London fashion scene, is Greece's most famous sartorial export. Following close on her heels
comes Angelos Frentzos, a master of tailoring fitted leather, whose creations are
also sold here. While in the store, check out the classic-with-a-twist silk and jer-
sey dresses by Filep Motwary, a young Greek talent who's just spreading his
wings Paris-wards. *Mon, Wed 10am-3pm, Tue, Thu-Fri 10am-8:30pm, Sat
10am-5pm.* Pindarou 40 & Anagnostopoulou 29, 210-339-2094

Cellier • Kolonaki • Shop
Think Greece's only wine is retsina? A quick tour through the shelves of this
well-stocked cellar by one of the helpful members of staff will soon show how
wrong you are. Here you can find some of the finest vintages from the vineyards
of Santorini (where the white assyrtiko varietal is grown), Nemea, Macedonia,
and Attica. *Mon, Wed 9am-5pm, Tue, Thu-Fri 9am-8:30pm, Sat 9am-5pm.*
Kriezotou 1 & Papdiamanti 10, 210-361-0040

DESTE Foundation of Contemporary Art • Neo Psihiko • Art Space
Best Art Spaces International art collector Dakis Ioannou can arguably claim to
have single-handedly brought top-end contemporary art to Athens, a city whose
first museum of contemporary art isn't set to open until sometime in 2006. The

center, set in a converted paper factory, has exhibited the likes of Chris Ofili, Maurizio Cattelan, and Cindy Sherman in a city known mainly for displays of 2,500-year-old marble sculptures. It's also been a major boost to Greek artists, sponsoring contests to find young talent and bring them to an international audience. In keeping with the hipness of its mission, the center has the happening bar-restaurant Cosmos and a saucy hot-pink-and-shag-rug-decorated gift shop. *Mon-Fri 10am-6pm, Sat noon-4pm. Closed for two to three weeks in Aug.* € Omirou 8, 210-672-9460, deste.gr

Fanourakis • Kolonaki • Shop

Greece is deservedly famous for its jewelry. Fanourakis is renowned for its intricate works combining gold or white gold with diamonds or other precious stones, so why not pop in here to buy that special souvenir for a loved one? The tiny brooches in the shapes of beetles and butterflies are a Fanourakis trademark, but the shop also offers plenty of more flamboyant designs, such as chunky gold and ruby bracelets and 22-karat gold chokers studded with diamonds. *Mon, Wed 9am-3pm, Tue, Thu-Fri 9am-2pm and 5-8:30pm, Sat 9am-3pm.* Patriarchou Ioakim 23, 210-721-1762, gofas.gr/fan.htm

Frissiras Museum • Plaka • Museum

Tucked into a pair of restored homes on one of Athens' most old-world streets is this fresh collection of some 3,000 paintings by modern European artists. The works are linked by the same theme—the human form—but otherwise offer a vibrant spectrum of the best art coming out of Europe, from established names to up-and-comers. *Wed-Fri 10am-5pm, Sat-Sun 11am-5pm; guided tours: Sat-Sun 12:30pm.* € Monis Asteriou 3 & Plaka 7, 210-323-4678, frissirasmuseum.com

Goulandris Museum of Cycladic Art • Kolonaki • Museum

Best Museums Little is known about the elegant 5,000-year-old female figures found on Greece's Cycladic islands, other than that they're believed to have been associated with a matriarchal goddess cult and possibly used in sacrificial fertility rites. If that's not enough to get you to take a look, at least stop by to wander through the Stathatos mansion, designed by Bavarian architect Earnst Ziller and filled with the crystal chandeliers and fairy tale icing details that characterized wealthy Athenian homes 100 years ago. The mansion also holds exhibits of artists like Picasso and Modigliani, whose work was heavily influenced by those Cycladic icons. *Mon, Wed-Fri 10am-4pm, Sat 10am-3pm.* € Neofytou Douka 4 & Irodotou, 210-722-8321, cycladic-m.gr

Goulandris Museum of Natural History • Kifissia • Museum

If you've had your fill of the astronomically priced boutiques and Olympic-caliber posing of Kifissia, stroll through this lovely chateau-style mini-palace, set on a leafy little side street. The extensive, excellently researched exhibits of Greece's rich, natural wildlife include a beautiful botanical collection of more than 200,000 species of Greek plants (145 of which were recently discovered, thanks to the museum's research), along with insects, mammals, birds, reptiles, shells, rocks, and fossils. *Mon-Thu and Sat-Sun 9am-2:30pm.* € Levidou 13, 210-801-5870, goulandris-nhm.gr

Kalogirou • Kolonaki and Kifissia • Shop

The windows of this shoe institution are always lined with would-be Imelda Marcoses eyeing their next bargain. As well as the shop's own-label footwear, which usually consists of designer copies at marginally lower prices, Kalogirou also stocks gorgeous but expensive shoes from the real designers. A word of warning: Customer service can be downright rude—especially if the salesgirls decide you can't really afford to be browsing there. *Mon, Wed 9am-3:30pm, Tue, Thu, Fri 9am-8:30pm, Sat 9am-5pm.* Patriarchou Ioakim 4, Kolonaki, 210-335-6401; Panagitsas 5, Kifissia, 210-335-6404

Kem • Kolonaki • Shop

One of Greece's finest homegrown fashion brands, Kem can be relied on for its finely crafted and always up-to-the-minute leather handbags, totes, and luggage. The Kolonaki outlet, which has been in place over 10 years, suits the sophisticated, chic local clientele. Each distinctive, color-coordinated design comes in various shapes and sizes, in a synthetic make or leather. Smaller items such as wallets and change purses are displayed in the store's glass cases. *Mon 8:30am-3pm, Tue, Thu-Fri 8:30am-8:30pm, Wed, Sat 8:30am-3:30pm.* Patriarchou Ioakim 2, 210-721-9230, kemgroup.gr

Mastic Spa • Kolonaki • Shop

A small shop with a long history, Mastic Spa specializes in products that use mastic, the resin of the mastic tree, which only grows on the island of Chios. Ioannis Sodis, a renowned pharmacist with a thing for Chios, experimented in the late 1970s with mastic, mastic oil, and mastic water (derived from mastic leaves, which he distilled). He researched for years before introducing the first mastic product, a toothpaste called Masticdent. Since then, it's been used in everything from digestive remedies to burn salves, tooth whiteners, and skin creams. Mastic Spa continues the tradition with shelves of mastic-based products like shaving foam and sunscreen. *Mon, Wed, Sat 9am-3pm, Tue, Thu-Fri 9am-9pm.* Irakleitou 1 & Solonos, 210-360-3413, masticspa.com

Mt. Lycabettus • Kolonaki • Park

The pine-clad slopes of Athens' highest hill, rising up from the center of its poshest neighborhood, make a welcome retreat from Kolonaki's bustling streets. At the peak (reached by funicular, 210-722-7092), there's a great view. On clear days you can even see the Saronic Gulf and the Peloponnese. You can also light a candle in the tiny church of St. George, reserve a terrace table with a view at the restaurant Orizondes, or catch a sunset concert at the amphitheater. *Funicular runs daily, every 30 mins, 9am-11:45pm. The Chapel of St. George holds services every Sun.* Aristippou & Ploutarchou, 210-722-7092

Old Athens • Kolonaki • Shop

Former fashion stylist Vassilis Zoulias sells elegant shoes, bags, and gloves inspired by the ladylike designs of the '50s and '60s. The walls of this nostalgic parlor dedicated to the glamour of yesteryear are festooned with black-and-white photos of Audrey Hepburn, Grace Kelly, and Greek stars like Aliki Vouyouklaki. Zoulias' pointy, kitten-heeled slingbacks and dainty ostrich-skin clutches are hand-stitched by the few remaining maestros left from Athens' days as the leather capital of Europe. *Tue, Thu-Fri 9:30am-9pm, Wed 9:30am-3:30pm, Sat 9:30am-6pm.* Kanari 17, 210-361-4762

Preview • Kolonaki and Kifissia • Shop

This high-fashion spot sells glamorous shoes by Alessandro Dell'Acqua, Rodolphe Menudier, Michel Perry, and others. If you've got a foot fetish and a high credit line, this is the place to do some serious damage. *Mon, Wed, Sat 10am-4pm, Tue, Thu-Fri 10am-9pm, Sat 9:45am-4pm.* Patriarchou Ioakim 19, Kolonaki, 210-722-4731; Panagitsas 6, Kifissia, 210-801-1120

Zoumboulakis • Kolonaki and Kriezotou • Art Gallery/Shop

Zoumboulakis is the elder statesman of Athens' art galleries—among other coups, it claims to have been the first gallery in Greece to show Picasso. The main space in Kolonaki is not the hippest, but it's a good place to look at some of the best work by today's Greek artists. The more fun and funky shop is a good place to pick up cool silk-screens, sketches, and objets d'art. *Tue, Thu-Fri 10am-8pm, Mon, Wed, Sat 10am-3pm.* Exhibition space, Plateia Kolonaki; Shop: Kriezotou 7, 210-363-4454, zoumboulakis.gr

Downtown Athens

You've seen the glories of the Acropolis and walked the quaint, tourist-clogged streets of Plaka—now head to the gritty, throbbing heart of downtown Athens. Browse the city's colorful, chaotic markets, as vital today as they were when the Ottomans founded them, and up your cool quotient exploring the once-crumbling warehouse district, now blooming into a white-hot center of cutting-edge art galleries, fusion restaurants, rave clubs, and some of the most happening (and latest) nightlife in Europe. Of course, because this is Athens, all this modernity still rubs shoulders with ancient marble ruins and frescoed Byzantine churches, which suddenly appear next to cement apartment blocks and on taxi-laden 21st-century streets. It's all part of the inimitable texture and energy of this layered city.

*Note: Venues in bold in the itinerary are described in detail in the listings that follow. Venues followed by an * asterisk are those we recommend as both a restaurant and a destination bar.*

Downtown Athens:
The Perfect Plan (3 Days and Nights)

Highlights

Friday

Breakfast	Air Lounge*
Morning	Central Market
Lunch	Diporto
Afternoon	Artower
Cocktails	Gazaki
Dinner	Aristera-Dexia, Thalatta
Nighttime	Nipiagogio, Mikra Asia
Late-Night	Mao

Saturday

Breakfast	The Fresh Hotel
Morning	Exarchia Market
Lunch	Giantes, Cookou Food
Afternoon	Free time
Dinner	Kostoyiannis, Alexandria
Nighttime	Stoa Ton Athanaton, Taximi
Late-Night	Kavouras

Sunday

Breakfast	Adrianou Street
Morning	Monastiraki Flea Market
Lunch	Cafe Avyssinia
Afternoon	Shopping, Sport Spa
Cocktails	Stavlos*
Dinner	Oineas, Hytra
Nighttime	Soul, Inoteka
Late-Night	Ilias, Central Market

Hotel: The Fresh Hotel

Friday

9am Start the day with breakfast at the **Fresh Hotel's Air Lounge***. True to its name, the rooftop spot offers a breath of open air in Athens' urban jungle.

11am Walk down Athinas to the sensory overload that is Athens' **Central Market**. Poke through stalls to buy the best goodies to sample or bring home—olives, cheese, vine leaves, sweet baklava, and rich, aromatic olive oil. Leaving the market, head west on Evripidou, the most fragrant street in Athens, lined with spice shops purveying everything from Greek mountain thyme to North African saffron. Don't miss Athens' quirkiest church, the **Church of St. John of the Column**—a tiny Orthodox structure, built around an ancient Corinthian pillar.

1pm Lunch Head back toward the market and duck into **Diporto** for a traditional meal washed down by barrel wine. Or grab a meal on the go from the stalls and make your way to your next stop, **Artower**, a gallery space rising over the Central Market, and have lunch on its steps while the colorful crowds go by.

DOWNTOWN

3pm Walk back up Evripidou, turning left on Aristophanous, which takes you into the heart of Psirri, one of Athens' oldest and most interesting neighborhoods, blending authentic workshops, neoclassical houses, and graceful historic churches with a happening arts and nightlife scene. An afternoon coffee at any one of the cafes in its main square, Plateia Iroon, gives a view of its vibrant daytime personality. Then wander through Psirri's narrow streets, heading west to the **Benaki Museum of Islamic Art**, which has more than 8,000 pieces. You'll leave Psirri on Ermou—once a clogged traffic artery, now transformed into a stone-paved walkway. Head west and you'll see the graceful marble sculptures of Keramikos, ancient Athens' cemetery.

8pm Make for Gazi. Like Psirri, this area was once an abandoned downtown wasteland. Its name translates as "gaslands," referring to the soot that poured from its factories. These have been transformed into performance complexes, theaters, restaurants, and vast arts spaces. The king of these is **Technopolis**, a former foundry that hosts everything from exhibits of trash art to indie-pop concerts. Check out what's happening tonight, but first, warm up with a cocktail at nearby **Gazaki**.

11pm Dinner Then, for a meal to remember, cab it down the street to **Aristera-Dexia**, arguably Athens'

first and still most beloved Greek fusion temple. Or for some of Athens' best seafood, cross the street to **Thalatta**—don't miss the raw bar or the grilled octopus topped with pumpkin puree and sun-dried tomatoes.

1am After dinner, Gazi is your oyster. You can't swing a cat without hitting hot nightlife. A couple of places to try are trippy **Nipiagogio**, a former kindergarten turned into a cheerful lounge; the Turkish-inspired **Mikra Asia**; or, for the very out-there, **Bios**, a bar-slash-"art experience" filled with interesting installations. This is also the best place in town for some late-night dancing.

3am Onwards to the vast converted warehouse of **Mao** for dancing until dawn. If you're still feeling arty, grab a cab to avant-garde **Club 22** to check out its decadent theme parties. The most happening gay dance club in town, glittery and glam **Lamda**, is also nearby.

Saturday

10am After breakfast at the hotel, walk a few blocks to the bohemian neighborhood of Exarchia, aiming for Kallidromiou. On Saturdays, this is the scene of a bustling street market; on any day, it's full of colorful, old-fashioned cafes, and it's a great place to caffeinate and people-watch (especially if you overdid it last night).

11am Throbbing head quieted, go down to Stournari, where you'll see the **Athens Polytechnic** (Panepistimiou University). In 1973, dozens of university students were murdered here while demonstrating against the country's hated military dictatorship. The university still stands as a monument to the students, to rebellion, and to freedom.

1pm Lunch If all this history is simply too heavy, trot up pretty pedestrian Valtetsiou to lunch in the courtyard of **Giantes**—there's no more charming place in all of Exarchia. If it's cloudy, try hip **Cookou Food**, around the corner.

3pm Choose an activity from one of the other itineraries. If you are staying in Exarchia, the National Archaeological Museum is a good place to spend an afternoon. Afterward, grab a newspaper and head to Plateia Exarchia, favorite haunt of Athens' musicians, students, lefties, and punks.

9pm Dinner Come back to Exarchia for dinner at lively **Kostoyiannis'**, one of the oldest tavernas in Athens. For something a little different, head to the starlit courtyard of **Alexandria** for great Middle Eastern food.

11pm After dinner, it's time for a wild night of rembetika, the Turkish-tinged "Balkan blues." Reserve a table at Athens' top rembetika venue, **Stoa Ton Athanaton**. For a more mellow take on the experience, try the intimate **Taximi**, or the communist-China-themed bar-club **Floral Liberal**. If you're in the mood for something with a modern edge, see who is playing at **An**. You might also hop in a cab and head out to Athens' grooviest, smokiest (and smallest) jazz club, the **Half Note**. In summer when Exarchia's music venues are closed, take in an under-the-stars flick at **Riviera**, which screens classic black-and-whites and serves cocktails.

2am No matter where you go out in Exarchia, make your last stop a hot, sauce-soaked souvlaki at **Kavouras** on the way home.

 Sunday

10am Start at the recently pedestrianized Adrianou, once a grungy stretch, but now one of the most attractive streets in Athens, overlooking the Acropolis and Agora. Grab a coffee and hang out.

11am Don't miss one of the highlights of downtown Athens: the colorful **Monastiraki Flea Market** on Sundays, where peddlers sell everything from antique furniture to frilly lace underwear.

1pm Lunch For lunch, there's only one option: **Cafe Avyssinia**, with live musicians singing Greek folk songs, and a menu of simple and tasty favorites.

3pm Wander through Monastiraki, and check out some cool shops from our Classic itinerary: Pick up some custom-fit Greek-god sandals at The Poet (p.72) or hand-painted island ceramics at the Center of Hellenic Tradition (p.70). Or try the **Sport Academy Spa** at the Athens Hilton, with more treatments than any other spa in the city, plus superb workout facilities and a pool.

6pm Late afternoons, the buzziest scene is on Iraklidon, a tiny pedestrian street lined with hip cafes. The coolest has always been **Stavlos***, in the former Greek royal stables, now converted to an arts space and colorful courtyard bar that always draws a fun crowd. If you're feeling high-minded, go to the end of the street and check out the **Melina Mercouri Cultural Center**, an art gallery housed in a restored top-hat factory.

10pm Dinner It's time for a night out in Psirri. Your first stop should be either **Oineas** or **Zeidoron**. Both are fun, modern tavernas with outdoor tables that have views of all the Psirri action. In winter, try **El Pecado**, with its Spanish-church-turned-bordello décor and nightly surprises like magicians, DJs, and belly dancers. For foodies, try **Hytra**, which serves inspired new takes on Greek seafood dishes.

1am After dinner, check out **Soul** for fresh-fruit cocktails in a palm-filled garden or the candlelit maze of stone rooms and jazz at **Thirio**. The trendy gay scenes at **Playback** and **Bee** are great for an alternative, or try electronica at **Inoteka** if you're in the mood to groove. For a kicked-back option, have a beer at the 1am movie under the stars in the garden of **Cine Psirri**.

4am No matter what, your last night in Athens should end like an Athenian's. Find Karaiskaki and follow your nose to the hole-in-the-wall bakery/factory **Ilias** where hungry clubbers end their evenings. Or, follow the post-4am crowd to the all-night options at the Central Market (**Papandreou's Taverna** is the most popular). For an authentic experience, order patsas—a soup made of pig intestines, which Greeks swear is the best hangover prevention around.

Downtown Athens:
The Key Neighborhoods

Slogans spray-painted on **Exarchia**'s alleys by radical students conjure the city's politically charged past, while sparkling shopping arcades just meters from the university hint at its future. This is a youthful area, where passionate intellectuals share space with hippies, drug addicts, and artists.

Gazi is home of Technolopolis, one of the trendiest art spots in town. It's also the epicenter of downtown's revival.

Athens never really had an inner city, but an influx of immigrants has changed the color and hue of neighborhoods around **Omonia**, and its neighbors of **Rouf**, **Metaxourgio**, and **Neos Kosmos**. Here, it's not unusual to see multiethnic delis stocking feta, fresh-made hummus, coconut milk, and bamboo shoots, or find passionfruit and mangoes at the weekly farmer's markets.

Not so long ago, **Psirri**, the once down-and-out district between Athinas and Ermou, wouldn't have won a mention from us. But today, it's a buzzing hotbed of trendy cafes, restaurants, and clubs, thanks to low rents and the nearby Gazi.

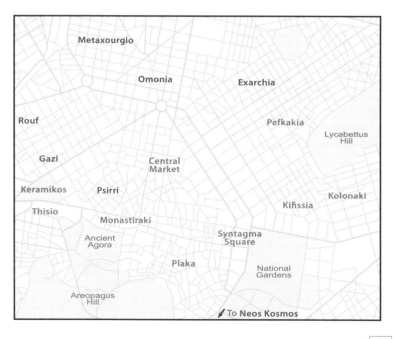

Downtown Athens:
The Shopping Blocks

Exarchia

Bohemian and fun, Exarchia is the place to come for the youthful, carefree fashions of Athens' 20-something set, and the accoutrements of the intellectual life.

Anavasi Map nirvana, from poster-sized surveys of Greece, to GPS devices to make your own. Stoa Arsakiou 6a, 210-321-8104

Psaltiri Hand-crafted musical instruments, even custom-made ones by Spiros Mamais. Emmanuil Benaki 101, 210-330-4198

Tsaknis Roasted pistachios to snack on when you get home, to remind you of those rembetika nights. Panepistimiou 49, 210-322-0716

Tsitouras Collection Decorative objects with the imperial flair you'd find at the Tsitouras Collection's exclusive retreat on Santorini. Solonos 80, 210-362-2326

Psirri

Often quirky and cutting edge, this is the place to head if you're looking for the ground zero of cool boutiques, new designers, and lots of cafes to rest your weary hands after signing all those credit card receipts.

Bahar Pick up mountain tea and saffron from Kozani at this rowdy spice market. Evripidou 31, 210-321-7225

Christoforos Kotentos An up-and-coming designer featured in international fashion mags and a growing number of exclusive boutiques around the world. Sahtouri 13, 210-325-5434

Closet Trendy women's clothing with an edge. Sarri 28, 210-331-1286

Ochi Original, often one-of-a-kind clothes and accessories in a warehouse setting. Sarri 35, 210-321-3298

Downtown Athens:
The Hotels

Athens Acropol • Omonia • Trendy (167 Rooms)

Local entrepreneurs have brought serious design to Greek accommodations, led by the forward-thinking Grecotel chain. Their star Athens property is the pricey N.J.V. Athens Plaza (see Hip & Cool Hotels p. 82), set in the fail-safe center of Syntagma Square. But their real gamble—and pay-off—came with the smaller Athens Acropol and Omonia Grand (see Downtown Hotels p.109) in the once-questionable center of Plateia Omonia—now just steps from the white-hot gallery and nightlife districts of Gazi and Psirri. The Athens Acropol is a perfect starting point for visiting both, with its arty lobby full of beaded fuchsia cushions, funky cylindrical light fixtures, and modern Japanese ceramics. Rooms are spacious and quiet, done in olive and cream with patterned-wood coffee tables, Art Deco armchairs, and other retro details. The best have balconies overlooking Omonia Square, but since it's on a busy street, request a higher floor for less noise at night. There's a good range of business services, along with baby-sitting, and the Omonia metro station outside is a hub that can whisk you away to meetings in minutes. €€ Pireos 1, 210-528-2100, grecotel.com

Athens Park Hotel • Exarchia • Timeless (152 Rooms)

For years, this hotel was a fallback for Greek business travelers. But a head-to-toe renovation, savvy P.R., and the addition of restaurant St'Astra, have sparked a total transformation. To be near bohemian Exarchia and the National Archaeological Museum, this is the best option. From the traffic-congested chaos of Alexandras, you enter a luxurious lobby with a crystal chandelier, buttery leather sofas, and the sounds of quiet piano and clinking glasses from the lounge. Upstairs, half the rooms have views to the Acropolis and half to Pedion Tou Areos, Athens' biggest park (we prefer the Acropolis view). All are comfortable with coral and midnight-blue furnishings, marble baths, Internet ports, and satellite TV. There's a gym with sauna, massage, and personal trainers, good conference facilities, and the Park Cafe, a meeting point for Athens society. But the indisputable star is the rooftop St'Astra restaurant (See Hip & Cool Restaurants p.90), with its Italian designer lounge, cowhide rugs, Murano glass chandeliers, and sublime cuisine from internationally acclaimed chef Herve Pronzato. €€€€ Alexandras 10, 210-889-4500, athensparkhotel.gr

Central Hotel • Plaka • Trendy (84 Rooms)

In early 2003, someone in Athens decided that "cool design" meant white, white, and more white—oh, and a bit of minimalism. Since then, this look has swept through the city's restaurants, bars, and hotels like a virus. The Central is one of the latest incarnations of this trend, and while it wins zero points for originality, it does fill a niche: the simple, central, but also sleek and chic little city hotel. So, yes, everything's white—marble lobby with white kidney-shaped sofa, cool white rooms with pale wood and glass accents, puffy white duvets, tatami floors, and windows overlooking a pale gray rock garden. The classic building carries off the look, and though minimal, the materials are high quality. Services are limited but friendly, and bonus points are given for the fantastic Acropolis views above the fourth floor and from the roof garden bar and rooftop Jacuzzi. € Apollonos 18, 210-323-4357, centralhotel.gr

Eridanus Luxury Art Hotel • Keramikos • Timeless (38 Rooms)

For many, the perfect hotel wouldn't be a hotel at all but a tasteful home among rich friends. For those of us without such friends, the Eridanus is a fine runner-up. The newly restored building with a typical Athenian neoclassical-era style has a lobby that feels like a salon, full of designer furnishings, walls peppered with contemporary art, couches and armchairs, and an area to enjoy the proprietor's fine espressos. A fitness center and steam bath add to the pleasures, while the rooms—each uniquely decorated and showcasing different works from rising and established Greek artists—make guests feel distinct. Most have tasteful dark green marble bathrooms, and eastward-facing rooms have Acropolis views. The only drawback is traffic noise in the neighborhood, but good sound-proofing cuts the buzz. €€ Pireos 78, 210-520-5360, eridanus.gr

The Fresh Hotel • Omonia • Trendy (133 Rooms)

The Fresh Hotel has brought something new to the downtown scene. Its claim that its arrival meant Athens would "finally have its own hip hotel centerpiece" has indeed proven to be true. Its design is at once peaceful and positively electric, since earth tones and organic touches like rock gardens throughout are offset with a neo-'70s design scheme with shocks of neon in the rooms and lobby. Rooms with Plaka-facing southern views and upper-floor rooms are best. The hotel is populated with 30-something Greeks entertaining their friends and clients in the art world, and is one of the few gay-friendly hotels in the city. The Fresh Hotel also houses one of the city's only urban spas, and the rooftop pool and Air Lounge, with dark wooden decks, have been buzz spots for downtown Athenians ever since they opened just before the Olympics. The hotel's restaurant and cafe are also notable. One drawback: The neighborhood is still gritty. When you leave your hotel, the area can seem a bit bleak, with auto shops, old stores, and a very inner city feel. €€ Sofokleous 26 & Klisthenous 2, 210-524-8511, thefreshhotel.gr

King George II Palace • Syntagma • Timeless (102 Rooms)

A former playground for kings, princes, presidents, and celebrities, the King George II prided itself on luxury. Built in 1936, it even hosted Grace Kelly and Prince Rainier for a month while she suffered complications from a pregnancy. But in the '80s, the King George shut its doors for nearly 15 years. Thanks to a recent renovation, completed in 2004 under current owners the Grecotel chain, the hotel, now called the King George II Palace, has been returned to its original glamorous state, and enjoys elite status as one of the Leading Hotels of the World. Overlooking Syntagma Square, this five-star property makes a royal first impression with Murano glass chandeliers and classic furniture. Each of the rooms is individually designed and decorated with hand-crafted armoires, custom raw-silk upholstery, and satin-fringed drapes. Bathrooms have deep sunken tubs and Bulgari toiletries. Rooms in the front and on the fourth floor sport views of the Acropolis. Don't be surprised to spot the likes of Diana Ross or Christina Aguilera here, as the hotel attracts a steady stream of film and music stars. The gourmet Tudor Hall restaurant is located on the seventh floor, a meeting ground for politicians, diplomats, corporate executives, and international celebrities. The King George has conference facilities, and its own fitness club and spa, offering massages, facials, and a variety of treatments. €€€ Vasileos Georgiou A 3, 210-322-2210, grecotel.com

Omonia Grand • Omonia • Trendy (115 Rooms)

Like its sister hotel, the Athens Acropol, the Grecotel-owned Omonia Grand is an oasis of fashionable designer cool in the middle of grungy, traffic-snarled Omonia, and bumps against the city's hippest neighborhoods. Granted, the designers may have gone a little overboard in the lobby—a mix of antique-print wallpaper and neon bug sculptures—but never fear, the rooms show an assured sense of designer detail mixed with traditional comforts: mod light fixtures alongside velvet drapes, wine-colored leather chairs, and marble bathrooms. The most lively rooms are the suites, decorated in lilac and silver. Some rooms have balconies overlooking Omonia Square, a hectic urban snarl that can be a fun view. Higher floors are better if you're after quiet, though double-glazed windows keep noise down in all rooms. The best part about staying here may be knowing that if it were just a few blocks away in Kolonaki, you'd probably be paying twice as much—and with no arty urban cachet.
€€ Pireos 2, 210-528-2100, grecotel.com

Residence Georgio • Omonia • Modern (136 Rooms)

At Residence Georgio, a new, distinguished large hotel near Omonia Square, the beauty lies in the details: warm pearwood room décor, exquisite bed linens and pillows, Jacuzzis and boutique-brand cosmetics in every marble-swathed bathroom, lights installed in closets, and complimentary custom-label wine and baskets of fruit placed in rooms. Suites are the real attraction, being exceptionally roomy and each with 30-inch plasma TVs. Rooms with southern views face the historical center of the city. An atrium-like fitness center is adjacent to a cool rooftop pool that includes an Acropolis view. The hotel clientele varies in age, and tends to include many elegant Cypriots and Italians engaged in conversation among the large lobby's clusters of sitting areas, as well as in the hotel's bustling sidewalk cafe.
€€ 28 Oktovriou & Halkokondili 14, 210-332-0100, residencegeorgio.com

DOWNTOWN

Downtown Athens:
The Restaurants

Alexandria • Exarchia • Middle Eastern
The Egyptian city of Alexandria was founded by Hellenes, and for centuries it was home to a lot of Greeks. Alexandria reflects the Hellenistic-Egyptian connection with a savory and sophisticated array of North African-cum-Med flavors. In the flowery courtyard in summer or in the cozy dining room lined with old, glass spice boxes in winter, feast with a bohemian crowd on dishes like octopus with eggplant, tomato, and tangy yogurt sauce. *Mon-Sat 8:30pm-1am. Closed in Aug.* €€ ▤ Metsovou 13 & Rethymnou 7, 210-821-0004

Aristera-Dexia • Rouf • Contemporary (G)
Best Nouveau Greek Dining It's been years since Chrysanthos Karamolengos pioneered Greek fusion (and put Athens on the foodie map) by imagining what would happen if a Greek mama's favorite dishes took a tour through Paris, New York, and Tokyo. He served up the results to a stylish and cool crowd in a funky industrial warehouse with a glass catwalk and Campari-bottle chandeliers. His experiment, Aristera-Dexia, is still one of the most name-dropped and best-loved restaurants in town. The menu is always changing, but recent favorites include seafood tempura with fig vinaigrette and crayfish dressed in lavender sauce, and the wine cellar is one of the finest in Greece. In summer it opens into an outdoor courtyard and serves simpler, post-modern taverna fare at lower prices. *Mon-Sat 8:30pm-1:30am.* €€€ ▤ Pireos 140 & Andronikou 3, 210-342-2606, aristera-dexia.gr

Cafe Avyssinia • Monastiraki • Meze
There's no better place to be on a Sunday afternoon in central Athens, when the little red tables at this family-run institution spill out into Plateia Abyssinia, offering front-row views to the colorful chaos of the flea market. Everyone who's anyone has lunched here, so sit back and order another carafe of wine, listen to the accordions and gypsy singers, and feast on delicious food that pays its respects to Greece's Middle Eastern ties: couscous with chutney, roast chicken with cumin, and grilled haloumi cheese from Cyprus. *Sept.-July Tue-Fri 10:30am-2am, Sat-Sun 10:30am-7pm; July-mid-Aug. Tue-Sun noon-1am.* € ▤ Kinetou 7, 210-321-7047

Cookou Food • Exarchia • Traditional
Artists and literary types hang out at this modern take on the old-fashioned taverna, just off the buzzing square of bohemian Exarchia. It's partly just that the space feels good—sunny yellow walls, eggplants hanging from the ceiling, and pictures and poem fragments painted on every table. But it's also the food, which is reassuringly old-school—hearty Greek village stews and piquant salatas—but there are a few fun additions, and everything is served by friendly, tattooed waitstaff. *Mon-Sat 1pm-1am. Closed 2 weeks in Aug.* € ▤ Themistokleous 66, 210-383-1955

Diporto • Central Market • Taverna

Ducking into this wine-barrel-lined cellar is like entering another world. The white-paper-topped tables are always packed with Greeks of every walk of life—blood-spattered butchers from the nearby Central Market rub shoulders with suit-clad brokers from the stock exchange, artists, journalists, and even ladies who lunch. There's no menu, but Barba Mitsos keeps everyone happy with his handful of delicious daily specials—the city's best horiatiki, buttery gigantes, fresh-from-the-market fish, and great barrel wine. If it's busy, you may be asked to draw your own. *Mon-Sat 8am-9pm.* € ≡ Sokratous 9, 210-321-1463

El Pecado • Psirri • International

El Pecado ("The Sin") resulted when a medieval Spanish-style church was mixed with erotic Bible-themed murals, dark-velvet thrones, wax-dripping candelabras, and a DJ soundtrack that blends flamenco with techno remixes of Damn Yankees. The result is delicious, audacious, and very fun. The menu runs from honey-barbecued chicken to truffles with pasta, but the real draw is the naughty-but-nice vibe and the like-minded crowd. *Oct.-mid-May Mon-Sat 10pm-3am. Moves to Mykonos in summer.* €€ ≡ Tournavitou 11 and Sarri, 210-324-4049

Giantes • Exarchia • Modern

Giantes is a hip but respectful update to the age-old tavernas that line cobble-stoned Valtetsiou, sleek and airy, with a fun menu of fusion starters. And no old-timer could find fault with the beautiful stone-paved courtyard smothered in bougainvillaea. Main courses like the Byzantine pork and chicken with honey, raisins, and coriander please the cool, arty 30-somethings, who like knowing that the owner heads Greece's foremost organic farmers' association. *Mon 8pm-1am, Tue-Sun 1:30pm-1am.* €€ ≡ Valtetsiou 44, 210-330-1369

Hytra • Psirri and Lagonissi • Contemporary (G)

Best Trendy Tables This cozy eatery draws a food-savvy crowd, mostly in its 30s and 40s. Some of the tasty offerings from chef Yiannis Baxevannis include seafood starters like fisherman's soup with bitter chicory, and calamari and spinach salad with julienne beets in a berry-filled sweet and sour sauce. Mains also often focus on fish, such as snapper served on a bed of raw grated squash and saffron potatoes. Save room for dessert, namely the shredded wheat pastry kataifi, filled with a bitter orange cream and served with poached dried apricots. In summer, Hytra moves to the sea at Grand Resort Lagonissi. *Mon-Sat 8pm-1am.* €€€ ≡ Winter: Navarchou Apostoli 7, Psirri, 210-331-6767; Summer: 40th km of the Athens-Sounio Hwy., Grand Resort Lagonissi, Lagonissi, 229-107-6000, lagonissiresort.gr

Ilias • Psirri • Bakery

The fresh baked scents from Ilias fill the entire block around this hole-in-the-wall institution. Ilias churns out hot, fresh koulouri (bagel-shaped, sesame-seed coated bread), raisin bread rolls, and doughnuts to hungry clubbers ending their evenings the way most Greeks start their mornings. It doesn't have a sign—look for the line. *24/7.* € Karaiskaki 23, 210-321-6797

DOWNTOWN

Interni • Thisio • International

Best Bar-Restaurants When a decadent bar-lounge-restaurant in the heart of the city's warehouse-and-art district is filled with models and hangers-on and is famous for a weekly hip-hop party known as "Booty Call," it's no surprise that the place is booked solid. What is a surprise is that the food is actually fantastic: Exquisite little purses of wild mushroom ragout and red onion confit with chive sauce or filleted red snapper stuffed with pine nuts and spinach are easily up to par with the city's haute cuisine offerings. Go on a Wednesday for the wildest scene. *Sept.-June daily 8:30pm-4am. Moves to Mykonos for summer.* €€€ 🆇🅱≡ Ermou 152, 210-346-8900, internirestaurant.gr

Kavouras • Exarchia • Souvlaki

Best Late-Late-Night Eats Liveliest after 3am, this is the place for your post-rembetika souvlaki fix. A ten-minute walk from Exarchia's prime music dives, here's where you'll see old Greek bouzoukia singers, Brit-pop indie stars, and fans of both loading up on hot slices of beef, wrapped in soft pita and slathered in tzatziki, after eight or ten beers and a night of grooving. Souvlaki was invented just for this, and Kavouras does it right. *Daily 10am-5am.* € ≡ Themistokleous 64, 210-383-7981

Kostoyiannis • Exarchia • Modern

Get far away from your fellow tourists at this authentic post-theater haunt that has lots of dark wood, barrel wine, sophisticated regulars, and a wide array of delicious Greek classics. Order from the menu, or just pick from the display in front—sure winners are the fresh fish, shrimp with ouzo, and warming, earthy stews, especially the rabbit stifado, made with sweet caramelized onions, cinnamon, and spices. *Sept.-mid-July Mon-Sat 8pm-2am. Closed mid-July-Aug.* € ≡ Zaimi 37, behind the Archaeological Museum, 210-822-0624

Mamacas • Gazi • Contemporary

Mamacas kick-started a trend that has transformed Athens' restaurant scene and its gritty downtown. The city's first "modern" taverna was a simple concept: hearty Greek village fare with a few new twists served in the then-fledgling Gazi district. The lure of great food with an arty edge brought out foodies and trendoids in droves and led to the opening of many copycats and to the burst of cool nightpots and fusion restaurants that have turned Gazi into the hippest part of town. Now the original has branched out into a late-night lounge next door. *Daily 2pm-2am.* €€ ≡ Persefonis 41, 210-346-4984

Oineas • Psirri • Contemporary

Everything about Oineas has a good vibe, from the 1950s Greek movie posters lining the inside, to the lights, music, and tables that spill out onto the streets of Psirri on warm nights. Oineas is both stylish and friendly, in a neighborhood that is sometimes too cool for school. The same spirit carries over to the food, which is ideally suited to sharing. Split a huge arugula and sesame chicken salad or plate of pasta, and pass around bite-size spanokopites. *Mon-Fri 6pm-2am, Sat-Sun noon-2am.* €€ ≡ Aisopou 9, 210-321-5614, oineas.gr

Papandreou's Taverna • Central Market • Taverna

Best Late-Late-Night Eats Deep in the Central Market's maze of alleys, this 24-hour taverna stays open long after the butchers and fishmongers have closed shop. Wander in at any time and pick from the hearty stews, casseroles, and kebabs, but peak hours are after 3am, when everyone from designer-suited scions to grizzled old rembetes and 16-year-old club kids packs in for a post-night-out nosh. The after-hours entree of choice (it's meant to prevent hang-overs) is patsas, but take care—the main ingredient is pig intestines. *24/7.* € ≡ Central Market, Aristogeitonos 1, 210-321-4970

Stavlos* • Thisio • International
Best Cafes The 19th-century royal stables have been converted into an all-day cafe-bar on this new stretch of walkway. In the stone-paved courtyard, student-types linger over coffees, cocktails, and board games, while 20- and 30-somethings grab seats out front to view the colorful street scene. As evening sets in, DJs kick up the tone with acid jazz, salsa, and electronica beats. Artwork is often displayed inside. *Daily 9am-3am.* €€ ℬ≡ Irakleidon 10, 210-345-2502, stavlos.gr

Ta Agrafa • Exarchia • Souvlaki
Best Souvlaki Purple-haired students, elbow-patched academics, tight-jeaned rockers, and every other Exarchia social type throng to this no-frills souvlaki joint on Valtetsiou for grilled pork and lamb sliced off the rotating spit, packed into home-made pitas, and smothered with garlicky tzatziki. Said by souvlaki aficionados to be among the very best in town. *Mon-Sat noon-2:30am.* € ≡ Valtesiou 50-52 & Benaki, 210-380-3144

Thalatta • Gazi • Mediterranean
Walking into this restored little house off the factory-lined streets of Gazi feels like stumbling into a wonderful secret. It's not just the island-y feel of the tile-paved, flower-filled courtyard—it's also discovering some of Athens' most delicious seafood in the heart of this trendy urban district. Start with fresh sea urchins from the raw bar, then move on to monkfish carpaccio with wild fennel, or salmon with cham-pagne sauce. *Mon-Sat 8pm-1:30am.* €€€ ≡ Koustantinopoleos 84, 210-346-4204

Zeidoron • Psirri • Meze
Dinner at this rambling multistory house in the center of Psirri is a perfect start to a night out in Athens' funkiest quarter. In winter, sit inside the stone-and-wood din-ing room; in summer, enjoy the open-air courtyard, or grab a table on the street to enjoy the picturesque old church across the way. The mostly mezedes menu is unsurprising but good, with a few very worthy offerings like lamb roasted with plums and port. *Daily noon-2am.* €€ ≡ Taki 10-12, 210-321-5368, zidoron.gr

Downtown Athens:
The Nightlife

An • Exarchia • Live Music
This small, smoky den is one of Athens' oldest and most beloved live music joints; it's hosted thousands of top European rock and jazz acts on their way to the top. The shows are always good, and there's usually an eclectic range, from Swedish rockers to jazzy takes on Greek traditional music. Check the sign outside the door for the occasional post-1am rave parties. *Mid-Sept.-mid–June Fri-Sat 9pm-4am.* Ⓒ≣ Solomou 13-15, 210-330-5056

Bee • Psirri • Bar/Cafe
A longtime meeting-place for starting a night in Psirri, Bee is no longer quite as edgy as it once was, but it's still loved by a mixed gay and straight crowd of 30-something magazine writers, fashionistas, and stylish Athenians who know it's never cool to try too hard. Everyone likes the shabby-chic painted pastel tables, colorful cube-shaped light fixtures, and groovy lounge tunes. On weekend nights, the gossipy cocktail-and-cigarette-clutching party nonchalantly over-flows out to the street. *Mon-Wed, Sun noon-3am, Thu-Sat noon-5am.* Ⓒ≣ Miaouli 6, 210-321-2624

Bios • Metaxourgio • Bar/Nightclub
Now that the former industrial wasteland of Gazi is firmly established as Athens' epicenter of art-gallery and warehouse-dance-space cool, the cutting edge needs to press on to something new. The prime contender is the still-gritty district of Metaxourgio, slowly waking up with the beginnings of a hip underground scene. Bios is the pioneer in this new frontier, and it's the place to say you've been if you want authentic downtown street cred with the supercool artist-and-DJ crowd. Set in an echoing 19th-century complex among artists' studios, Bios is often filled with funky installations set up by the neighbors—you may get lost in a forest of plastic flowers hanging from the ceiling or turn a corner and be confronted with a series of slides of nudes dancing on the wall. The music varies from house and trance to art rock and emo depending on the DJ—but like the crowd, it's bound to be very hip and high energy. *Daily 10am-about 3am.* ≣ Pireos 84, 210-342-5335

Cine Psirri • Psirri • Cinema
Best Summer Cinemas Funky Psirri's only outdoor cinema eschews mainstream fare for a diet of Hitchcock, Jarmusch, Chaplin, and the like under the stars. All movies are shown in their original language, with Greek subtitles, accompanied by ice-cold beers or cocktails from the bar. Within a two-minute walk of a dozen hip little nightspots and mezedopolia, it's the perfect start for a night out in Psirri—the last show ends at 1am, just as the rest of the neighborhood is gearing up. *May-Sept.* Ⓒ≣ Sarri 40-44, 210-321-2476

Club 22 • Neos Kosmos • Nightclub
Home to Athens' most spirited and fun-loving crowd, this trend-setting hot spot became famous for its theme-based parties. From Eurovision night and its Bollywood bash to the Bond ball and the notorious Kitscherella parties, a visit

here is an adventure in itself. Hosting everything from stand-up comedy, theater, and film screenings to concerts and exhibits, this multipurpose venue bursts at the seams with a hip 30-something crowd (and a smattering of stars) that takes the club's motto "Express Yourself" seriously. A place with personality that changes décor every now and then but retains a neon-lit touch of Pop-Art culture. *Wed-Sun from 11:30pm. Check listings for seasonal whereabouts.* ⒸΞ Vouliagmenis 22, 210-924-9814, club22.gr

Danza • Psirri • Nightclub
Best Dance Clubs True to its name, Danza is a dance extravaganza, with slinky dance teams set against an industrial backdrop touched with stained glass for color. At the heart of the city's entertainment district, Danza is downright sexy, swarming with a beautiful bunch of 20-somethings, and music and media folk. Action picks up after hours, when flocks of scenesters move upstairs to the funky gay club Playback. The club warms up earlier on Sundays thanks to the Defsoul R&B parties. *Tue-Sat. 9pm-4am.* ⒸΞ Aristopanous 11, 210-331-7105

Floral Liberal • Exarchia • Bar/Cafe
Is it a bar, an art gallery, or a club? It's hard to imagine kooky Floral Liberal being anywhere in Athens other than offbeat Exarchia. Its odd theme (military-rule communist China) is brilliantly executed with clever takes on proletarian slogans posted on the mirrored columns, giant Mao Tse Tung portraits looming overhead, camouflage tables and chairs, and splashes of red throughout. The spacious ground-floor bar-cafe area is open all day, frequented by a chatty, approachable crowd in their late 20s and early 30s. In the evening the slightly smaller subterranean club area of Floral Liberal fills up with a much flashier and energetic crowd at mirror-topped tables lining the dance floor. *Mon-Sat noon-about 3am.* ⒸⒷΞ Themistokleous 80, Exarchia Square, 210-330-0938

Fresh Hotel's Air Lounge* • Omonia • Bar/Restaurant
What serves as the Fresh Hotel's swimming pool area by day, replete with Acropolis views, transforms into a hot spot for young trendies after 8pm. The Air Lounge folds up its poolside sun beds and sets up tables and chairs for its fulll menu of Mediterranean-style cuisine. Dishes range from terrific buffalo milk mozzarella salad to penne rigate with smoked salmon in orange and vodka sauce. Burgers are also available, as are a full range of cocktails. Locals outnumber hotel guests from Thursday through Saturday when DJs spin '80s and '90s club music. When it rains, Air Lounge heads downstairs to Fresh Hotel's intimate Orange Bar. *Daily 8pm-1:30am, bar open until 2am.* ⒸⒻΞ Sofokleous 26 & Klisthenous 2, 210-524-8511, freshhotel.gr

Gazaki • Gazi • Bar
It might be small, but this cozy haunt has built a reputation that's bigger than its tiny wooden porch can possibly hold. Dim lights, flickering candles, alternative pop, plenty of popcorn, and lots of cool folks (with a touch of pretense) sitting, standing, and staring make this the place to be if you're of the arts, into the arts, or just plain artsy. Instead of walls, cardboard artworks depict the gasworks company that lent this bar its name. In the snug embrace of the once-industrial-now-turned-hip zone of Athens, this baby bar is all about seeing and being seen. *Daily 9pm-about 3:30am.* ⒸΞ Triptolemou 31, 210-346-0901

Half Note • Pangrati • Live Music

Best Live Music Venues The best spot to tune in to the ethnic/jazz scene—local and international—is dark, sensual, and sophisticated. A tad small, with vantage points only for the lucky few who get there early, this established house of jazz plays host to a top-notch lineup of artists and draws baby boomers and the eclectic bunch of uptown execs who want to sharpen their listening skills. Big-name gigs sell out quickly, so securing tix in advance is a must. Local bands play on calmer nights. *Daily 9pm, showtimes vary.* C☰ Trivonianou 17, 210-921-3310, halfnote.gr

Home Lounge/Home Club • Elliniko and Gazi • Bar/Restaurant

One of the city's most popular new nightspots, Home is quite tourist-friendly, and it's one of the only year-round clubs to offer city views from its pleasant terrace, which booms with electronica and house sounds. It calls itself "the first virtual club in the world," a curious and almost unintelligible description, with video projections changing nightly. Early in the evening, it has more of a loungey feel, and light meals are available. Later on, around 1am, the whiter-than-white minimalist space takes on a decidedly more clubby atmosphere, as the DJ console heats up and its youthful patrons start packing in. Its summer location on the coast in Elliniko is shared with Kolonaki's Voyage restaurant. *Daily 7pm-about 3:30am.* B☰ Home Club, Posidonos 5, Elliniko, 210-894-4138; Home Lounge, Voutadon 34, Gazi, 210-346-0347

Inoteka • Monastiraki • Wine Bar

When the electronica-loving hipsters who run Inoteka took over this jewelbox of a space from the previous owners—an old-fashioned, exclusive restaurant—they effected a full transformation, with cherry-red walls, funky lounges, and the addition of their vast catalog of trance, ambient, and trip-hop vinyl on the turntables. But they kept the extensively stocked wine cellar downstairs, which means you can still enjoy a refreshing vintage Bordeaux with your Chemical Brothers. Inside, music lovers get geeky over the sound system, but for a mellow vibe, come in summer when candlelit tables are set up in the cobblestoned plateia. *Daily 8pm-6am.* ☰ Plateia Abyssinia 3, 210-324-6446, inoteka.com

Interni • Thisio • Bar/Restaurant

This chic, über-designed lounge—black leather beanbags and giant wine-red lanterns—transforms into a heaving crush of pretty people (including a sinfully high number of international models) during the Wednesday night dance parties, delicately known as "Booty Call." *(See Downtown Restaurants, p.112, for description).* No cover except Wed. C☰F☰ Ermou 152, 210-346-8900

Lamda • Makrigianni • Bar/Nightclub

Best Gay Bars Athens' longest-running gay dance club is a standard-looking but well-executed cocktail of shiny silver-and-glass walls, colored strobe lights, well-gelled shirtless men, and Europop, Greek and dance hits du jour. The bar is packed with cruisers who adjourn to the dimly-lit back room. A few women occasionally come to dance as well. *Daily 11pm-about 5am.* C☰ Lembessi 15, 210-922-4202, lamdaclub.gr

Mao • Psirri • Nightclub

Best Dance Clubs There's no lack of hot dance clubs in Psirri, but Mao manages to stand out and stay packed night after very long night. The highlight of the cavernous space, with dramatic eastern motif, is a Kodo drummer who is lowered onto a platform, pounding and thumping the crowd into a frenzy whenever spirits start to flag. In back, a raised dais is a hangout for those looking to get noticed, and also clubbers who want a break. Like many clubs, Mao moves oceanside in summer, but doesn't have a fixed location, so check local listings. *Wed-Sun 9pm-4am.* C≡ Ayion Anaryiorn & Agatharou 3, 210-331-7639.

Mikra Asia • Rouf • Bar/Lounge

The name means "Asia Minor," and this Turkish-themed lounge has the appropriate low couches, beaded cushions, red lighting, colored tiles, and a wall-size picture of the city Greeks still call Constantinople. The crowd is sophisticated, mellow, and over 30, but definitely still enjoys lazing on the harem-y chaises and stuffing bills into the sparkling costumes of the excellent belly dancers. *Daily 7pm-4am.* C≡ Konstantinopoleous 70, 210-346-3851

Nipiagogio • Gazi • Bar/Cafe

The name means "kindergarten," which is clear as soon as you walk into this old well, kindergarten. With pint-size silhouette paintings on the wall, stained-glass flower windows, and a balloon-and-fairy-light-filled courtyard, this place just manages the balance between whimsy and cool. The soundtrack, which bounces between acid jazz, trip-hop, and '80s pop, the arty 30-something crowd, and the downtown Gazi location keep it fun instead of cloying. *Daily 9pm-about 4am.* ≡ Elasidon & Kleanthous 8, 210-345-8534

Playback • Psirri • Bar/Nightclub

Best Gay and Lesbian Bars The bar that was once legend ventures back into the public eye, not on Mykonos, but in one of the loudest and hippest blocks in Athens. Pierro's people are back in action. This gay-friendly haunt in gaudy colors and kinky bits and pieces cranks up the volume after midnight with solid servings of hip-hop, house, and progressive, offering 30-something scenesters a view to the other side ... through a glass interface. The party migrates between next door club Danza, and back. *Thu-Sun 11pm-about 5am. Things get going around 2am.* C≡ Aristophanous 11, 210-331-7105

Riviera • Exarchia • Bar/Cafe

Set in a bower of bougainvillaea on a cobblestone pedestrian street, the Riveria is easily one of Athens' prettiest summer cinemas. It shows good movies, too, tending toward arty and independent flicks. However, because it's in the middle of a residential neighborhood, the speakers are turned down for later showings. Come around 9pm and relax with a drink from the bar, and then head out to a night of bohemian fun in Exarchia, starting with dinner in the courtyard of Giantes next door. *May-Sept. Showtimes from about 9pm.* C B ⊟ Valtetsiou 46, 210-383-7716

DOWNTOWN

Soul • Psirri • Bar/Club

Best See-and-Be-Seen Bars Soul is hip minus the attitude. Despite its popularity, there's still no snooty bouncer or impenetrable velvet rope. It's at its best in summer, when fashion-and-writer types fill the courtyard, sheltered by lush palms and lit by Chinese lanterns. Reserve a table and order up a tray full of spicy Asian finger food and fresh-fruit cocktails—the lemon daiquiris and Bloody Marys are the best in town. After 1am, the indoor dance floor—a lipstick-red cube—heats up to fever pitch. *Daily 9pm-4am. Closed for three weeks in Aug.* B≡ Evripidou 65, 210-331-0907

Stavros tou Notou • Neos Kosmos • Live Music

Best Live Music Venues Athens' premier indie club draws a casual crowd more likely to show up in worn denim than designer anything. A large venue with multiple stages, Stavros tou Notou lures international bands as well as local groups. For music lovers, the smaller stages are favorites for discovering the next big Greek thing. *May-Oct. Wed-Sat from about 8pm.* CF≡ Frantzi & Tharipou 37, 210-922-6975

Stoa Ton Athanaton • Central Market • Rembetika

Best Rembetika Clubs Athens' best known rembetika club is a rollicking all-day all-night party set in the middle of the city's Central Market. If you only spend one day or night taking in the "Balkan blues," do it at this old-time classic. Reservations at night are a must, but it's also fun to drop in on a cold winter afternoon, when the carved-wood hall is slightly less packed. *May-Oct. Mon-Sat 3:30-7:30pm and 10:30pm-8am.* CF≡ Central Market, Sophokleous 19, 210-321-4362

Taximi • Exarchia • Rembetika

Best Rembetika Clubs This bohemian rembetika haunt is a step into another world, with its devoted clientele of old-time music-lovers and musicians, students, and elbow-patched academics. It's got smoke-stained walls, signed black-and-white photos of the greats, red candles on tiny cafe tables, and the best, most bluesy performers in Greece. *Mid-Sept.-Apr. Wed-Sun 10pm-3am.* CF≡ Harilau Trikoupi & Isavron 29, 210-363-9919

Thirio • Psirri • Bar/Lounge

Walking into this old stone house feels like falling into a dream. Small rooms flow endlessly into one another, lit by flickering candles in wall sconces. World jazz plays, tucked-away couches beckon, and hipsters, lovers, and jazz fans get to know each other over glasses of red wine and warm honeyed raki. *Sun-Thu 8pm-3:30am, Fri-Sat 8pm-5:30am.* CB≡ Lepeniotou 1, 210-321-7836

Venue • Psirri and Varkiza • Nightclub

Best Dance Clubs Hot spots in Athens come and go, but this favorite has stayed at the top for years by constantly reinventing itself. There are always top DJs—both local and international, and patrons are among the sexiest you'll see in Europe. When you reserve a table, you'll get not only a bottle, but also unlimited mixers and free cigarettes. As for the coveted VIP room, it has harem-style beds, sushi, and model-perfect staff. *Sept.-May Wed-Sun 11pm-about 5am. Moves to Varkiza for summer.* CB≡ Winter: Agias Eleousis 3, 210-331-7801; Summer: Athens-Sounio Coastal Hwy., Varkiza, 210-897-1163

Downtown Athens:
The Attractions

Artower • Omonia • Art Gallery

Set right in the heart of the gritty, chaotic Central Market area, Artower combines eight floors of contemporary art, unimpeachable downtown street cred, and ravishing Acropolis views, all in one very cool new package. Each floor has a different gallery with its own distinct style—for example, sixth-floor Ourania hangs avant-garde paintings, the fifth-floor Erato is devoted to architecture and design, and the fourth-floor Clio focuses more on representative and figural art. There's also a shop and a funky new cafe, Art + Taste. *Wed-Fri 3-8pm, Sat noon-4pm.* Athinas & Armodiou 10, 210-324-6100, artower.gr

Athens Polytechnic • Exarchia • Historical Site

While Greeks are proud of the Acropolis, this building makes them truly misty-eyed. The events that happened here are arguably the most important in modern Greek history. In 1973, when the country was run by a military dictatorship, students from Athens Polytechnic protested acts of random jailing and torture. In response, the colonels rolled out tanks and shot many to death in the streets and buildings around the Polytechnic—the exact numbers are still unknown. The protest led to the overthrow of the junta the next year and the return of democracy to the country of its birth. The university, an impressive structure in its own right, stands as a monument to the rebellion. Inside its gates is a marble sculpture honoring the students who were killed. On November 17, the anniversary of the protest, Greeks turn out en masse to lay flowers before it. And every day, students keep with the spirit by leafleting for the leftist cause du jour in front of the Polytechnic's gates. Patission & Stournari, ntua.gr

Benaki Museum of Islamic Art • Psirri • Museum

Kolonaki's Benaki Museum, founded by one of Greece's wealthiest art dynasties, has a first-rate collection of Greek art displayed in a rich marble mansion that draws Athens' most well-heeled socialites. Just in time for the Olympics, the museum opened a new branch amidst the workshops, nightclubs, and art-student haunts of Psirri. Located in a renovated neoclassical house, the museum displays highlights from Antonis Benaki's collection of 8,000 pieces of Islamic art, including an extraordinary filigreed 10th-century gold belt from Samarra, Iraq; a 14th-century universal astrolabe (the only known example of medieval astronomical equipment of its kind); and the entire marble-lined reception room of a 17th-century Egyptian mansion, transported from Cairo. *Fri-Sun, Tue 9am-3pm, Wed 9am-9pm.* € Corner of Ayion Assomaton & Dipilou, 210-325-1311, benaki.gr/collections/islamic/en/

Central Market • Central Athens • Market

For the truest taste (and smell) of Athens, there's only one place to go: the sensory overload that is the Central Market. The enormous covered marketplace was built in 1870 and in many ways has remained unchanged since. On the blood-spattered, yellow-lit north side, butchers stand among carcasses of every description, barking out prices while hacking expertly with massive cleavers just centimeters from their fingers. The adjacent fish market is actually rather beautiful, with sunlight streaking in from the high glass roof glittering off fish scales of every color. This is the place to feel the heart of the city and to stock up on everything from artisanal olive oil to wedges of fragrant feta or sweet, flaky hunks of baklava. *Mon-Sat 7am-3pm.* € Sofokleous & Evripidou

Church of St. John of the Column • Central Athens • Church

Athens' quirkiest church is a perfect paradigm of the city's layers of history. The tiny Christian basilica, believed to date back as early as the 6th century AD, is built around a marble Corinthian column left over from an ancient pagan temple, most likely dedicated to the god Apollo. It's set on Evripidou, a street where spices introduced in Ottoman times are sold and that is now filled with shops run by Greece's new waves of migrants, desperate to assimilate in a modern European Union country. *Daily mid-morning to early-evening.* Evripidou 72

Keramikos • Central Athens • Archaeological Site

This rambling green-gladed oasis in the heart of central Athens was actually at the far outskirts of the city in Classical times. Running through the site are the foundations of the Themistoclean wall, the 5th-century BC barrier hastily built at the city's edge as the Spartans threatened to invade. Inside the wall are the poetic remains of ancient Attica's largest cemetery, filled with huge marble tombs built for statesmen and heroes. This was also home to prostitutes and even had an old marble brothel built on site. In the small but fascinating museum, you can see evidence of that past in the 2,500-year-old erotic engravings on display. Other quirky artifacts include small bits of stone carved with curses, which ancient Athenians slipped into the tombs of their enemies. *Daily 8am-5pm, but call to confirm hours.* € Ermou 148, 210-346-3552

Melina Mercouri Cultural Center • Thisio • Art Space

Once a top-hat factory, this steel-and-stone structure has been converted into a lovely art space displaying works by Greece's finest painters and photographers. The center, at the end of trendy Iraklidon and at the edge of Gazi, can claim credit for helping transform this part of town from industrial wasteland to up-and-coming art district. Its one permanent exhibit is a re-creation of a street from turn-of-the-19th-century Athens, using all authentic antiques and miscellanea to create storefronts, a mayor's office, and more. *Tue-Sat 9am-1pm and 5-9pm, Sun 9am-1pm.* Iraklidon 66, 210-345-2150

Monastiraki Flea Market • Monastiraki • Market

Whether you're searching for a one-of-a-kind Hellenistic antiquity or just a few dirty postcards and a bottle of ouzo, you won't want to miss Athens' best flea market. Sunday afternoons, when the rest of the city is closed up, little Plateia Abyssinia comes alive with peddlers selling everything from marble-topped Rococo dressing tables and 18th-century editions of the *Iliad* to Turkish liquor bottles, Russian nesting dolls, satin G-strings, and glow-in-the-dark Jesus figures. You're bound to find something you never knew you needed. Bring your haggling skills. *Sun around 8am-3:30pm.* Plateia Abyssinias & Ifestou

Sport Academy & Sport Academy Spa • Ilisia • Gym/Spa

A truly full-service spa and fitness center, Sport Academy has everything you need, whether it's revving up at the state-of-the-art gym and aerobics studio, or decompressing with the "hydrotherapy" facilities, like the atmospherically lit pool featuring underwater lighting, water-massage devices, and "water curtains." You can also wind down in the sauna or meditation room, take an "event shower" with exotic scents and sounds, or relax at the foot-spa stations. Treatments are extensive, and include aromatherapy, acupuncture, and massage. There is also a full salon. €€€ Athens Hilton, Vassilissis Sofias 46, 210-725-7070, hilton.com

Technopolis • Gazi • Art Space

Best Art Spaces When the city of Athens bought this abandoned foundry and converted it into a multipurpose arts complex, it kick-started the transformation of the surrounding neighborhood, Gazi (named for the gas that once spewed from the factory), into Athens' hippest art and nightlife district. Today Technopolis' smokestacks are illuminated in red neon, drawing the cooler-than-thou crowd to exhibitions of everything from trash art to photographs of Iraqi children. It also hosts a European jazz festival, indie concerts, and avant-garde theater performances in its vast courtyard. The one permanent exhibit is the Maria Callas Museum, a small collection of the diva's personal items. Check local listings for exhibits and evening events. *10am-9pm during exhibitions.* Pireos 100, 210-346-7322, cityofathens.gr

By-the-Water Athens

Come June, most of the city's nightclubs close down and migrate south to Attica's beaches, shedding their winter locations like overstuffed parkas in a crowded room. Stick around Athens' sweltering heat and you'll quickly understand why. But along the Aegean coast, you'll find herds of thong bunnies and bare-chested he-babes intensely going about the business of a Greek summer: drinking, tanning, and resting up for a long evening of carousing. When the glorious sunset has fallen below the horizon, made almost spiritual in its beauty by that last daiquiri, the crowd slinks away to don its Choos and Cavalli, then returns for an open-air club scene that lasts until dawn. But this isn't the soulless Hamptons: There's culture to be had, with the magnificent ancient Temple of Poseidon, the god who inspired it all, presiding over the cliffs. Check it out. And then it's time for a Bloody Mary, and another tough day on the sand.

*Note: Venues in bold in the itinerary are described in detail in the listings that follow. Venues followed by an * asterisk are those we recommend as both a restaurant and a destination bar.*

By-the-Water Athens:
The Perfect Plan (3 Days and Nights)

Highlights

Thursday

Breakfast	**Café Freddo**
Morning	**Hellenic Maritime Museum**
Lunch	**Achinos**
Afternoon	**Arti Themistokleous**
Cocktails	**Istioploikos**
Dinner	**Jimmy and the Fish**
Nighttime	**Neon, Love Cafe**
Late-Night	**Romeo**

Friday

Morning	**Scuba dive, Apollon Spa**
Lunch	**Oceanis**
Afternoon	**Grand Beach Lagonissi**
Dinner	**Varoulko**
Nighttime	**Passa**

Saturday

Breakfast	**Ghiolman Yachts, Patroklos**
Lunch	**Patroklos Taverna**
Afternoon	**Sounio**
Evening	**Temple of Poseidon**
Dinner	**Ithaki**
Nighttime	**Privilege**

Hotel: Astir Palace Resort

Thursday

10am Hop a taxi from the hotel and plunge into the waterfront of Piraeus, Greece's biggest harbor. Founded in the 5th century BC by the Athenian general-statesman Themistocles, it has grown today into a sister city to Athens, but one with a distinct character. The harbor is a mix of glamorous yachts, humble fishing boats, ferries disgorging tanned tourists, and tankers and cruise ships embarking on cross-Atlantic odysseys. The surrounding area is filled with ouzeries, rembetika joints, and ancient ruins. Start your exploration of the port with a coffee on the garden terrace of **Cafe Freddo**, which overlooks the sweeping bay of Passalimani, the harbor of 60-foot yachts and flashy gin palace cruisers.

11am Then stroll up to the **Hellenic Maritime Museum** to zip through the history of this seafaring country's long relationship with Poseidon. From here, a ten-minute walk inland will bring you to the **Archaeological Museum of Piraeus**, which is home to some of the most magnificent works of Classical Greek art in existence.

1pm Lunch If you're a seafood fan, it's hard to go wrong. At chic **Achinos**, views and fresh fish are embellished with refined mezedes and a well-chosen wine list. About a mile up the coast is **Diasimos**, loved for its barbecued fish and barrel wine. Or take a taxi to the cult favorite **Margaro**, where there's huge portions of the catch of the day.

3pm Work off lunch by taking the coastal promenade, **Akti Themistokleous,** all the way back to Passalimani, continuing on to the pretty harbor of Mikrolimano, filled with fishing boats and lined with tavernas. Head up the steep slope behind the harbor, which leads to the historic hilltop neighborhood of Kastella, a picturesque jumble of narrow streets, neoclassical mansions, and a perfect panorama. At the peak, marked by the white-domed Church of Profitis Ilias, have a drink on the terrace of the **Bowling Center Cafe**. If you're not up to the hike, taxi back to the **Astir Palace Resort Beaches** and try the resort's abundant water sports, from jet-skiing to snorkeling. Or you can work on that swimsuit body by booking a private Pilates session.

9pm After a siesta, head back to Mikrolimano, which comes alive with music drifting from seafront cafes. Take in the view over drinks at the Yacht Club rooftop bar **Istioploikos**, peopled by true sailors and a fair share of glam-orous wannabes. In summer, head to Kastella's ancient **Veakio Theatre**, to see a concert or dance performance as the sun sets over the sea.

11pm Dinner You'll want a waterside table at friendly **Jimmy and the Fish**, famous for its grilled fish and sesame-crusted shrimp cooked in ouzo. Next door, chic **Plous Podilato** does a designer take on seaside dining, with a sophisticated kitchen turning out grilled baby octopus with fennel or cuttlefish over white-beet risotto. Further inland, everyone from local fishermen to politicians shares benches at **Dourabeis** for fresh lobster and red mullet pulled from the sea.

1am In summer, check out open-air lounge **Neon**, where you can sit with cocktails on white leather sofas under the stars or join the pretty people grooving to ambient house on the dance floor. For late-night drinks by the water, try the neo-'70s-inspired **Love Cafe**, and for something mellow, retreat to Kastella for a nightcap in the candlelit **Don Quixote's**.

3am Head to the main coastal road of Posidonos and roll into the early hours at a glitzy seaside bouzoukia club—**Romeo**, **Thalassa**, and **Posidonio**, all longtime favorites of Greek bouzoukia fans.

Friday

9am There's taking a dip at the beach, and then there's plunging in the Big Blue (which, remember, was also the name of a film shot near Greece's sapphire waters). Go all the way with a half-day scuba trip arranged by the **Aegean Dive Center**, which organizes dives for swimmers of all levels of experience. If submerging doesn't appeal to you, then there's also "taking the waters," which you can do in high style at the seaside **Apollon Divani Thalassotherapy Spa**—one of the best spas in Greece and the only one around Athens to offer the trademark Greek treatment of thalassotherapy, which uses fresh, heated seawater. Afterward, get wrapped in seaweed, scrubbed by sea salts, and rubbed down by the best masseuses in the country.

1pm Lunch Emerge like Aphrodite from the waves and sail into **Oceanis**, a trendy palm-fringed cafe whose terrace opens out to Vouliagmeni Bay. Or take a seat at the sleek new **Kitchen Bar** overlooking Alimos Marina, and have calamari or Caesar salad with a view of sailing students trying their first skiffs.

3pm Don your designer pareo and taxi down the coast to the **Grand Beach Lagonissi**. Spend the afternoon lounging on linen chaises,

having a Shiatsu massage by the pool, sipping cocktails and nibbling gourmet finger food, playing on a jet ski, checking out the crowd, or maybe even taking a swim. In the cooler months, water babies may also be drawn to **Vouliagmeni Lake**, a clear, blue-green thermal spring that stays warm year round and is said to have extraordinary healing powers. Or bypass the water altogether in favor of a few rounds at the coastal **Glyfada Golf Club**, the only place near Athens to swing a nine-iron.

10pm Dinner Head to **Varoulko**, where foodies flock to taste chef Lefteris Lazarou's creations. Let him choose for you, picking from the likes of crab salad with mango, grapes, and leeks, or honey-laced mullet roe. The urban branch of this restaurant is set in Piraeus, but in summer it moves here to a seaside terrace in Vouliagmeni. For Saronic Gulf views accompanied by groovy DJ beats, reserve a table on one of the three seafront balconies at trendy but mellow **Vive Mar**.

Midnight It's a short drive down the coast to happening, hot-pink **Passa**, where you'll be engaging in prime people-watching, posing, and even some dancing as the night wears on.

Saturday

9am From Odysseus to Onassis, there's never been any question that the best way to explore Greece's greatest asset is from the deck of your own boat. Book a private charter and board one of the crafts at **Ghiolman Yachts**. They'll provide everything you need, from a skipper and crew to a luxurious lunch. You can also chart your own course by renting a car for a drive along the coast to the village of Thymari. Once there, take the first turn on the right and follow the sign to **Patroklos**. You'll end at a beach where a water taxi leaves every ten minutes for this pristine island, with a magical shoreline and sparkling water. Call the boatman in advance and he'll be waiting for you when you arrive.

1pm Lunch After a swim, you'll definitely want to fill up on the catch of the day and some retsina at the island's only structure, the wonderfully rustic **Patroklos Taverna**. Or, if you stayed on the mainland in your rented wheels, continue along the coast towards Sounio. Stop on the way at **Syrtaki** for a traditional taverna meal on the sea view terrace.

6pm Get back out on the road to Sounio, aiming to arrive at the **Temple of Poseidon** about an hour before sunset. Take some time to explore the site—it's at its most

sublime as the sun dips down over the dazzling waters. Watching the sky fade from rose to wine behind the marble columns is one of the most memorable moments to be had in Greece.

10pm Dinner After all that sun, salt, and sea air (and hopefully a shower), head to the glass-and-wood **Ithaki**, built into a cliff jutting over the Agean, so every table has a sea view. Relax over caviar and grilled sea bass in its lily-filled dining room. Farther down the coast, you might also go for sushi and sinful chocolate desserts on the beautiful terrace of **Island** before moving on to cocktails and dancing by the sea with a glamorous crowd.

Midnight Close out the night—or, rather, the early morning—by making an appearance at one of Athens' most famous downtown nightclubs in their summer seaside incarnations. Sip champagne among soccer stars and their model wives at **Privilege**, or dance to the dark, throbbing beats at **Venue**. End with a splash—toss yourself into the sea as the sun rises.

By-the-Water Athens:
The Key Neighborhoods

Glyfada is part of the eastern coast from Elliniko to Sounio that forms a very cosmopolitian riviera with its mix of moderate apartment buildings, luxurious villas, modest restaurants, and trendy nightclubs that all have one thing in common: the laid-back attitude of the seaside.

Piraeus has the quicker, tenser pulse of a large port with its attached city. Here wealth and poverty float side by side like oil and water, bumping up against one another, but never mixing. One of this area's most lively waterfront districts is **Mikrolimano**, where you'll find dozens of cafes, bars, and shops.

The southern coast is all about fishing lines strung with octopus left to dry in the Aegean breeze, brightly colored beach umbrellas, waterfront bars, and palm trees tracing the stunning shores—not to mention that its golden sands are an adult playground dotted with swingsets and basketball courts for daytime, and the hottest dance clubs for nighttime revelry.

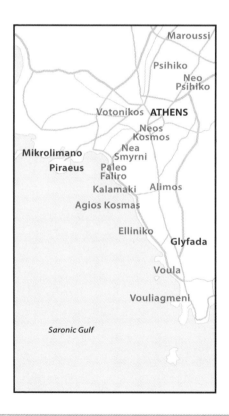

By-the-Water Athens:
The Shopping Blocks

Glyfada

Glyfada is a delightful mix of high-end brands and boutiques, especially around Metaxa Street.

Achilleas Accessories Look for Greek designs in the piles of scarves, bags, baubles, and sandals in this local chain. Andreou Metaxa 13, 210-323-9970

First Super-sexy styles from a designer who's the pet of the city's fashionistas. Grigoriou Lambraki 16, 210-898-2423

Soho Soho Private Head here for the season's must-have additions to your wardrobe. Gounari 112, 210-961-6688

Piraeus

Window-shop international designer labels like Longchamp and Furla on Iroon Polytechniou or poke around smaller streets like Notara for exotic teas, spices, and knickknacks.

Fresh Line Fresh-made cosmetics inspired by the Greek gods. Try an Aphrodite moisturizer or Poseidon bath bomb. Sotiros Dios 31, 210-413-7038

Ice Cube Discount outlet for one of Kolonaki's hottest designer emporiums with labels like Deux Hommes and Aesthetic Theory. Pireos 76, 210-483-8230

Parthenis Wonderfully baggy unisex drawstring linen pants, flowing tunics, and breezy and chic clothes perfect for an island summer. Praxitelous 143, 210-413-2325

Vardas Bargainhunter paradise for shop-label tailored suits and last season's designer items. Pireos 76, 210-483-1802

By-the-Water Athens:
The Hotels

Astir Palace Resort • Vouliagmeni • Modern (3 Hotels; 508 Rooms)
Best Rooms with a View This is the hotel of Greeks' fantasies, and the backdrop for scores of movies from the Greek cinema's golden era. The guest list is an eclectic mix of jet-setting moguls and media stars, executives, and foreign dignitaries who like to relax away from prying eyes but without going into seclusion. Jane Fonda and Ted Turner are rumored to have stayed here, but the hotel won't confirm that (sleep-and-tell is so tacky). Set on 75 acres of private grounds on a peninsula with spectacular sunsets over the sea, this resort is 25km southeast of the city center, which is served by a shuttle, limousine service, and even a heliport. The complex encompasses three modern hotels—the Arion, the Nafsika, and the Aphrodite. It was remodeled in 2004 by the world's top hospitality interior design firm, Hirsch Bedner Associates, whose work you'll be familiar with if you've visited the Fullerton Hotel in Singapore, the Mandarin Oriental in Miami, or the Bacara Resort in Santa Barbara. Rooms now boast modern furniture, high-tech facilities, and 24-hour room service. There are three beaches complete with chaises and parasols, three outdoor pools, floodlit tennis courts, and a great choice of bars and restaurants. All rooms in Nafsika have sea views. Arion sea-view rooms are arranged so that the bathtubs have prime water views. A new Astir Spa is scheduled to open in 2006. €€€ Apollonos 40, 210-890-2000 / 800-888-1199, astir-palace.com

Divani Apollon Palace & Spa • Vouliagmeni • Modern (286 Rooms)
This seven-story 1970s concrete-and-glass structure overlooks Kavouri Bay, 18km from the city center, which is served by a hotel shuttle bus. A member of Leading Hotels of the World, its big, new attraction is the luxury Spa & Thalasso Center, with a large indoor seawater pool lined with emerald-blue mosaic tiles. Hotel guests and nonguests alike come here to wallow, steam, and indulge in massage and beauty treatments. The spacious rooms all have balconies with sea views and are adorned with modern oak furniture and sophisticated Italian designer fabrics. Each room has a TV Internet connection and a sleek, green marble bathroom. The complex opens onto a private beach with water sports facilities, and there's also a garden with two outdoor pools rimmed with white chaise longues, served by the Meltemi Snack Bar. An American buffet breakfast can be enjoyed overlooking the pools, while the Mythos seafood restaurant looks directly onto the beach (and can be reached through an underground tunnel). The Pelagos Bar opens each night to the sounds of live piano music and the shaking of some of the city's best cocktails. €€€€ Aghiou Nikolaou 10, Iliou, 210-891-1100, divaniapollon.gr

Grand Resort Lagonissi • Southwest of Vouliagmeni • Modern (318 Rooms)
It doesn't get much more indulgent than this. Depending on which level you'd like to book (Comfort Club, Premium Club, Exclusive Club, or Platinum Club), you'll get niceties here that range from simply swell (sea-view rooms, verandas, CD players, satellite TV, marble bathrooms, computer connections) to totally knock-your-socks-off (personal trainer, butler, chef, and even pianist). Villas have heated seafront pools, the royal suite has both indoor and outdoor pools, and you can be chauffeured in a limousine, Lear jet, or helicopter, after spending time enjoying the 120-some acres of prime coastline (with extravagantly showy beach scenes, *see Best Beaches, p.19*), browsing the shopping center, getting pampered in the spa, or lighting a candle in the Lagonissi chapel. On site restaurants cover all the bases: an ouzerie, an Italian restaurant, a Polynesian and sushi joint, and even a floating bar, among others (oh, and nutritional consultation is also available if all this becomes a problem). Rooms in the main building can be a bit small. Opt for a seaside bungalow with private pool, instead. €€€€ 15km (9mi) southwest of Vouliagmeni on the Athens-Sounio Rd., Lagonissi, 229-107-6000, lagonissiresort.gr

The Margi • Vouliagmeni • Timeless (90 Rooms)
Indisputably one of the coolest hotels you'll find in Greater Athens, this six-story rose-pink building with balconies shaded by green-and-white striped awnings is just a five-minute walk from the beach at Vouliagmeni Bay. The reception lounge has wooden floors, Persian rugs, and an open fireplace. The staff is young and good-looking and dressed entirely in black, and ethnic music sets the mood in all the public spaces. The guest rooms are done up in warm hues with 19th-century antiques, including a wardrobe and desk, and gray marble bathrooms are supplied with Bulgari products. Some have views of the pine forest, but the ones with views of the bay are spectacular. All rooms have a DVD player, and you'll find a DVD library at reception. The ground-floor Cafe Tabac is a mellow bar-restaurant serving Mediterranean dishes, plus sushi and finger food, and remains open until 2am. There's a small pool in the garden (also open to non-residents for a fee), and a poolside bar serving cocktails, malt whiskeys, and cigars into the early hours. An American buffet breakfast is served each morning overlooking the pool. The Margi is popular with Greek couples on romantic weekend retreats and with glamorous Americans and Europeans on longer stays. €€€ Litous 11, 210-896-2061, themargi.gr

By-the-Water Athens:
The Restaurants

Achinos • Piraeus • Seafood
Reminiscent of the best of Santorini, this split-level bar-restaurant is built into a cliff overlooking the sea, just a ten-minute walk from Passalimani. The restaurant is on two levels, with fantastic views across the water, especially at sunset, and is done up with blue-and-white checkered tablecloths, white sofas, and blue wooden chairs with wicker seats. The menu changes seasonally but always features regional specialties like the delicious grilled haloumi cheese from Cyprus, barbecued fish, hearty casseroles, and a tempting range of colorful, beautifully presented salads. Achinos means "sea urchin," and indeed sea urchin eggs are on offer here too. The staff provides professional service, there's a great wine list, and there's live music in the winter on Saturday night and Sunday afternoon. *Daily 10am-midnight.* €€ ⊺⨍▤ Akti Themostokleous 51, 210-452-6944

Bowling Center Cafe • Piraeus • Cafe
If you make the stiff uphill climb through Kastella to arrive at the highest point, Profitis Ilias, you more than deserve a break. The Bowling Center Cafe has a vast terrace with stunning views across the bay to Athens and all the way along the coast, including the Peace and Friendship Stadium and the Olympic seaside complex at Faliro. The '70s interior is impersonal and dated, but that doesn't keep locals from flocking there for standard Greek fare, pizza, ice cream, coffee, and drinks. *Daily 10am-3am.* € ▤ Profitis Ilias, Kastella, 210-412-0271

Cafe Freddo • Pasalimani • Cafe
Overlooking the flashy motorboats that cruise in and out of Passalimani harbor, the Cafe Freddo garden is laid out with marble-top tables, comfy wicker chairs, and potted palms. It stays open all day for coffee and drinks, and also serves a tempting selection of toasted sandwiches, cakes, pastries, and ice cream. *Daily 8am-2am.* € ▤ Plateia Alexandras 14, 210-422-6637

Diasimos • Piraeus • Seafood
A one-mile walk following the meandering coastline along the seafront promenade from Freatida brings you to this popular psarotaverna (fish restaurant) and ouzerie that's a taste of the islands. The blue frontage has large windows opening onto a seafront terrace (often lined with octopus hanging out to dry), filled with wooden tables and chairs, and locals indulging in a late lunch on a summer afternoon. They serve up delicious fried calamari, barbecued fish, and retsina wine straight from the barrel. The waiters don't speak much English, so just remember barbouni (red mullet), gavros (anchovy), tsipouro (gilt-head sea bream), xifias (swordfish)—and kali orexi (enjoy your meal). *Daily 10am-1am.* €€ ⨍▤ Akti Themostokleous 306, 210-451-4887

Dourabeis • Piraeus • Seafood
Members of the Spanish royal family ate here recently and apparently loved it. On the go since 1932, Dourabeis is totally unassuming, with a small terrace with wood-and-wicker-seat chairs and blue-and-white striped awnings out front,

and down-to-earth service inside. However, it's also one of the top places to eat straightforward grilled, fresh fish, dressed with olive oil and lemon. Look for tsipouro (gilt-head sea bream), barbouni (red mullet) and astakos (lobster), to be accompanied by a decent bottle of white wine. Round it all off with Greek coffee and loukoumades (honey-soaked Greek doughnuts) for dessert. *Daily noon-5pm and 7pm-12:30am.* €€€ ≡ Akti Dilaveri 29, 210-412-2092

Island • Varkiza • Mediterranean (G)
Seafood as good as the view from celebrity chef Yannis Geldis. Stay for one of the hottest club scenes on the coast. *See By-the-Water Nightlife, p.135 for description.* €€ ⅩⒷ≡ Limanakia Vouliagmenis, 210-965-3563

Ithaki • Vouliagmeni • Mediterranean (G)
This swank restaurant is housed in a modern wood-and-glass structure on a cliff overlooking the Astir Palace Resort public beach. The parquet-floored dining room is on three levels, with a glazed facade opening onto a terrace so all tables have a sea view. Tablecloths and cushions are cream, fawn, and brown, and large glass vases of lilies are on display, as well as a smattering of movie stars. Fish predominates, but there are several interesting meat dishes. Kick things off with Russian red caviar, follow it up with either grilled sea bass with sautéed spinach or duck breast with raspberry and redcurrant sauce, and finish with pavlova with berries and whipped cream. *Daily 12:30pm-1:30am.* €€€€ ⅩⒷ≡ Apollonos 28, Laimos Vouliagmeni, 210-896-3747, ithakirestaurantbar.gr

Jimmy and the Fish • Piraeus • Seafood
Best Seafood Restaurants Long hailed a classic seafood favorite, Jimmy and the Fish affords a prime position overlooking the postcard-perfect fishing harbor of Mikrolimano. On the waterside terrace—complete with blue-and-white striped canvas fold-up chairs and retractable white awnings—you can see anyone from bearded Orthodox priests to celebrities. Waiters run to and fro with silver ice-buckets for chilling the wine, platters of grilled fish, and huge black frying pans of lobster with linguini pasta. *Daily 12:30pm-1:30am.* €€€ ≡ Akti Koumoundourou 46, 210-412-4417, jimmyandthefish.gr

Kitchen Bar • Paleo Faliro • Cafe
Overlooking the sailboats of Alimos Marina, this new cafe-restaurant from the outside seems more like a factory than an eatery. However, the cool spacious interior offers respite from the midday sun—the furniture is all wood, and there's a central open-plan kitchen area so you can see the cooks at work. The menu includes club sandwiches, Caesar salad, stuffed potatoes, pasta dishes, and grilled meats, making it an ideal lunchtime spot. Or, take a table on the terrace and opt for coffee or a cocktail. *Sun-Thu 9am-2am, Fri-Sat 9am-4am.* € ≡ Posidonos 3, Alimos Marina, 210-981-2004

Margaro • Piraeus • Seafood
So, so simple, yet so good. Fish is the only entrée item here, but no need to dig deep in your pockets. Margaro is unique in that it serves a limited selection of fried fish, fresher than fresh. Expect whitebait, mullet, bream, and shrimp, depending on the night's catch. Also basic but wholesome horiatiki (Greek salad) with the season's best tomatoes and cucumber, Kalamata black olives, and feta cheese, served with a sprinkling of oregano and a dash of olive oil. Take

a marble-topped table on the terrace, order a carafe of retsina, then sit back and wait for the goodies to arrive. Margaro's located next to the Naval Academy, but it's difficult to find, so you're probably better off taking a taxi. *Mon-Sat noon-midnight, Sun noon-5:30pm. Closed Aug.* € ≡ Hatzikyriakou 126, 210-451-4226

Oceanis • Vouliagmeni • International
Great for a light lunch before an afternoon on the beach, this cafe-restaurant looks directly onto the rolling sands of Vouliagmeni Bay. Outside there's an open-air terrace planted with palms and shrubs and lined with tables, while indoors the double-height space and mezzanine has a glazed facade with sea views. The interior is furnished with '70s retro orange, brown, and beige leather sofas. Choose from a menu of sandwiches and salads plus a limited selection of pasta and risotto dishes. *Daily 8am-2am.* €€ ≡ Apollonos 1, 210-896-1133

Patroklos Taverna • Patroklos • Taverna
Each summer, this tiny informal taverna opens up on the castaway island of Patroklos. The menu is simple, featuring locally caught fish cooked over glowing charcoal, plus seasonal salads, fresh bread, and hima (barrel wine). As there is no fresh water supply, this is one of the few places where you'll be obliged to fork out for bottled mineral water. Also, no espresso machine—so it's hard core ellinikos kafes for your afternoon caffeine fix. *Daily late-June-early-Sept.* Call contact at Patroklos ahead of time to make sure taverna is open. € ≡ Island of Patroklos, near Thimari, on Athens-Sounio Rd., 229-103-7326

Plous Podilato • Mikrolimano • Seafood (G)
Best Seafood Restaurants Overlooking the fishing boats of Mikrolimano, this restaurant is a great surprise: Finally, something funky, fusion, and refined. It's only been here since 2002, but it's already won the hearts of many seafood connoisseurs. The dining room is minimalist chic, the terrace overlooking the water likewise. But the menu is full of creative delights, with an experimental touch. Choose from crayfish tails sautéed with ouzo and anise and served on a warm salad with ginger, or stuffed grouper with spinach and lemon. Ask the waiter to recommend a wine compatible with the dishes you've ordered. *Daily 12:30pm-12:30am.* €€€ ≡ Akti Koumoundourou 42, 210-413-7910

Syrtaki • Sounio • Traditional
This family-run restaurant makes an ideal stop if you're visiting the Temple of Poseidon at Sounio. There's a cozy tiled-floor dining room with wooden furniture and shelves stacked with wine bottles, but the main pull is the outdoor seating on two terraces with sea views. The menu features barbecued fish (look for red mullet and sea bream, and excellent lobster) and spit-roast meats (delicious lamb). The fries are made from real potatoes and the salads are colorful and tasty—they even use roka (arugula) in the horiatiki (Greek salad). The service is slow, but then in a place like this, who's in a hurry? *Daily 12:30pm-midnight.* €€ ≡ 2km north of the Temple of Poseidon, 229-203-9125, syrtaki.gr

Varoulko • Piraeus/Keramikos/Vouliagmeni • Seafood (G)
Best Seafood Restaurants Scoring a prestigious Michelin star in 2002, owner-cook Lefteris Lazarou earned the respect of Athens' most avid foodies with Varoulko, a superb fish restaurant located in a former warehouse in Piraeus. In 2004, he scored another success when he opened another Varoulko in a

gorgeously renovated building with a contemporary, bistro-like atmosphere in a newly-trendy downtown location. The menu changes daily, but look for beautifully-presented creative seafood dishes like baby squid with pesto and monkfish cooked in wild celery and topped with sautéed hot peppers. *Mon-Sat 8:30pm-1am.* €€€€ B≣ Winter: Deligeorgi 14, Piraeus, 210-411-2043; Summer: Marina Vouliagmenis, Vouliagmeni, 210-967-0659; Branch location: 80 Pireos, Keramikos, 210-522-8400 varoulko.gr/uk/varoulko.html

Vive Mar • Voula • Seafood
Best Tables with a View It's all about the view—the glittering Saronic Gulf, studded with vibrant green islands—at this seaside escape. Three levels of palm-shaded balconies make the most of the caressing sea breezes and super-soothing panorama. Linger over a long lunch of good creative Italian fare, or, for the most sublime scene, snag a table at sunset. *Sun-Thu 8am-2:30am, Fri-Sat 8am-4am.* €€€ ≣ Karamanli 18, 210-899-2453, vivemar.gr

By-the-Water Athens:
The Nightlife

Don Quixote's • Piraeus • Bar/Cafe

Best Candlelit Bars Warm, intimate, and seductive, this hideaway nighttime bar has been on the go since the 1970s. It's perched on the hillside overlooking Mikrolimano, with creaky wooden stairs leading to a candlelit rooftop terrace with views over the fishing harbor and yacht club. The atmosphere is friendly and informal, the music rock and soul plus a few old-time Greek favorites. *Daily 9pm-3am.* ▤ Vasileos Pavlou 68, Kastella, 210-413-7016

Island • Varkiza • Bar/Restaurant

Best Dance Clubs by the Sea Inspired by the simple white forms of Cycladic architecture, with a series of levels opening out onto the sea furnished with low-level sofas and coffee tables, Island has to be one of the most exclusive clubs in town. Red silk drapes are suggestive of a harem, while the palm trees and music—ethnic, Oriental, ambient, plus mainstream hits—recall places warm and exotic. This is a stunning place to eat, drink, dance, and name-drop—among the guests you're guaranteed to spot models, celebrities, and high-powered businesspeople. *May-Oct. Club: 11pm-about 3:30am; Restaurant: 9:30pm-2am.* ⒸⒷ▤ Limanakia Vouliagmenis, 210-965-3563

Istioploikos • Mikrolimano • Bar/Cafe

This smart rooftop bar, overlooking the sheltered marina with its sailing boats moored up with creaking ropes to one side and views out to the waves beating against the rocks to the other, is one of Piraeus' top see-and-be-seen spots. You may need a sailing license to rent a vessel, but looks and attitude are enough to get you a table here. The décor is trendy, minimalist white, with tables and chairs arranged to make the most of the views, and a central bar rimmed by high stools on four sides. The crowd is mostly ritzy-dress with plenty of gold, plus a few weather-beaten yachting types. *Daily noon-about 2:30am, kitchen closes midnight.* ▤ Yacht Club of Greece, 210-413-4084, istioploikos.gr

Love Cafe • Mikrolimano • Bar/Cafe

Maybe not where you'd expect to find it, squeezed between the rustic seafood tavernas of Mikrolimano, but Love Cafe has certainly brought a touch of the new millennium to this quaint fishing harbor. The interior is '70s retro minimalist white, from the flexiform plastic tables and chairs to the floor-to-ceiling drapes. Cushions and lampshades add the occasional splash of red, while the pulsing music keeps the energy high. The clientele is young, dressed-up, made-up, and ready to party—keeping the waterside terrace buzzing into the early hours. *Daily 10am-2:30am.* Ⓕ▤ Akti Koumoundourou 58, 210-417-7778

Neon • Piraeus • Bar/Cafe

With a vast open-air terrace and a three-level interior arranged like a stage set—white leather director's chairs, white leather sofas, a mezzanine, and a mirrored back wall—Neon is the place to look good. During the day, it functions as a mellow cafe, serving coffee and drinks to the easygoing sounds of Moby and Eros Ramazzotti, but after midnight you'll find the fantastic sound system has come into its own, pumping up the shiny, happy people with anything from sophisticated ambient to commercial dance music. Order a Neon Special (rum, amaretto, Cointreau, fresh strawberries, and lemon syrup on ice) and the night is yours. *Daily 10am-about 2am or 3am.* F≣ Akti Dilaveri 5, 210-347-5655

Passa • Voula and Kolona • Nightclub

Best Dance Clubs by the Sea Exclusive, and thus much-loved by the image-conscious Kolonaki-Kifissia crowd, Passa lives up to all expectations with a cool and airy white, minimalist interior opening directly onto the sea. Color is added with funky, pink-silk, hanging lampshades, lush Mediterranean plantings (lots of bougainvillaea), and of course, the people—upscale and fashionable. Music is mainstream—summer's latest hits plus cheerful hip-hop. An upmarket spot to drink, dance, and eat. *May-Sept. Club: 10:30pm-about 5:30am; Restaurant: 10pm-2am; Cafe: 11am-2:30am.* C F≣ Karamanli 14, 210-895-9645

Posidonio • Elliniko • Bouzoukia

Best Bouzoukia in Summer Where else in Athens would those rubbing against the bar get as clear a view as those occupying a table? This dome of delight along the trendy coastal strip is all about back-to-basics entertainment. Growing on the phenomenal success of Greek crooner Yiannis Ploutarchos, this circular '80s-style venue, dressed in subdued colors and lush carpet, swells up with hordes of tipsy latecomers in their mid-20s who plunge into the action in the small hours and party on until sunrise. Opt for Thursdays if you want to avoid the weekend push and shove—you'll get better service and a decent vantage point. *May-Sept. Wed-Sun 11pm-5am.* B≣ Posidonos 18, 210-894-1033

Privilege • Various • Bar/Nightclub

Best Glamorous Clubs Although it moves each summer, it's always on the beach and always a top-notch venue. Run by the same management who gave us Privilege in Kifissia, this is a stylish rich kids' affair, drawing in tanned blonds in mini-skirts and men slick enough to pick them up. Hard to get in, unless you know the right people or have reserved a table. Convertible BMWs and Range Rovers outside, mainstream music plus occasional Greek hits inside. *Daily mid-May-mid-June and Thu-Sun during winter, usually midnight-6am.* C F≣ Location changes; check local listings or ask your concierge for details. 210-801-8304 privilege-athens.com

Romeo • Glyfada • Bouzoukia

Best Bouzoukia in Summer Bouzoukia at the beach: What better way to blast through an Athens night? Romeo's summer incarnation sends upbeat Greek and Asian music of longing and desire wafting through the seaside air, while on the dance floor the young and restless dance with abandon and guys fling flowers at their gals. *Mid-May-mid-Sept. Wed-Sun 11pm-about 5:30am.* ≣ Ellinikou 1, Glyfada, 210-894-5345; Winter location changes yearly. Check local listings or hotel concierge for location.

Thalassa • Asteras Glyfadas • Bouzoukia

Best Bouzoukia in Summer Athens' restless 20-somethings head for the water-front in summer for their boisterous nights of bouzoukia by the sea. Thalassa, which actually translates as "sea," sits adjacent to the beach in trendy Glyfada, and on warm weekend nights spills over with young women confined by slinky skirts and skin-tight tops and men sporting white linen and slicked hair. This is not the sophisticated set. Thalassa brings in bouzoukia fans just as intent on ripping it up as listening to the singers perform. It's not unusual for the crowd to end up dancing on the tables as room on the floor gets too tight to move. *Tue-Sat 9:30pm-about 6am.* B≣ Posidonos 58, 210-898-2979

Veakio Theatre • Piraeus • Theater

Located at Profitis Ilias, the highest point of Kastella, this 2,000-seat open-air theater hosts the Piraeus Summer Festival each year, July-August. The program features classical theater and music, with performances given both by Greek artists and touring foreign groups. C≣ Profitis Ilias, Kastella, 210-419-4520

Venue • Varkiza and Psirri • Nightclub

One of central Athens' hottest winter clubs also brings us down to the beach at Varkiza for warm summer evenings below the stars, champagne cocktails, and mainstream hits softened by the sound of the waves. Be sure to look good, feel good, and, when you're finally overcome by the urge to cast Gucci sandals aside and take to the water, don't whisper a word to anyone. *June-Sept. from 11pm.* C≣ Summer location: Athens-Sounio Coastal Highway, Varkiza, 210-897-1163; Winter location: Agias Eleousis 3, Psirri, 210-331-7801

BY-THE-WATER

By-the-Water Athens:
The Attractions

Aegean Dive Center • Glyfada • Dive School
The Aegean Dive Center organizes daily morning dive trips (ranging from a few hours to all-day excursions). Boats depart from Glyfada (with a maximum of ten divers) and travel along the coast to Cape Sounio, offering chances to explore an underwater wreck, a cave, and a reef. Visibility is 30-100 feet, and water temperatures are around 26°C (78°F) in summer and 14°C (58°F) in winter, making diving possible all year. The staff speak excellent English, and for those with no experience, the center runs introductory courses. €€€€ Zamanou 53 & Pandhoras, 210-894-5409, adc.gr

Akti Themistokleous • Piraeus • Neighborhood
With the open sea and views to the islands of Aegina and Salamina on one side and modern apartment blocks and psarotavernas (fish restaurants) to the other, this lamp-lined coastal promenade follows the course of the ancient seaward walls, which date back to the 5th century BC.

Apollon Divani Thalassotherapy Spa • Vouliagmeni • Spa
One of Greece's premier spas, the seaside Apollon Divani is blissful just to look at—all marble whirlpools, waterfalls, and sun streaming in from windows that open straight out to the sea. Services center on Greece's signature technique, thalassotherapy—a system of rejuvenation and healing based on the properties of seawater. The spa's treatments all use top-quality products from the sea. So splash in the vast seawater pool, have your skin buffed to velvety softness with a sea salt scrub or seaweed wrap, and follow it all up with a seaside massage from one of the country's top masseuses. All treatments are by appointment. *Mon-Fri 10am-10pm, Sat 10am-8pm, Sun 11am-7pm.* €€€ Aghiou Nikolaou 10 & Iliou, 210-891-1100, divanis.gr/hotels/view

Archaeological Museum of Piraeus • Piraeus • Museum
This treasure-trove of Piraeus' archaeological finds overlooks the semi-excavated 2nd century BC Theatre of Zea. On the ground floor is the highly ornate 4th century BC Kalithea funerary monument, a miniature temple (standing 20 feet tall) housing statues of the family it commemorates. In the next room is a collection of marble stele (gravestones) decorated with thought-provoking reliefs of the deceased—men depicted shaking hands with family or close friends, women seated and resigned to their destiny. *Tue-Sat 9am-3pm. Closed in Aug.* € Harilaou Trikoupi 32, 210-452-1598, culture.gr

Astir Palace Resort Beaches • Vouliagmeni • Beach
If you're lucky, you're staying here already. If not, be sure to check it out. With both a private and public beach, this resort is more than just a chic stretch of sand. Organized activities include water sports (jet-skiing, waterskiing, and windsurfing) as well as beach volleyball, yoga, and Pilates. Be sure to call in advance to check out the programs they offer and reserve a place. *10am-sunset.* €€ Apollonos 40, 210-890-2000 / 800-888-1199 astir-palace.com

Ghiolman Yachts • Syntagma • Boat Rental

All the rage with rich Russians, chartered boats do indeed offer the best way to experience the sea. Ghiolman Yachts can arrange anything from a small sailing boat to a high-powered motor cruiser for a private trip around the nearby islands, with lunch included. A compulsory skipper is part of the package unless at least two of your crew have sailing licenses. Most trips are scheduled to depart from Alimos Marina at 9am, with a welcome aboard drink and a visit to the island of Aegina, returning to the marina at 5:30pm. When you book your trip, you'll be asked what sort of lunch you'd like. They can lay on anything from diet-conscious summer salads to elaborate seafood and roast meat dishes served up on silver platters, and they also supply wines. €€€€ Filellinon 4, 210-323-0330, ghiolman.com

Glyfada Golf Club • Glyfada • Golf

Designed by noted Scottish architect Donald Harradine in 1962 and remodeled by American golf architect Robert Trent Jones in 1979, this professional 18-hole, 72-par course is set among lush greens and dense pine woods, cooled by a gentle sea breeze. In 1979 it hosted the World Cup Championship, in 1991 the Mediterranean Championship, and Greece's annual International Amateur Championship is held here as well. It is open year round. *Mon 1pm-sunset, Tue-Sun 7:30am-sunset.* €€€€ Panopis 15 & Kypros, 210-894-6820, athensgolfclub.com

Grand Beach Lagonissi • Lagonissi • Beach

Best Beaches Twelve sandy coves rim this peninsula, occupied by a luxury resort set on 72 acres of parkland. Beach amenities include chaise longues, towels, dressing rooms, showers, and lockers, plus water sports and beach volleyball, a floating bar, Thai and shiatsu massage, reflexology, body painting, and henna tattoos. There is a shop for beach equipment, and you can try your luck at the Grand Beach Lottery. *Summer daily 10am-9pm.* €€ 15km (9mi) southwest of Vouliagmeni on the Athens-Sounio Rd., 229-107-6000, lagonissiresort.gr

Hellenic Maritime Museum • Piraeus • Museum

On the western corner of Passalimani, in a 1960s building set in lovely gardens, this museum traces Hellenic naval power from the 5th century BC expansion of the ancient Greek empire up to the rise of today's Onassis-type shipping magnates (who still dominate international merchant shipping). On display are minutely detailed scale models of vessels including battleships, cruisers, and tankers, as well as uniforms, navigational equipment, maps, and big canvasses depicting ships on the ocean. *Tue-Sun 9am-2pm.* € Akti Themistokleous, 210-451-6264, greece.org/poseidon/work/museums/hmm

Kastella • Piraeus • Neighborhood

Pastel-colored neoclassical houses with ornate cornice details and wrought-iron balconies are arranged higgledy-piggledy on the hillside area of Kastella, overlooking the pretty fishing harbor of Mikrolimano. A series of pedestrian stairways and steep, winding streets bring you to the highest point, Profitis Ilias, crowned by a church, the Bowling Center Cafe (*see By-the-Water Restaurants p.131*), and the open-air Veakio Theatre (*see By-the-Water Nightlife p.137*).

Mikrolimano • Piraeus • Neighborhood
Seafood connoisseurs flock to this picturesque harbor rimmed by a string of top fish restaurants with open-air waterside terraces. Two-and three-story white cubic buildings rise up from the water's edge, forming an amphitheater-like space around this small circular bay. The bay itself is filled with dozens of colorful wooden boats belonging to local fishermen who hang their nets out to dry along the quayside on sunny afternoons. Mikrolimano buzzes with activity from lunchtime into the wee hours.

Passalimani • Piraeus • Neighborhood
Today surrounded by eight-story modern apartment blocks, with a waterside promenade lined with poplars, palms, and orange trees and overlooked by open-air cafes, this large, circular bay was the main port of ancient Athens. The 5th-century BC seaward walls remain partly intact, though the 200 wooden trireme (ancient battleships) that used to moor here have been replaced by countless luxury motor cruisers bearing flags from Greece, the U.S., the UK, and far-off Caribbean islands.

Patroklos • southeast of Vouliagmeni • Beach
Best Beaches Mainland beaches are glamorous—and crowded. For a real Robinson Crusoe experience, visit the tiny island of Patroklos, where you'll find glorious stretches of sand, crystal-clear water, and no development except for one little fish taverna. To get there, follow the coastal main road toward Sounio to the 60km mark, go about 300m beyond, then turn right at Kasidiara. From here, a taxi boat to Patroklos leaves regularly through peak season. *Boat operates late-June–early-Sept., every 10 min., 10am-8pm.* € 35km (22mi) southeast of Vouliagmeni, Sounio; Boatman: 229-103-7326 / 697-469-3323

Temple of Poseidon • Sounio • Archaeological Site
Poseidon, the Greek god of the sea, was worshipped at this 5th century BC temple. Built of white marble, it originally had 34 Doric columns, of which 16 are still standing. The columns create a dramatic silhouette on the highest point of a wind-swept promontory overlooking the waves from Attica's southernmost tip. The decadent 19th-century romantic British poet Lord Byron came here to carve his name into one of the columns and later lauded the site in his lyrical verses. Modern-day romantics come here to watch the sunset. *Daily 10am-sunset.* € 70km (44mi) southeast of Athens, 229-202-2817, culture.gr

Vouliagmeni Lake • Vouliagmeni • Hot Spring
One of nature's extraordinary surprises, this thermal lake is filled with warm therapeutic waters that maintain a steady temperature of 22°-25°C (68°-77°F), making bathing possible even on a chilly winter's day. Its mineral-rich waters are recommended for ailments from eczema to lumbago. Even if you're perfectly healthy, it's still a great place to swim, flanked by a rocky cliff on one side and pine woods on the other. Facilities include a snack bar, chaises, umbrellas, changing booths, and a "hydrotherapy center." *Summer: 7am-8pm; Winter: 7:30am-5pm.* € 210-896-2239

PRIME TIME ATHENS

Everything in life is timing (with a dash of serendipity thrown in). Would you want to arrive in Pamplona, Spain the day *after* the Running of the Bulls? Not if you have a choice, and you relish being a part of life's peak experiences. With our month-by-month calendar of events, there's no excuse to miss out on any of Athens' greatest moments. From the classic to the quirky, the sophisticated to the outrageous, you'll find all you need to know about the city's best events right here.

Prime Time Basics

Eating and Drinking

For Greeks, eating and drinking are social activities. Breakfast isn't a big deal (unless you count a morning cigarette), and most locals just munch on a toasted sandwich or pie around 11am. This is enough to tide them over until lunch—in winter at 2-3pm but in summer or weekends around 3-4pm, though restaurants begin serving as early as noon or 1pm, especially in tourist areas. Desserts or sweets are usually consumed in the afternoon with coffee—a great way to wake up from a nap. Dinner hits around 10pm, and often as late as midnight in summer and on weekends. Then it's off for drinks and clubbing: which explains why on some islands the dance spots don't open until 2am.

Weather and Tourism

Most people think of Greece as a summer destination, and with its great weather, spectacular beaches, and outdoor lifestyle, it does shine in summer. But the hot season might not be the best time to visit. If you can, arrive in mid- or late June or late August to mid-September. That's when you'll find all the fun, fewer crowds, and better prices.

During the peak tourist season, plan your day around rushhour: Visit museums late in the day to avoid crowds. There's little shade at most archaeological sites, so visit those early morning. (If you're a photography buff, don't take a tripod with you to museums or sites as its use is banned in most.)

Foreign residents often complain about the Greeks' lack of organization, but the only way to truly enjoy yourself is to go with the

Seasonal Changes

Month	Fahrenheit High	Fahrenheit Low	Celsius High	Celsius Low	Hotel Rates
Jan.	56	44	13	7	L
Feb.	57	45	14	7	L
Mar.	60	47	16	8	L
Apr.	66	53	19	12	S
May	75	60	24	16	S
June	83	68	28	20	S
July	88	72	31	23	H
Aug.	88	72	31	22	H
Sept.	82	67	28	19	H
Oct.	73	59	23	15	S
Nov.	55	53	19	12	L
Dec.	59	48	15	9	L

H-High Season; S-Shoulder; L-Low

flow. Almost everything is ruled by personal relationships, so if you chat up the bank teller or waiter you'll get better service.

Jan.-Mar.: January and February are typically cold, and March can be cool and rainy. It's a great time to visit for clubbing and bouzoukia, as this is their busiest time. There's Rio-style partying in Patras during Apokries (carnival) and hot after-ski action at resorts like Arahova. If you plan to tour the mainland, keep to the south and coastal areas; the mountains can be cut off by ice and snow.

Apr.-Jul.: The best time to visit, since you'll be able to hit the beaches and take in the sights too. There's a small crowd on the islands, but nothing like the August crush. The summer clubs start opening mid-May, so you'll get top DJs and parties at the beach before everyone goes off island-hopping. June is a good time to visit the islands: hotel rates are cheaper, but you may have to limit your clubbing to weekends.

Aug.-Dec.: Most everyone flees Athens in August, especially around the 15th, when many vacations begin. In September you'll still be able to swim and visit islands, but by late October it's too cool to really enjoy them. Expect some rain, although it rarely lasts more than a few days—and there's plenty indoors to keep you busy.

National Holidays

New Year's Day	January 1
Epiphany	January 6
Kathara Deftera	40 days before Easter
Easter Friday	March or April
Easter Monday	March or April
Whit Monday/Ascension	40 days after Easter
Independence Day	March 25
Labor Day	May 1
Assumption of the Virgin	August 15
'Ohi' Day	October 28
Christmas Day	December 25
Boxing Day	December 26

Listings in blue are major celebrations but not official holidays.

PRIME TIME

The Best Events Calendar

January	February	March
• Epiphany	• Apokries	• Clean Monday • The Greek Wine Forum and Oenorama

April	May	June
• Easter	• Art Athina • European Jazz Festival in Athens	• Acropolis Rally • Hellenic Festival • Maroussi Festival • Piraeus Festival • Rematia Festival • Rockwave • Vyronas Festival

July	August	September
• Athens International Dance Festival • International Aegean Sailing Regatta	• Full Moon Festival	• Athens International Film Festival • Trash Art • Vavel Comic Art Festival

October	November	December
	• Athens Marathon	

Night+Day's Top Five Events are in blue font.
High season is from July-September, represented by blue banner.

The Best Events

January

Epiphany

Ports in various locations

The Lowdown: The "Blessing of the Waters" is an age-old Orthodox tradition. At the start of the year, thousands gather at Greece's ports and beaches to watch priests bless the seas. After the sermon, the priest throws a cross in the water and local boys dive into the icy depths to retrieve it. The one who finds the cross gets a blessing from the priest. After the ceremony, everyone heads to the closest fish tavernas for a festive seafood meal. In Athens, the official ceremony is held in Piraeus; if you don't want to trek there, the Athens' mayor customarily attends the ceremony at Dexameni in Kolonaki. *January 6.* Free.

February

Apokries

Plaka, Patras, and various locations, spring 2007

The Lowdown: The Greek Orthodox Carnivale begins 58 days before Easter. Festivities—such as masquerade parties—can last for weeks, with the partying and boozing reaching a fever pitch in the last days before Lent. In Athens, the celebrations center in Plaka, with colorful parades, drunken revelers, and dancing girls in the streets. The city of Patras holds the country's most famous Apokries parties and parades. Saturdays and Sundays are the nights for masquerading, but modern tradition dictates following Tsiknopempti (smoky Thursday) barbecues with a night of bar-hopping and clubbing. *End of February or early March.* Free.

March

The Greek Wine Forum and Oenorama

The Greek Wine Forum: Zappeion, 210-766-0560, dionyssia.gr;
Oenorama: Eket Exhibition Center, oenorama.com

The Lowdown: The Greek Wine Forum, held in odd years, is an elegant three-day tasting session with exquisite and unusual wines from around the country displayed at a showpiece cultural center in central Athens. It's next set to happen in spring 2007 in Zappeion. Oenorama, held in even years, is a huge expo of wines—again, with plenty of opportunities to taste. The expo concludes with a competition to determine Greece's top wines, sommeliers, and restaurant wine cellars. This expo is next set to happen in spring 2008. *Dates vary.* Prices vary.

PRIME TIME

Clean Monday

All over the country

The Lowdown: After all that Apokries partying, Greeks spend Clean Monday doing something much more wholesome—kite-flying! In Athens, head to Philopappou Hill to see a sky full of fanciful wind-borne creations. Then follow the crowds to nearby tavernas for the requisite meatless dinners, though in Orthodoxy, there's never a ban on wine. *Monday before Lent.* Free.

April

Easter

All over the country

The Lowdown: Greece's most important holiday is steeped in rituals from Byzantine chants to echoes of pagan rites of spring. Celebrations are spread out over a full week, culminating late Saturday night before the big day. Worshippers gather at church for a chanting, candlelit procession through the streets behind a mock bier on which a wooden Christ figure has been laid. Especially pretty to watch from Lycabettus, where you can join the church's procession but also see lights snaking through other neighborhoods. Midnight is marked by fireworks, gunshots, and cries of *"Christos anesti*!*"* ("Christ is risen!"). In Athens, the best procession starts from Mitropoleos church through the streets and old chapels of Plaka. Sunday is for roasting lamb and eating eggs dyed red (symbolizing blood and rebirth). *Easter Sunday and the week prior.* Free.

May

Art Athina

HelExpo Center, Kifissias 39, Maroussi, 210-691-2331, helexpo.gr; festival: 210-691-3943

The Lowdown: Held over four days in May, Art Athina is centered at HelExpo, an exhibition center next door to Athens' main Olympic sports hub. But displays and events, which showcase work from cutting-edge Greek and international artists, are spread out among hip galleries all over town, along with plenty of parties and lots of art-world buzz. *Four days in May.* Prices vary.

European Jazz Festival in Athens

Technopolis, Pireos 100, Gazi, 210-346-7322

The Lowdown: Started in 2001, this festival looks set to become an institution on the Athens music scene. The free four-day concert, held at the end of May at Technopolis, brings in top European jazz musicians, with each set devoted to the jazz of a specific country. The festival promotes the music of whichever country holds the rotating European Union presidency, so in 2006, you'll hear jazz musicians from Austria and Finland, and in 2007, from Germany and Portugal, alongside Greek and international bands. *End of May.* Free.

June

Acropolis Rally

Acropolis starting point, acropolisrally.gr

The Lowdown: One of the most demanding race car routes in the world, this three-day off-road competition begins and ends under the Acropolis. Join the roadside spectators or rent your own vehicle to follow the race through Attica. *Dates vary. For 2006, race begins June 1.* Free.

Hellenic Festival

Odeon of Herodes Atticus and Mt. Lycabettus Theater, 210-928-2900, hellenicfestival.gr

The Lowdown: For the unforgettable beauty of its ancient marble amphitheater, the brilliance of its world-class performers, and the once-in-a-lifetime opportunity to see the great Greek dramas performed in the land of their birth, the Hellenic Festival ranks as one of the greatest experiences in Greece, and also in the world. The festival is based in the Odeon of Herodes Atticus. A typical season might include moonlit performances from the likes of Luciano Pavarotti, the Bolshoi Ballet, and the Harlem Gospel Choir. The Athens Festival also runs performances in the amphitheater atop lofty Mt. Lycabettus, hosting shows from the likes of Massive Attack, Philip Glass, and the surreal Momix dance company. *June to October.* Price varies from €15-90.

Maroussi Festival

Next to Athens Olympic Sports Complex, 210-876-0000, maroussi.gr

The Lowdown: The Maroussi Festival offers a good opportunity to see top Greek pop and folk singers perform, in free shows at its open-air park amphitheater. This festival, set right next door to the main Olympic stadium, got a big boost in funding and exposure after 2004, and the lineup gets stronger every year. *June to September.* Free.

Piraeus Festival

Veakio Theatre, 210-410-1750

The Lowdown: This top-quality local offering also got a big boost in profile and revenue due to its setting close to several Olympic venues. A relaxing night in the lovely Veakio Theatre, located in Piraeus' scenic hilltop Kastella district, has always been worth the journey. Enjoy arty international music and dance performances under the stars. *June to September.* Prices vary.

Rematia Festival

Rematia Theatre, Halandri, 210-680-0001

The Lowdown: This small but high-quality festival should be on serious music-lovers' agendas: It showcases folk music from Greece, the Balkans, and Asia Minor, in a cool northern-suburb amphitheater. *June to July.* Prices vary.

PRIME TIME

Rockwave

Location varies, 210-882-0426, didimusic.gr

The Lowdown: Who knew Greece was such a hotbed of Goths and metalheads? They come out in full leather-clad force at this three-day hard-rocking festival which brings some of the darkest acts around to one of the sunniest countries in the world. The concert usually takes place at an industrial venue—it was once held at an abandoned airport, transformed with booths vending everything from indie CDs to S&M gear. *Late June to early July.* Prices vary.

Vyronas Festival

Melina Mercouri Vrahon Theatre, Mt. Hymettos, 210-764-8675

The Lowdown: Held in a rocky amphitheater carved into the scenic slopes of Mt. Hymettos, this festival brings a good mix of Greek, international, and world music acts, from the classic old-school warblings of Dimitris Mitropanos and Dimitris Basis to the modern Brit-pop of Suede. If you can't get tickets to the Athens Festival, a show at this festival will give admirable consolation. *June to September.* Prices vary.

July

Athens International Dance Festival

Technopolis, Pireos 100, Gazi, 210-346-7322; festival: 210-346-0981

The Lowdown: This two-year-old festival already seems destined to become a fixture in Athens events. The modern dance showcase featuring around 20 performances debuted the summer Athens, which until very recently was off the map in terms of modern dance, hosted the Olympics, which helped draw foreign choreographers like Katja Wachter, Elio Gervasi, and Kitt Johnson. It's also, of course, a great way to get introduced to the work of Greek modern dance choreographers such as Yiannis Bougourdis and Konstantinos Rigos, whose work is increasingly noted internationally. Held yearly at the eclectic arts haven Technopolis. *Ten days in July.* Prices vary.

International Aegean Sailing Regatta

Piraeus, 210-412-3357, 210-411-3201, aegeanrally.gr, horc.gr

The Lowdown: Greece's oldest and most prestigious sailing regatta draws top competitors and spectators from all over the world. Its timing coincides with the arrival of Greece's meltemi (southern wind) and its sunniest days of the year, making for ideal sailing conditions. The boats start near Piraeus, and you can get a great view from any one of southern Athens' coastal clubs and cafes. For the best experience, wangle your way onto a yacht—the competitors here are the biggest and best in the Mediterranean. *End of July.* Free.

August

Full Moon Festival
Acropolis, Odeon, Roman Agora

The Lowdown: Every year, during the August full moon, the Greek Culture Ministry sponsors nighttime events at archaeological sites all over the country, so you can visit the Acropolis by night, watch traditional dancers perform in the Odeon of Herodes Atticus, and hear opera divas sing in the Roman Agora, all for free. Check local English-language papers for a listing of what's on where. *August full moon.* Free.

September

Athens International Film Festival
Attikon, Apollon Film Center, Danaos 1 & 2, 210-606-1363, aiff.gr

The Lowdown: Hardly in the league of Cannes or Venice, this quirky up-and-coming ten-day festival is still worth checking out, although some claim it's less a festival and more a series of screenings. It shows about 100 features and short films, a mix of mainstream Hollywood fare, old black-and-whites, and independent European flicks. The most interesting and oddball offerings are premieres of Greek films and pictures that are somehow connected to Greece—such as a movie about Maria Callas. *Ten days in September.* Prices vary.

Trash Art
Various locations, 210-338-7133

The Lowdown: A smorgasbord of funky events all linked by themes of trash and recycling—art installations, fashion shows of "recycled" clothes, open workshops where you can watch artists create trash sculptures, booths where you can buy jewelry made of trash, and parties in clubs decorated with trash art, hosted by the city's best DJs. *Dates vary.* Prices vary.

Vavel Comic Art Festival
Technopolis, Pireos 100, Gazi, 210-346-7322; festival: 210-382-5430

The Lowdown: Comic-book geeks, edgy new artists, the indie-rock crowd, and international hipsters flock to this renowned international event, which is getting bigger every year. There are parties, concerts, grafitti art contests, street performances, and—oh yeah—fabulously fun exhibits of all kinds of comic book art, from Yellow Kid homages to sexy Japanese manga. Most events and exhibitions happen at urban-art magnet Technopolis. *Dates vary.* Prices vary.

PRIME TIME

Athens Marathon
Marathon Route, 210-755-2888, athensmarathon.com

The Lowdown: There's nothing like the thrill of running the original marathon, starting—where else?—on the ancient, storied field of Marathon. In 490 BC, a vastly outnumbered army of Athenians defeated the invading Persians on the field of Marathon, in a battle that's gone down in world history as responsible for saving the first democracy. The messenger Pheidippides is said to have run the 26.2 miles back to Athens, announced the outcome ("Victory!"), then died of exhaustion. Today, runners from around the world retrace Pheidippides' steps, all the way to the finish line, at the 1896 Olympic Stadium. Even if you don't run, joining the crowds at the marble stadium is an exhilarating experience. *Date varies.* Spectators free.

HIT the GROUND RUNNING

With three millennia of history sitting concrete-upon-brick-upon-stone in today's modern city, Athens can appear to be an impenetrable labyrinth to even the most devoted Hellenophile. Which road leads to the sea? Why's my drink gone cloudy white? Why are all the shops closed? Whether you're a first-timer or a return visitor, you need local knowledge. Here are the most essential facts and figures, including our *Cheat Sheet*, a quick reference countdown of vital information that'll stand you in good stead for the challenges ahead.

City Essentials

Getting to Athens: By Air

Athens International Airport S.A. Eleftherios Venizelos (ATH)
Loutsa Ave., Spata, 210-353-0000, aia.gr

Newly opened in 2001, Athens International Airport (Eleftherios Venizelos) was designed as part of the improved national transport system in the run-up to the 2004 Olympics and saw more than 13 million passengers pass through its gates in 2005. It's 17mi (27km) northeast of the city center, approximately 40 minutes driving time, depending on the traffic, or a predictable 41 minutes via metro.

Amenities include banks, currency exchange, duty-free shops, bars, restaurants, a post office, and a GNTO tourist information desk in the arrivals hall,

Flying Times to Athens

From	Airport	Hours	Stop
Amsterdam	AMS	3 $^{1/2}$	
Atlanta	ATL	11 $^{1/4}$	
Cairo	CAI	2	
Chicago	ORD	12	Yes
Dallas	DFW	15	Yes
Frankfurt	FRA	2 $^{3/4}$	
London	LHR	3 $^{1/2}$	
Los Angeles	LAX	15	Yes
Madrid	MAD	3 $^{1/2}$	
Mexico City	MEX	15	Yes
Montreal	YUL	11	Yes
New York	JFK	10	
Paris	CDG	3 $^{1/2}$	
Rome	FCO	2	
San Francisco	SFO	15	Yes
Tel Aviv	TLV	2	

(210-353-0447 and 210-353-0445, open daily 9am-7pm). The restaurants are mostly typical airport fare. In the main terminal, Olive Tree Restaurant offers views over the runways with Greek-Med food, including vegetarian options. If you're truly trapped here for awhile, there is a retail and restaurant complex about 800 meters outside of the aiport, which ups the game slightly to include shopping options like Ikea, and a range of okay eating places like the Italian spot La Pateria. The airport also has a museum and rotating art exhibits. On permanent display at the museum on the departures level of the main terminal is a collection of archaeological findings dating from the Neolithic and Early Helladic through the Post-Byzantine period.

Airlines Serving Athens International Airport

Airlines	Website	800 Number
Air France	airfrance.us	800-237-2747
Aeroflot	aeroflot.org	800-736-4192
Alitalia	alitaliausa.com	800-223-5730
Austrian Airlines	aua.com	800-843-0002
British Airways	britishairways.com	800-247-9297
CZA-Czech Airlines	czechairlines.com	800-223-2365
Delta Airlines	delta.com	800-221-1212
Iberia Airlines	iberia.com	800-772-4642
KLM RoyalDutch Airlines	klm.com	800-447-4747
LOT Polish Airlines	lot.com	800-223-0593
Lufthansa	lufthansa.com	800-645-3880
Malev-Hungarian Airlines	malev.hu	800-223-6884
Olympic Airways	olympic-airways.gr	800-223-1226
SAS-Scandinavian Airlines	scandinavian.net	800-221-2350
Singapore Airlines	singaporeair.com	800-742-3333
Turkish Airlines	turkishairlines.com	800-874-8875

Car rental companies include Alamo, National, Avis, Budget, Europcar, Hertz and Sixt. (Many are also in town across from the Temple of Zeus, Syngrou Avenue.) Twenty-four-hour parking is available. The Sofitel Athens Airport Hotel (210-354-4000, sofitel.com) offers pricey but luxurious accommodation, and two restaurants, one billed as gourmet.

Into Town by Public Transport: The Athens Urban Transport Organization (OASA) runs three 24-hour bus shuttle services linking the airport to the city. Line E94 runs to Ethniki Amyna metro station (at the end of the Blue Line), E95 to Syntagma Square in the city center, E92 goes to the northern suburb of Kifissia, E93 to Kifissos and Liossion inter-city bus terminals, E97 to Dafni metro station, and E96 to Piraeus Port. Airport buses info: 185 or 210-820-0999. Tickets (available from the driver) cost €2.90 and allow for 24 hours of unlimited travel on all forms of public transit (buses, trolley buses, and metro), making this a much cheaper option than a taxi. The fastest way to get from the airport to the city center is via the metro, which whizzes to Syntagma Square in 41 minutes and Monastiraki Square in 43 minutes, stopping at all metro line stations. A ticket for one person costs €6 and €5 per ticket for two or more people. It leaves every 30 minutes from 5:30am-1:20am. Yellow taxis are also available; expect to pay around €25 to the city center.

HIT THE GROUND

Getting to Athens: By Land and By Water

Getting to Athens by Car: Athens can be reached overland from Patras (3 hrs.) and Thessaloniki (6 hrs. 45 min.). The three cities are joined by the PATHE (Patras, Athens, and Thessaloniki) motorway, running from Patras in the west via Athens to Thessaloniki in the north.

Getting to Athens by Train: Athens is served by the Greek railway service, run by the Hellenic Railways Organization (OSE), ose.gr. The rail service is rather limited, connecting the capital to the northern and eastern mainland (including Thessaloniki, 6 hrs.) and parts of the Peloponnese (including Patras, 4 hrs.). Trains from the Peloponnese arrive at Peloponnese Station, while those from northern Greece arrive at Larissa Station. Both stations are located on Theodorou Diligiani, a 20-minute walk from Omonia Square in the city center. Larissa Station is connected directly to the center (Syntagma) by metro (Red Line, 2). Facilities at these stations are minimal, and include left luggage, bars, and taxis. The most central OSE office is at Sina 6, Kolonaki, 210-362-7947, open Mon-Fri 8am-3pm.

Getting to Athens by Boat: Athens is served by the port of Piraeus, where amenities include left luggage, ATMs, banks, currency exchange, bars, restaurants, taxis, car hire, and rental and travel agencies selling ferry tickets. From Piraeus there are regular crossings to and from ports in the following island groups: the Dodecanese, Crete, the Cyclades, the Saronic islands, and the North Eastern Aegean. Ferry schedules (greek-ferries.gr) change frequently and services are reduced out of season. Tickets can be bought from the shipping lines' offices located around the quaysides, and the larger lines also have offices in the city center. Hydrofoils cost about twice as much and take half the time of regular ferries, but are often cancelled due to bad weather. The majority of hydrofoils serving Piraeus are run by Hellas Flying Dolphin (dolphins.gr). Reservations and tickets can be purchased at the main booking office at Akti Kondili in Piraeus or from authorized agents in the city center. Piraeus is connected to central Athens by metro (25 minutes). A taxi from the port to the center costs approximately €9.

Passports and Visas: U.S., Canadian, Australian, and New Zealand citizens need a valid passport to enter Greece and can then stay for up to 90 days. Exceeding this stay without obtaining a visa extension risks deportation and a hefty fine. EU nationals need only a valid passport or national ID card to enter the country and can stay indefinitely.

Athens: Lay of the Land

Athens, at ground level, presents a totally different picture than it does when viewed from the air. What appears from above to be a viscous concrete mass, spreading further and further from the sea toward the mountain ridges that cradle the Attica basin, at close range dissolves into self-contained neighborhoods. This is the secret of the city's charm: its capacity to surprise even its most jaded resident. The heart of Athens has changed little from ancient times, with central districts like the Plaka and Syntagma Square luring the most tourists. But in the eighties, the city's hot young things were not just upwardly mobile, but geographically too, as they left this center to build villas and swank apartments in Kifissia, to the north, and the Glyfada-Voula-Vouliagmeni zone along the coast. Chic restaurants and boutiques followed in their wake. But the city's old money remained firmly ensconced around Irodou Attikou, where the official residences of the president and prime minister are located, as well as in Kavouri by the sea, and to the city's north, Paleo Psychico and Filothei. New money, showier and glitzier, has settled around Kefalari, Ekali, and Politia, with their exclusive tennis clubs—racket not necessarily required. In the city center, Exarchia is still a hotbed of students, left politics, and publishing, while the edgier arts scene has migrated from Kolonaki's environs to Psirri, Thissio, and the corridor off Pireos Street, drawn by the relocation there of the School of Fine Arts and venerable Benaki Museum's annex. Thanks to the metro's expansion, the blue-collar districts of western Athens, especially Peristeri and Bournazi, have also developed distinctive clublands—clusters of cafe-bars and dance clubs often cruised by prep-school youth on a walk on the wild side.

Getting Around Athens

By Car: If you're staying in the city center, you can get around Athens comfortably without a car. Public transit is cheap and frequent (though often overcrowded), while having a vehicle brings with it the headache of traffic and the eternal challenge of finding a parking space.

If you do decide to rent a car, remember that traffic drives on the right and the minimum age for driving is 18 (though many car rental companies stipulate the minimum age for renting as 21 or 25). U.S., Canadian, Australian, and New Zealand passport holders need an International Driving Permit, while for EU passport holders, a national driving license will suffice. The maximum speed limit is 120kmh (70mph) on motorways, 110kmh (60mph) outside built-up areas, and

HIT THE GROUND

Rental Cars

Agency	Website	Local Number
Avis	avis.com	210-322-4951
		210-322-4958
Budget	budget.com	210-921-4771
		210-921-4773
European Car Rental	european-rentacar.com	210-923-3200
Hertz	hertz.com	210-922-0102
		210-922-0104
Sixt	sixt.gr	210-922-0171

Rental Scooters

Rental Moto	motorrent.gr	210-923-4939

50kmh (31mph) in built-up areas. Penalties for drinking and driving over the limit are severe—the maximum legal alcohol to blood ratio is 0.05%, and above 0.08% is considered a criminal offense.

By Trolley, Bus, and Tram: The city center and Greater Athens are served by some 320 bus and trolley bus lines, operated by the Athens Urban Transport Organization (OASA), oasa.gr. Yellow trolley buses run in the city center, linking most major sights, while white-blue-and-yellow buses run from the center out to the suburbs. Most daytime services run 4:30am-midnight, with very few lines running at night. In addition, a new tram line now links the city center to Glyfada on the coast. A weekly ticket for all major public transport costs €10.

Tickets, which cost €0.45 and are valid for one journey only, can be purchased at the ubiquitous periptero (street kiosks) as well as at the special kiosks near bus line terminals. Upon boarding, stamp your ticket in the validation machine. It's also possible to buy a day-ticket costing €2.90 which allows 24 hours of unlimited travel by all forms of public transit (buses, trams, trolley cars, all metro lines, and suburban railway) and one trip to or from the airport. Also available are a 1.5 hour transfer ticket for bus, trolley, all metro, tram and Proastiakos (€1 except for airport), 24-hour ticket for all the above (€3), and 7-day ticket for all the above (€10).

By Suburban Railway: The new Proastiakos (suburban railway) train (proastiakos.gr, 210-527-2000) links Athens' airport to major areas in northern Athens and the central railway station. From the airport it stops at Doukissis Plakendias metro station, Kifissias Avenue, the Olympic

Stadium (Neratziotissa station where passengers can transer to metro line 1) and ends at Larissa railway station (where passengers can transfer to metro line 2). Journeys anywhere between the railway station and Doukissis Plakendias cost €0.70, and increase incrementally from there to the airport.

By Metro: Athens is served by a network of three metro lines (ametro.gr). The three lines are:

• Green Line (1) runs north-south from Kifissia to Piraeus, passing through Omonia, and is referred to as "ilektriko" (electric train). It runs 5am-midnight.

• Red Line (2) runs from Aghios Anhtonios to Aghios Dimitrios, passing through Syntagma and Omonia. It runs 5:30am-11:50pm.

• Blue Line (3) runs from Monastiraki to Doukissis Plakendias, passing through Syntagma. Select trains continue from Doukissis Plakendias to the airport. It runs 5:30am-midnight.

Tickets, which cost €0.60 for the green line and €0.70 for the red and blue lines, can be purchased at the automatic vending machines and staffed kiosks within the metro stations.

By Taxi: Official yellow taxis with red-on-white number plates can be hailed from the street. When the roads are busy and taxis are in heavy demand, it's not unusual to share a ride (but not the fare) with other passengers who are going in a similar direction (if there are four passengers, it's also normal for one person to sit in the front). Athens' taxis are probably the cheapest among European capitals—the meter starts at €.86 (nonnegotiable), and extra charges for baggage, late-night journeys (midnight-5am) and trips to the airport are explained in English on placards inside the vehicles. The minimum fare is €1.80. As of 2004, taxis are required to give receipts on request, although some may still be reluctant to do so. Expect to give the driver directions for anywhere but major landmarks and squares. Tipping is not customary, although drivers may expect to keep the change.

Another taxi option in Athens is George the Taxi Driver. A former mechanical engineer who shucked the corporate life, George now runs a small fleet of super-high-tech Mercedes taxis that charge somewhere between limo and taxi prices. What you get for the extra expense are knowledgeable drivers in smoke-free cars that are equipped with everything from DVDs to wireless connections to GPS. This is the favorite mode of travel for visiting technofiles. Contact George at georgetaxitours@yahoo.com or by phone at 210-963-7030 or mobile phone at 693-220-5887.

HIT THE GROUND

Other Practical Information

Money Matters (Currency, Taxes, Tipping and Service Charges): All service taxes and VAT (value added tax, or fi-pi-a in Greek) are included on bills and in prices at most stores, unless noted. VAT is 19 percent for most goods and services; 4.5 percent for books; lower in some areas and islands. If you plan to make big-ticket purchases, consult with the Greek consulate or a travel agent on how to apply for VAT refunds.

Metric Conversion

From	To	Multiply by
Cm	Inches	0.39
Meters	Yards	1.1
Km	Miles	0.62
Liters	Gallons	0.26
Kg	Pounds	2.2

All payments are cash or credit card: Few places take travelers' checks and you won't be able to use personal checks at all. There are ATMs everywhere. Ask your bank if it has a local affiliate to lower charges.

A gratuity is included in restaurants, cafes, and bars, so tipping is optional, but expected. Ten to 15 percent is average. Taxi drivers often keep change, assuming you'll want to tip them—if you don't, insist on getting change and don't let their scowling or muttering put you off. Taxi fees are posted on a card—in Greek and in English—in the cab. At Christmas and Easter, a holiday bonus is tacked on to taxi fares, as well as bills at hairdressing salons, and some restaurants. The amount and dates this applies are posted in a prominent place.

Safety: Like any other major European city, Athens is as safe as you make it. In tourist areas such as Plaka, the major dangers are pickpockets and con artists—beware of being invited to drinks by strangers as this is often a trick to trap you into a large bar bill. Athens does have rough spots, especially in up-and-coming areas like Rouf, where you need to be more cautious. And like everywhere, make sure the meter in the taxi is running, or you agree on the fare, before your drive.

Numbers to Know (Hotlines)

Police	100
Ambulance	166
Fire Department	199
Tourist Police	171
Hospitals	
Hospitals / Clinics	1434
Pharmacies	1434

Gay and Lesbian Travel: Despite the wild and colorful gay scene found on the island of Mykonos, Greeks remain conservative when it comes to homosexuality, especially outside Athens. For listings of gay-friendly bars, restaurants, clubs, and beaches in Athens and on the islands, visit gaygreece.gr, a gay and lesbian tourist guide to Greece, in Greek and English. The following U.S. organizations offer information about travel and accommodation in Greece:

• Damron Company, damron.com
• International Gay/Lesbian Travel Associations, iglta.org

Traveling with Disabilities: According to statistics, approximately 10% of the total Greek population suffers from some sort of disability. However, as the city is so difficult to move about in, you'll very seldom see people in wheelchairs. Fortunately, the 2004 Olympic Games, and especially the Paralympic Games, have brought heightened awareness to the issue. The city council added ramps and platforms to bus stops, railway stations, and ports, while sports venues and metro stations are almost all accessible to those with disabilities. Most central Athens streets, sites, and metro stations also feature special sidewalks to aid the visually impaired.

The following U.S. organizations provide useful information:

• Access-Able, access-able.com
• Mobility International USA, miusa.org
• Society for the Advancement of Travelers with Handicaps (SATH), sath.org
• Wheels Up, wheelsup.com

Women Traveling Alone: Greece is a perfectly safe place for women traveling alone—indeed, it's actually statistically safer than most other countries. Greek men are extremely open about showing interest in women, however; a disconcerting habit for those not used to such displays. If you're not impressed, a withering look is usually enough to stop them.

Print Media: The weekly *Athens News* (athensnews.gr) is the most popular English-language newspaper in town. The monthly *Insider* (insider-magazine.gr) is aimed at foreigners living in and visiting Athens, with articles about culture, shopping, and recreational activities, plus a decent section of listings. The glossy bimonthly *Odyssey* (odyssey.gr) has some good feature stories about Greece and the Greek diaspora. *The International Herald Tribune* carries an English-language condensed version of the Greek daily *Kathimerini* (ekathimerini.gr) bringing international news and Greek current affairs to its readers. *Athinorama* is also an excellent weekly culture guide but is published in Greek only.

HIT THE GROUND

Websites: The Ministry of Culture's culture.gr is a good (but seldom updated) destination with listings of museums, archaeological sites, and cultural activities.

The Hellenic Festival (Athens and Epidaurus festivals) summer programs can be found at greekfestival.gr.

Greece Now, funded by the Greek Ministry of Foreign Affairs, provides information about Greece at greece.gr.

English-Language Bookshops:

- Eleftheroudakis, Panepistimiou 17, Syntagma. Vast bookshop extending onto eight floors, with a cafe.

- Compendium, Nikis 28, Syntagma. New and used books.

- Folia tou Vivliou (The Book Nest), Panepistimiou 25, Syntagma. Modern shopping arcade filled with bookstores.

- Reymondos, Voukouristiou 18, Syntagma. Small but good selection of books and foreign magazines.

- Road, Ippokratous 39, Exarchia. Road Editions-brand maps and other travel guides.

Maps: The best maps to use when traveling throughout Greece are by Road Editions. These can be bought at their shop, Road, and the main branch of Eleftheroudakis, both in Athens, and sometimes (though do not rely on this) in tourist bookshops outside the capital.

Internet Cafes: Athens is as Internet-friendly as any other European capital city, though some of the Internet cafes in touristy Plaka are small, expensive, and poorly run. The city's best Internet cafes are:

- Museum Internet Cafe, Patission 46, next door to the National Archaeological Museum

- Cafe4u, Ippokratous 44, Exarchia (open 24 hours)

- Netmania, Vasileos Pavlou 135, Kastella, Piraeus

Shopping: Shopping hours vary from store to store (with the traditional afternoon siesta breaking the day), but as a general rule you should find shops open: Mon 9am-2:30pm; Tue 9am-2pm and 5-8pm; Wed 9am-2:30pm; Thu 9am-2pm and 5-8pm; Fri 9am-2pm and 5-8pm; Sat 9am-2:30pm.

Size Conversion

Dress Sizes

US	6	8	10	12	14	16
UK	8	10	12	14	16	18
France	36	38	40	42	44	46
Italy	38	40	42	44	46	48
Europe	34	36	38	40	42	44

Women's Shoes

US	6	6½	7	7½	8	8½
UK	4½	5	5½	6	6½	7
Europe	38	38	39	39	40	41

Men's Suits

US	36	38	40	42	44	46
UK	36	38	40	42	44	46
Europe	46	48	50	52	54	56

Men's Shirts

US	14½	15	15½	16	16½	17
UK	14½	15	15½	16	16½	17
Europe	38	39	39-40	41	42	43

Men's Shoes

US	8	8½	9½	10½	11½	12
UK	7	7½	8½	9½	10½	11
Europe	41	42	43	44	45	46

Attire: Greeks are informal but stylish, with women especially dressing to kill when going out for the night. In summer, light clothes suffice, though you may need a hat and long-sleeved cotton shirts and trousers if you are prone to sunburn. On a winter visit, pack plenty of warm clothes. A decent pair of walking shoes is essential if you plan to spend much time sightseeing.

Drinking: Greeks drink wine or beer with meals (heed the Greek folk adage that advises you to add water to wine in months without an "r" in them). Clear spirits like raki, tsikoudia, and ouzo are sipped before lunch or in early afternoon, while whiskey, vodka, gin, tequila, and so on are ordered at bars and clubs. The legal drinking age is 18, but this is only loosely enforced in clubs; teens will be served wine or beer at family meals, especially on holidays.

Greeks do drink a lot, but they don't go on drinking binges. Alcohol is consumed slowly with food and conversation. If it's your birthday, anniversary, or other milestone, you'll be expected to buy a round.

HIT THE GROUND

Greek Nightlife

Bouzoukia

Your Greek friends' excited chatter about the *pistes* has nothing to do with downhill skiing. A pista is a nightclub stage, and twice a year the media goes into a frenzy trying to guess the season's hot *schemata* (marquee). Smashing plates has been replaced by the safer tossing of flowers or napkins, but the idea is the same: you rain them over your singer or partner to express admiration. Here's a crash course in Greece's nightclub scene:

Bouzoukia: A generic term used to describe nightclubs with floor-shows built around two or three top names, some promising younger singers, a tacky dance group, and a live orchestra whose centerpiece was the bouzoukia. Today, the *bouzoukia* are more likely to be either *pistes* or *programata*.

Pistes: Cavernous nightclubs with large stages and smallish tables crammed together. The draw are one or two big name stars who don't emerge until the wee hours of the morning, after audiences have been warmed up by other acts, often pop to appeal to younger patrons. As the night heats up, people get up and dance on tabletops or, if you're a celebrity, on stage.

Megala Programata: A variation of the pista with a more elaborate stage show. Express admiration by buying straw trays of flowers to be rained over the performers. The music is supposed to be live but there have been instances of singers being caught using playback.

Musikes Skines: Musical stages featuring either Greek or rock music. Such venues usually feature *entechno laiko*, the musical equivalent of literary fiction to the pistes' pulp fiction. Venues are still large but have a more intimate atmosphere than the sprawling nightclubs.

Skyladika: Apply the expression "gone to the dogs" to bouzoukia and you have your *skyladika*, literally place frequented by dogs. Located on the city's outskirts, often along the highway, these dives have rougher edges and gaudier décor. Buxom, earthy, bottle-blonds in provocative gowns and less-polished male singers than you'll see in the pistes coax patrons onto the stage for a zeibekiko turn or two.

Smoking: Anti-smoking laws go back to the '50s, but enforcement is new. Restaurants and cafes are required to have non-smoking sections, but often that's no more than a couple of tables next to chain-smokers. Bars and restaurants usually have better ventilation than cafes, but if smoke really bothers you, then plan to visit in the warmer months when everything's happening outside. Also, query your hotel about its non-smoking rooms: Those with mostly foreign guests are very conscientious, even smaller hotels. Those with a mix of Greek and foreign guests are less so. As one manager said, "if you don't smoke in the room, then it's non-smoking."

Drugs: Greek law doesn't distinguish between hard and soft drugs, but it is more lenient with addicts than with users or dealers. The bottom line is, don't bring drugs into Greece and don't do drugs in Greece.

Time Zone: Greece is two hours ahead of Greenwich Mean Time. If it's noon in London and 7am in New York, it's 2pm in Athens. "Summer time," or daylight savings, is a two-hour jump. It begins on 1am on the last Sunday in March and lasts until 2am on the last Sunday in October.

General Information for Visitors

Greek National Tourist Organization (GNTO)
Mon-Fri 8am-3pm. Tsoha 7, Ambelokipi, Athens, 210-870-7000, gnto.gr
GNTO walk-in information center
Mon-Fri 9am-3:30pm with extended hours through peak season.
Amalias 26, Syntagma, 210-331-0392 / 210-331-0716 / 210-331-0640
GNTO desk at airport arrivals hall
Mon-Sat 9am-7pm, Sun 10am-4pm. Athens International Airport (Eleftherios Venizelos), 210-353-0445
Hellenic-American Union HAU organizes cultural events, offers English and Greek language courses, and also has a library open to the public. Massalias 22, Kolonaki, 210-368-0000, hau.gr
Foreign Visitors
U.S. Embassy: *8:30am-5pm.* Vas Sofias 91, Ambelokipi, 210-721-2951/2959, usembassy.gr
Passport requirements: U.S. visitors need a passport only, no visa, for stays under 90 days.
Cell phones: Check with your service provider for a local affiliate; interconnection charges can be a nasty surprise when you get your bill. It's cheaper to buy a local pre-paid card (*kartokiniti*, available at electronics stores and many kiosks) rather than routing calls through your home provider.
Electrical: 220 volts/50 Hz. Converters needed for most US appliances.
The latest-info websites: athensnews.gr, ekathimerini.com, or ana.gr for news. And of course, pulseguides.com.

HIT THE GROUND

Greek Language

It's easy to get through your stay in Athens without a word of Greek; most street signs are written in Latin characters and most tourist sites have information in English. But learning the Greek alphabet and a few phrases will considerably ease your stay. The following will help you cheat your way through asking directions, recognizing street names, and ordering food. If need be, it's worth a try to ask in English—most Athenians speak at least a bit.

The Alphabet

	Name	Sound
α	alpha	apple
β	vita	victory
γ	gamma	yard
δ	delta	this
ε	epsilon	bet
ζ	zita	zone
η	ita	bin
θ	thita	thin
ι	yota	bin
κ	kappa	cook
λ	lamda	lemon
μ	mi	mother
ν	ni	no
ξ	xi	ax
ο	omicron	on
π	pi	pot
ρ	rho	real
σ	sigma	see
τ	taf	two
υ	ipsilon	bin
φ	fi	leaf
χ	hi	hear
ψ	psi	lips
ω	omega	on

Combination Vowels

	Name	Sound
αι	eh	= as bet
οι	ih	= as bin
ει	ih	= as bin
ου	oo	= as boot
αυ	afz	= as affection
αυ	av	= as cavalry
ευ	ef	= as effect
ευ	ev	= as every

Combination Consonants

	Name	Sound
μπ	b	= as ball
ντ	d	= as doll
τζ	g	= as jar
τσ	ch	= as children
γγ	g	= as gear
γκ	g	= as gear

Numbers

1	ena
2	thio
3	tria
4	tessera
5	pende
6	exi
7	epta
8	okto
9	enea
10	theka
20	ikosi
30	trianda
40	saranda
50	peninda
60	exinda
70	evthominda
80	oghthonda
90	eneninda
100	ekato
200	thiakosia
300	triakosia
1000	hilia
2000	dio thiliades
3000	tris hiliades
5000	pende hiliades

Key Words and Phrases

English	*Greek*
Yes	*Ne*
No	*Ohi*
Hello (formal)	*Herete*
Hi (informal)	*Ghia sou*
Good Morning	*Kalimera*
Good Afternoon	*Kalispera*
Good Night	*Kalinihta*
Goodbye	*Andio*
Please / You're welcome	*Parakalo*
Thank you	*Efharisto*
Thank you very much	*Efharisto poli*
What's your name? (informal)	*Pos se lene?*
What is your name? (formal)	*Pos sas lene?*
My name is ... (informal)	*Me lene ...*
Do you speak English?	*Milas Aglika?*
I don't understand	*Then katalaveno*
OK	*Endaxi*
Excuse me	*Signomi*
Down the hatch	*Stin ighia sas*
Where is the restrooom?	*Pou ine i tooaleta*
How much does it cost?	*Posso kani?*
Monday	*Theftera*
Tuesday	*Triti*
Wednesday	*Tetarti*
Thursday	*Pempti*
Friday	*Paraskevi*
Saturday	*Savato*
Sunday	*Kiriaki*
Open	*Anikto*
Closed	*Klisto*
How much?	*Posso?*
Where?	*Pou?*
When?	*Pote?*
May I have a menu?	*Ton katalogo, parakalo*
I would like to eat ...	*Tha ithela na fao ...*
The bill, please	*Ton logariasmo, parakalo*

Areas / Neighborhoods

English	Greek
Akti Themistokleous	Ακτη Θεμιστοκλεους
Alimos Marina	Αλιμος Μαρινα
Ambelokipi	Αμπελοκηποι
Anafiotika	Αναφιωτικα
Athens	Αθηνα
Exarchia	Εξαρχεια
Faliro	Φαληρο
Filomouson Square	Πλατεια Φιλομουσων
Filopappos	Φιλοπαππου
Gazi	Γκαζι
Glyfada	Γλυφαδα
Kastella	Καστελα
Kifissia	Κηφησια
Kolonaki	Κολονακι
Koukaki	Κουκακι
Makrigiani	Μακρυγιαννη
Metropolis Square	Πλατεια Μητροπολεως
Monastiraki	Μοναστηρακι
Mt. Lycabettus	Λυκαβητος
Paleo Faliro	Παλαιο Φαληρο
Pangrati	Παγκρατι
Piraeus	Πειραιας
Plaka	Πλακα
Plateia Kefalari	Πλατεια Κεφαλαριου
Plateia Kolonaki	Πλατεια Κολονακιου
Plateia Omonia	Πλατεια Ομονοιας
Psirri	Ψυρι
Omonia	Ομονοια
Syntagma Square	Πλατεια Συνταγματος
Syngrou	Συγγρου
Thimari	Θυμαρι
Thisio	Θησειο
Voula	Βουλα
Vouliagmeni	Βουλιαγμενη
Zea	Ζεα

Street Names

English	Greek
Adrianou	Αδριανου
Akademias	Ακαδημιας
Aristophanous	Αριστοφανους
Ermou	Ερμου
Evripidou	Ευριπιδου
Iraklidon	Ηρακλειδων
Kallidromiou	Καλιδρομιου
Kydathineon	Κυδαθηναιων
Mnisikleous	Μνησικλεους
Panepistimiou	Πανεπιστημιου
Patission	Πατησιων
Pireos	Πειραιως
Stadiou	Σταδιου
Stournari	Στουρναρη
Valtetsiou	Βαλτετσιου
Vassilissis Sofias	Βασιλισσης Σοφιας

Best Hotels

English	Greek	English	Greek
Astir Palace Resort	Αστηρ Παλας	Hotel Grande Bretagne	Μεγαλη Βρετανια
Divani Palace Acropolis	Ντιβανι Παλας	The Margi	Μαρτζυ
Electra Palace	Ηλεκτρα Παλας	The St. George Lycabettus	Σαιντ Τζωρτζ Λυκαβητος

Best Restaurants

English	Greek	English	Greek
Aiolis	Αιολις	48	Σαραντα Οκτω
Archeon Gefsis	Αρχαιων Γευσεις	Frame	Φρειμ
Aristera-Dexia	Αριστερα- Δεξια	Freud Oriental	Φροιντ Οριενταλ
Athinaikon	Αθηναικον	Interni	Ιντερνι
Balthazar	Μπαλταζαρ	Island	Αιλαντ
Central	Σεντραλ	Jimmy and the Fish	Ο Τζιμης και το Ψαρι
Daphne's	Δαφνης		
Edodi	Εδωδη	Karavitis	Καραβιτης
Estiatorio 24	Εστιατοριο εικοσιτ εσσερα	Kavouras	Καβουρας
		Kiku	Κικου
Filistron	Φιλιστρων	Mamacas	Μαμακας

Best Restaurants (cont.)

English	Greek	English	Greek
O Kostas	Ο Κωστας	Septem	Σεπτεμ
O Platanos	Ο Πλατανος	Square Sushi	Σκουερ Σουσι
Orea Ellas	Ωραια Ελλας	Stavlos	Σταυλος
Orizontes	Οριζοντες	Ta Agrafa	Τα Αγραφα
Ouzadiko	Ουζαδικο	Thanassis	Θανασης
Papandreou's Taverna	Ταβερνατου Παπανδρεου	Tou Psarra	Του Ψαρα
		Varoulko	Βαρουλκο
Pil-Poul	Πιλ-Πουλε	Vassilenas	Βασιλαινας
Plous Podilato	Πλους Ποδηλατο	Vive Mar	Βιβε Μαρ
Red	Ρεντ	Vlassis	Βλασσης

Best Nightlife

English	Greek	English	Greek
Aegli Village Cool	Αιγλη Βιλλατζ Κουλ	Mt. Lycabettus Theater	Θεατρο Λυκαβητου
Akrotiri	Ακροτηρι	Neraida	Νεραιδα
Bedlam	Μπεντλαμ	Odeon of Herodes Atticus	Ωδειον Ηρωδου Αττικου
Cine Paris	Σινε Παρι		
Cine Psirri	Σινε Ψυρι	Playback	Πλαιυ Μπακ
Diogenis Studio	Στουντιο Διογενης	Posidonio	Ποσειδωνειον
Don Quixote's	Δον Κιχωτης	Privilege	Πριβιλεντζ
Dora Stratou Dance Theatre	Δωρα Στρατου	Rex	Ρεξ
		Romeo's	Ρομεο
Dragoste	Ντραγκοστ	Soul	Σοουλ
Half Note	Χαφ Νοουτ	Stavlos	Σταυλος
Island	Αιλαντ	Stoa Ton Athanaton	Στοα των Αθανατων
Kidathineon	Κυδαθηναιων	Taximi	Ταξιμι
Lambda	Λαμδα	Thirio	Θηριο
Megaron Mousikis	Μεγαρο Μουσικης	Venue	Βενιου
Melina	Μελινα		
Mnisikleous	Μνησικλεους		
Mommy	Μαμμυ		

Best Attractions

English	Greek	Englsih	Greek
Acropolis	Ακροπολις	Grand Beach Lagonissi	Παραλια Λαγονησιου
Ancient Agora	Αρχαια Αγορα	Kapnikarea	Καπνικαρεα
Asteria Seaside Beach	Παραλια Αστεριρ	Kessariani	Καισαριανη
Athinais	Αθηναις	National Archeological Museum	Εθνικο Αρχαιολογικο Μουσειο
Benaki Museum	Μουσειο Μπενακι		
Byzantine Museum	Βυζαντινο Μουσειο	Roman Agora	Ρωμαικη Αγορα
DESTE Foundation of Contemporary Art	ΔΕΣΤΕ Ιδρυμα Συγχρωνης Τεχνης	Technopolis	Τεχνοπολης
Goulandris Museum of Cycladic Art	Μουσειο Κυκλαδικης Τεχνης Γουλανδρη		

Party Conversation—A Few Surprising Facts

- Greeks are Europe's heaviest smokers, with 45% of the adult population lighting up regularly. In 2003, it consumed 4,313 cigarettes per person, an average of 12 cigarettes each day for every man, woman, and child.

- Greeks drink more Scotch whiskey per person than any other nation in the world. In 2001, Greece consumed more than 45 million bottles, an average of four for each citizen. Also worth mentioning: The legal drinking age is 16.

- Greek male life expectancy is 74.6 years, the ninth highest in the world, as compared with the U.S., where it is 70, ranking 24th. And that's despite all the whiskey and cigarettes.

- Greece has the lowest crime rate in the European Union.

- There are half as many Greeks outside Greece as inside. Melbourne (Australia) has the second largest Greek population in the world.

- In the English language, about a third of the words are either transliterated Greek or of Greek origin.

- The yo-yo was invented and popularized in Greece more than 3,000 years ago, and is the world's second-oldest known toy (dolls are the first).

- The Greek merchant marine fleet is the largest in the world, representing 16% of the world's total fleet.

- Greece's coastline spans a total of 9,300 miles, just a bit less than America's 11,800 miles of coastline—incredible when one considers that Greece's land mass is roughly the size of Alabama.

- *Malacas* is the most-often-uttered word in Athens. Literally it means "wanker," or "jerk," but really it's a multipurpose insult; if used on a friend, it can be almost affectionate, while if used in an argument with a stranger it can be very potent. It's often used as a curse word, say, when the person in front of you is not driving fast enough. But then it's always accompanied by a raised hand ("eh") and a smile.

The Cheat Sheet
(The Very Least You Ought to Know
About Athens)

If you're going to survive the taxi drivers, you'd better have some insider knowledge about Athens. Here's a countdown of the ten most important facts you need to keep you looking and sounding like a local.

Neighborhoods

Exarchia is the slightly grungy student quarter, with a somewhat exaggerated reputation for anarchists, drugs, and a secret terrorist organization.

Gazi was once the home of the city gasworks and is now a happening area, with industrial art spaces, restaurants, and late-night bars.

Keramikos centers on ancient Athens' main cemetery, which is just outside the 5th-century city walls.

Kolonaki is the domain of wealthy Greeks, foreign embassy staffers, designer stores, and hip bar-restaurants—moneyed, chic, and trendy.

Makrigianni is located south of Plaka and is a peaceful residential quarter with several high-class restaurants and some decent hotels.

Monastiraki is best known for its central metro station, at the foot of Plaka, and its Sunday flea market.

Pangrati is middle class and middle-aged. Pangrati is safe and respectable, with several reliable tavernas and restaurants.

Plaka is the oldest residential part of town, quaint and touristy, in the shadow of the Acropolis.

Psirri is a gritty quarter close to Monastiraki. Psirri has recently undergone a revival to bring in tavernas, late-night bars, and clubs.

Thisio has smart neoclassical houses that accommodate some high-end bars and cafes overlooking the Ancient Agora.

Streets

Akademias runs from the National Gardens, below Kolonaki and Exarchia, to Kaningos Square, after which it joins Patission.

Ermou runs from Syntagma Square past Monastiraki to meet Pireos in Gazi. From Syntagma Square to Monastiraki, it is a cobblestoned pedestrian zone.

Leoforos Alexandras runs from Patission to meet Vassilissis Sofias.

Panepistimiou (or Eleftheriou Venizelou) runs from Syntagma to Omonia.

Patission (also known as 28 Oktovriou) runs past the National Archaeological Museum and Polytechnic.

Pireos runs from Gazi in the center to Piraeus on the coast.

Stadiou runs from Omonia to Syntagma.

Syngrou runs from the city center to the sea, hitting the coastal road at Kalithea, between Paleo Faliro and Neo Faliro.

Vassilissis Sofias is often referred to as "Museum Row" and runs from Syntagma Square past the Hilton to meet Leoforos Alexandras.

Typical Greek Dishes

Baklava Countless layers of filo pastry filled with ground walnuts and almonds, baked and then soaked in a rich, sweet syrup.

Dolmades Rolled vine leaves filled with rice, grated onion, and mint.

Fassolada White (haricot) beans cooked with tomato, carrots, onions, and oregano.

Horiatiki (Greek salad) Tomatoes, cucumber, green peppers, olives, feta cheese, olive oil, and oregano—best in summer when its ingredients are in season.

Keftedes Ground meat and onion meatballs, fried or in saltsa (rich tomato sauce).

Moussaka Layered eggplant and potato, ground meat, and tomato, topped with béchamel sauce and oven-baked.

Taramosalata A rich spread of fish roe, oil, lemon, onion, and breadcrumbs.

Tzatziki A sauce made of yogurt, grated cucumber, and garlic.

Island Groups

Crete Greece's largest island, with a population of 500,000, 2,456m-high mountains (which have snow from Nov.-May), and a huge repertoire of local customs.

Cyclades Arid, rocky islands with characteristic white cubic architecture; the most visited islands are Mykonos and Santorini.

Dodecanese The most distant island group, close to Turkey. Dodeka means twelve, and indeed there are a dozen of these.

Ionian Islands Six green, fertile islands on the Adriatic Sea, off the mainland west coast, the largest of which is Corfu.

North Eastern Aegean Islands This group is between northeastern Greece and Turkey.

Saronic Islands South of Athens off the Peloponnese east coast, the most exclusive of these islands is Hydra.

Sporades Known for their pretty pine forests and even more beautiful beaches, this group includes Skiathos.

Drinks

Coffee Kafe elliniko (Greek coffee) is short, strong, and gritty. The famous Greek frappe (iced coffee) is made from Nescafe and is taken as a long, tall drink served with a straw. Order your coffee gliko, metrio, or sketo (sweet, medium, or without sugar).

Metaxa A Greek brandy, of varying quality, rated by stars.

Ouzo An aniseed-flavored spirit, drunk with or without iced water (which makes it turn white and cloudy), traditionally accompanied by mezedes (appetizers).

Raki A potent distilled spirit, made from grapes, often taken as a shot.

Tea It's available but rarely drunk in cafes, though tsay vounou (Greek mountain tea) and a wide variety of herbal teas are available in shops and markets.

Wine Though little known abroad, Greek wines are currently enjoying a renaissance. Some of the bottled wines are of exceptional quality, and several vineyards recently have begun opening their gates to the public for wine-tasting sessions.

HIT THE GROUND

5 Hills

Acropolis Rises above Plaka.

Lycabettus Rises behind Kolonaki.

Philopappou Rises southwest of the Acropolis.

Pnyx Rises west of the Acropolis.

Strefi Rises behind Exarchia.

4 Deities

Athena Daughter of Zeus, goddess of wisdom, and protectress of Athens.

Hera Queen of the gods, wife (and sister) of Zeus, and goddess of women and marriage.

Poseidon God of the sea and earthquakes, the younger brother of Zeus.

Zeus God of gods, ruler of the skies, and father of many heroes.

3 Things to Avoid

Accepting drinks from strangers on Syntagma A long-standing scam, with foreign men the victims. A man asks you the time, then offers a drink, taking you to a dubious bar. You're bullied into paying the huge bill.

Entering churches in skimpy clothing Out of respect, be sure to have shoulders and legs covered when visiting churches and religious institutions.

Getting ripped off by taxi drivers Although they have a very bad reputation, Athens' taxi drivers are generally honest. Make sure the meter is on.

Sports Teams

Olympiakos of Piraeus Soccer team that plays at Karaiskaki Stadium in Neo Faliro. National rating: top of the Hellenic National League.

Panathinaikos of Athens play at Apostolos Nikolaidis Stadium. National rating: second place on the Hellenic National League.

Singular Sensation

Parthenon This icon of Western democracy symbolizes the spirit of Athens.

Coffee (quick stops for a java jolt)

Da Capo More deals have been brokered over a quick cup of espresso—the best you'll find in Athens—at Da Capo than the backrooms of Parliament. It's all politics and business in the morning, marketing and fashion by early afternoon. (Kolonaki Square)

Platis serves arguably the best cafe latte in Athens to patrons ranging from retired politicians to tourists. Ianos (inside Ianos books) is a hotbed of publishing gossip and favorite hangout of writers. (in Eleftheroudakis Bookstore)

Polis Popular among actors and students, this rooftop cafe-bar is loud and filled with nervous energy. Pass on the tea or cappuccino and order a Greek coffee, brewed to perfection on a small hearth and served in a copper *briki*. (Stoa Vivliou rooftop)

Vivliothiki Da Capo's counterweight draws the same heady mix of politicians and businessmen, along with a sprinkling of writers and artists, who enjoy the more leisurely pace and pride themselves on a more intellectual outlook on life. (Kolonaki Square)

HIT THE GROUND

Just for Business and Conventions

If you're in Athens for a trade show or conference at one of the major convention centers—all of which are in the northern and more rural eastern suburbs—you face a problem: Staying near the Attiki Odos highway and the airport to be closer to business means being far from Athens' exciting nightlife. For travelers who want both, staying in chic Kifissia or nearby Ekali is a reasonable compromise; Kifissia is home to many glamorous restaurants, bars, clubs, and shops yet is about a 15-minute drive from convention centers.

Addresses to Know

Convention Centers
- Helexpo Palace
  Attica Exhibition & Conference Center
  39 Kifissias, Maroussi
  210-616-8888, helexpo.gr
- EXPO Athens
  2 Drafiou, Attiki Odos exit 14, Anthousa
  210-685-4885, expoathens.gr
- EKEP Exposition Center
  12 km Athens-Lamia Hwy., Metamorphosis
  210-284-6060
- M.E.C. (Mediterranean Exhibition Center)
  301 Lavrio, Peania
  210-604-1410, mec.gr

City Information
- City of Athens
  Athinas 63, Kotzia Square
  210-372-2001, cityofathens.gr
- Athens Tourist Information
  24-hour hotline for visitor information
  Tel: 171

Business and Convention Hotels

These business-friendly spots are all a reasonable distance to convention centers.

Airport Area

Holiday Inn Athens Brand-new standard five-star populated with fellow conventioneers. Light, airy rooms and an atrium-like indoor pool. Avenue Attiki Odos, 40th km, between exits 17 & 18, Peania, 210-668-9000, holiday-inn.com

Sofitel Athens Airport Among the most luxurious airport hotels in Europe, not so much near the airport as in the airport. Eleftherios Venizelos Intl. Airport, Spata, 210-354-4000, sofitel.com

Northern Suburbs

Hotel Caterina Converted rustic country inn caters to working stiffs with its den-like rooms. Mikonou 3, Kifissia, 210-801-8495, hotelcaterina.com

Hotel 21 Hyper-modern business hotel with an artsy, independent, techno-savvy crowd. Kolokotrini 21 & Mykonou, Kifissia, 210-623-3521, twentyone.gr

Life Gallery Offers body-and-soul soothing with its state-of-the-art spa. Thiseos 103, 14565 Ekali, 210-626-0400, blue.gr

Pentelikon The taste of grand old luxury, this is a '20s-era estate-like hotel. Deligianni 66, Kifissia, 210-623-0650, hotelpentelikon.gr

Business Entertaining

Need to impress a client? These places will help seal the deal.

Avenue 103 Notable newcomer serves Greek-French cuisine to powerbrokers. Life Gallery hotel/spa, Thiseos 103, Ekali, 210-626-0400, blue.gr

Jaipur Palace Athens' best Indian restaurant honors clients with elegant décor and cuisine. Aghiou Konstantinou 73 & Themidos, Maroussi, 210-805-2762

Karavi Inspired French cuisine, ideally enjoyed from the ninth-floor perc h . Sofitel Athens Airport (9th floor), Spata, 210-354-4000

Kastelorizo Wow them with fresh fish grilled to perfection at this seafood restaurant. Platanon 2, Nea Kifissia, 210-807-5408

Piazza Mela Award-winning Italian cuisine served to wheelers and dealers. Kifissias 238 (Mela Shopping Center), Kifissia, 210-623-6596

Ta Kioupia Decadent prix-fixe menu of Greek cuisine. Olimpionikon 2 & Dexameni, Politia, 210-620-0005, takioupia.gr

Ducking Out for a Half Day

Athenians know leisure time is serious business. Follow their lead and leave work behind for a few hours of fun.

Acropolis How could you visit Athens without seeing this temple of democracy and having a stroll around Plaka and Monastiraki?

Head to the beach Whiz from business to a beach in the north (Nea Makri, Porto Rafti, or Schinias) or south (Vouliagmeni, Varkiza, or Lagonissi) in 30 minutes.

Kefalari Square Sip a frappe, shop, and stroll around Kefalari Square in Kifissia, Athens most fashionable suburb—15 minutes from the convention centers.

Gifts to Bring Home

Don't leave Athens without a tasteful (or tacky, if you prefer) souvenir, even if you haven't left your convention center.

Eleftherios Venizelos (Athens International Airport) Gifts on the fly—literally: Impressive coffee-table books, Greek music CDs, fine komboloi (worry beads), and high-design Greek jewelry are among the offerings. Spata, 210-353-0000

Inopantopoleion A quick detour via Attiki Odos rewards you with the best Greek honey, olives, cheeses, wild teas, and even monastery beers in convenient small sizes. 76 Ag. Antoniou, Patima Halandri, 210-600-9199

HIT THE GROUND

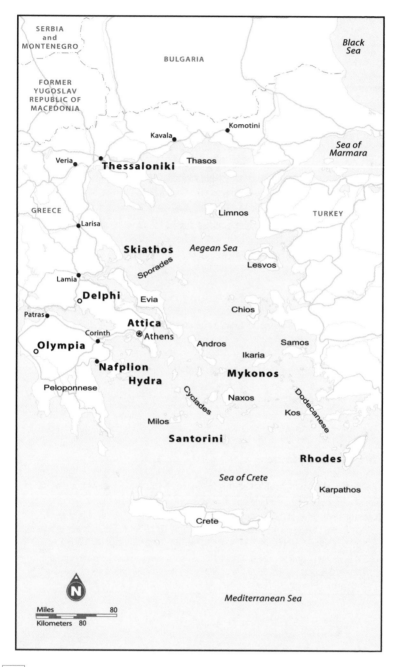

SERBIA and MONTENEGRO

BULGARIA

Black Sea

FORMER YUGOSLAV REPUBLIC OF MACEDONIA

Komotini

Kavala

Sea of Marmara

Veria

Thessaloniki

Thasos

GREECE

Larisa

Limnos

TURKEY

Skiathos

Aegean Sea

Lesvos

Sporades

Lamia

Delphi

Evia

Chios

Patras

Attica

⊛ Athens

Corinth

Olympia

Andros

Samos

Ikaria

Nafplion

Mykonos

Hydra

Peloponnese

Cyclades

Naxos

Dodecanese

Kos

Milos

Santorini

Rhodes

Sea of Crete

Karpathos

Crete

N

Miles   80
Kilometers   80

Mediterranean Sea

LEAVING ATHENS

Just because you've had your fill of urban Athens doesn't mean you're done. Pack an overnight case and get ready for islands, oracles, and adventures, like a walk through the ancient castle of Agamemnon or a decadent stay in a beachfront villa. From destinations on the mainland to those legendary Greek isles, there's plenty worth doing only a few hours from the country's cosmopolitan capital.

Delphi

Hot Tip: April to October are the best weather months, but you can double your fun on winter weekends, enjoying the ruins and skiing by day, and trying Arahova's all-night clubbing after a nap.

The Lowdown: Delphi has just about everything: It's perhaps the most beautiful and fascinating ancient site in all of Greece, with a history full of myths and mystics. It has dozens of classical temples, a top-notch museum, and stunning natural beauty. It's also set halfway between the mountains and the sea, which both offer fashionable resort scenes packed with pretty Athenians along with plenty of opportunities for swimming and hiking.

When Zeus wanted to find the center of the world, he released two eagles from the ends of the universe. They met over Delphi, marking the place the ancient Greeks called the ompahlos (navel). They associated great mystic powers with the site, whose jutting mountain, gaping chasms, and rushing springs still give the feeling that this could indeed be where the seams of the earth came together. An oracle gave prophecies at Delphi, presided over by Apollo. Marble shrines were built to honor the god and to house his priestesses, who chewed mind-altering herbs before giving their abstruse prophecies (they told Lydia's King Croesus that if he invaded Persia he would destroy a great empire, neglecting to mention that the empire would be his own). Despite these lapses in detail, pilgrims came from around the world to consult the oracle. Heads of state brought treasures (which were not unknown to lead to favorable prophecies). The site was one of the most important in the ancient world, and although it declined after Roman times, it is still among Greece's greatest treasures.

While exploring Delphi is memorable enough in itself, it would be a mistake to overlook the rest of the area—the oracle knew how to pick good real estate. Above Delphi is lofty Mount Parnassus and the trendy ski resort Arahova, while below it is the chic beach town of Galaxidhi. Depending on the season, Athens' rich and pretty pack both these spots on weekends.

Delphi itself is at its most magical in spring, when the mountains and marbles are blanketed with flowers. Hikers will want to climb up Mount Parnassus on the many trails leading up from Delphi.

Best Attractions

Arahova Tourist Office Information about the ski resort filled with rich Athenians, cozy inns, and bars. 226-703-1630

Delphi Museum Contains exclusive finds from the site of Delphi; an integral part of the sanctuary. 226-508-2312, culture.gr

Galaxidhi Tourist Office Filled with 19th-century mansions, good beaches and cool waterfront bars, this mellow, friendly resort is the prettiest and most fashionable town on the Gulf of Corinth. 226-504-1262

Mount Parnassus Ski Centre Hiking and skiing for all levels, from springtime walks to black diamond ski trails. 226-702-2689

Best Hotels

Arhontiko Visithra Themed rooms include the "Bridal" (white-linen canopy bed), the "At Sea" (driftwood), and the "Conception" (round bed and mirrored ceiling!). Close to the harbor, Galaxidhi, 226-504-1788, gto.gr

Delphi Palace Comfortable, classic rooms with splendid views of the olive groves below Delphi, plus an indoor pool and fitness club. Delphi, 226-508-2151, delphi-hotels.gr

Elatos Resort, Arahova Greece's only Alpine resort, with wood chalets, fireplaces, a health club, and stylish Greeks who may never strap on skis but know that this is the place to be seen. At Itamos, 25km from Arahova on the road to Agoriani, 223-406-1162 / 210-459-8131, elatos.com

Hotel Ganimede Genteel Italians run this 19th-century mansion with simple but elegant rooms and sumptuous breakfasts in a flower-filled courtyard—very romantic. Gourgouri 16, Galaxidhi, 226-504-1328, gfp.gr/ganimede.gr

Best Restaurants

Babis Kalyvia Parnassou Very mountain villagey—a crackling fireplace and soul-warming bowls of hot stifado. Arahova, 226-703-2155

Barko tis Maritsas The most popular taverna on the beach specializes in mussels—baked, fried, or in sauce. Ianthis on the beach, Amfissa, Galaxidhi, 226-504-1059

Epicouros Vas. Traditional Greek dishes, including the house specialty, wild boar, are just the backdrop for the fine view of the alpine valley below. Pavlou 22, Delphi, 226-508-3250

Taverna Vakhos The exception to Delphi's generally bland tourist tavernas has sweeping gulf views. Apollonos 31, Delphi, 226-508-3186

Best Nightlife

Emboriko Where everyone goes for après-ski cocktails. Arahova, 226-703-2467

To Kioski In summer, this harborside cafe is buzzing with fashionable young things weekending it away from Kolonaki. In winter, there's a dark wood interior, glowing fireplace, and good jazz. Waterfront, Galaxidi, 226-504-1930

Getting There: There are six daily buses from Athens to Delphi; the journey takes three hours. Buses leave from Liosion terminal; call 210-831-7096 for exact times. By car, take the Athens-Thessaloniki National Highway to the Thebes turnoff. Continue west, following signs to Arachova and Delphi at the 84th kilometer.

LEAVING

Nafplion

Hot Tip: Traffic can be brutal. In high season from April to October, avoid the weekend crush heading back to Athens by arriving earlier in the week and checking out on Saturday morning.

The Lowdown: With its bougainvillaea-draped 19th-century mansions, cobblestone streets, fairy-tale Venetian fortress, and azure-water beach, Nafplion is an easy contender for the prettiest city in Greece. But what makes it a must-see—at least for fans of Homer, myths, and marble—is its proximity to some of the most important sites in the ancient world. Here you can actually walk in the castle of Agamemnon and see the citadels of Homer's "well-built Mycenae, rich in gold." You can also watch classical Greek dramas (replete with lust, murder, and incest) at Epidavros, the spectacular 4th-century BC amphitheater where they were originally produced. If ancient cities and Oedipal complexes just aren't your thing, Nafplion's also just a short hop away from any number of hard-partying beach resorts as well as being in the heart of Greece's best wine country, where up-and-coming vintners give tours and tastings of the ruby-red local product, known since ancient times as "Hercules' blood."

Nafplion has an Old City and New City, and deciding which one to stay in is a no-brainer: pastel neoclassical mansions and tavernas under flowered trellises or '60s cement apartment blocks and neon fast-food sprawl? Stay in the heart of the Old City and most of your trip will be taken care of—just walking around Nafplion is enchanting. From the junction between the Old and New cities, buses leave several times a day to the surrounding archaeological sites of Mycenae, Nemea, Tiryns, and Argos, all of which date from around the 16th–13th centuries BC. Of these, the most impressive is Mycenae, likely home of the same Myceneans who fought the Trojan War and were immortalized in the *Iliad*. You may also want to take a day trip to Epidavros, Greece's best-preserved ancient amphitheater, and try the acoustics for yourself. If you don't go by day, though, it's imperative that you see a performance by night. Tickets are available at the Hellenic Festival box offices in Athens and Nafplion. Reserve up to two weeks in advance. Beachgoers may be perfectly happy at the local beach or they may want to take the hour-long bus ride to the G-string-friendly resort of Tolo. Among the many nearby wineries that offer tours are the superb Gaia and Skouros vineyards.

Best Attractions

Gaia Wines Gaia's gorgeous Nemean vineyards produce deep, velvety reds that have won high international kudos. Koutsi, Upper Nemea, 274-602-2057

Hellenic Festival Box Office Watch Oedipus gouge his eyes out in the same theater as the ancients did. (Tickets for performances at Epidavros) Panepistimiou 39, off Syntagma Sq., Athens, 210-929-2900

Mycenae An irresistible blend of history, myth, literature, and legend. culture.gr

Best Hotels

Amphitryon Hotel Newly renovated, this is the only really smart, elegant, full-service hotel in town—not as charming as some of the family-run inns, but still smallish and personal at 42 rooms. All rooms have panoramic sea views and a great view of the islet. Spiliadou 21, Nafplion, 275-207-0700, nafplionhotels.gr

Byron Hotel Marble-topped tables, lace bedspreads, blue shutters, and sea views, in a pretty pink house at the top of the Old City. Plateia Aghiou Spiridona, 275-202-2351, byronhotel.gr

Hotel Nafsimedon Tasteful, old-fashioned rooms in an elegant mansion overlooking a palm-filled park. Sideras Merarhias 9, 275-202-5060, nafsimedon.gr

Nafplia Palace Nafplion's nicest hotel is set superbly on the hill within the ancient fortress walls and has large wood-and-marble rooms and airy bungalows. Acronafplia, 275-202-8981, nafplionhotels.gr

Best Restaurants

Kanaris (Karamanli) Greece's former president Constantine Karamanlis liked this cheerful taverna so much that they added his name to the sign. Wash down the stuffed cabbage leaves and yiouvetsi with barrel retsina. Bouboulinas 1, 275-202-7668

Noufara Good Italian fare and good people-watching offer a nice break from tavernas. Plateia Syntagma, 275-202-3648

Spilia Savor braised lamb and seasonal baby artichokes accompanied by magnificent wine from local Nemea vineyards in one of the best tavernas in Greece. Tripleos 165, Kefalari, Argolida, 12km outside Nafplion, 275-106-2300

Getting There: There are three or four buses daily from Athens to Nafplion departing from the bus station at 100 Kifissiou (210-513-4110). The bus takes about four hours and should be reserved in advance. Two trains per day leave Athens' Piraeus train station for Nafplion; call 275-202-9380 for details. By car, head south from Athens on the Athens-Corinth national road (E94), then take E65 toward Tripoli. Follow signs to the Argos exit, driving through Argos and following signs for the Nafplion road, which will take you straight through to Nafplion. The drive takes about one hour.

205
miles
W

Olympia

Hot Tip: High season is May to September. In summer, arrive the night before and hit the ruins early, moving on to the museum as the sun starts to climb. Later, cool off with a swim and enjoy the western Peloponnese coast's gorgeous sand beaches.

The Lowdown: This is what all the fuss is about every four years. From a foot race linked to the worship of Zeus, king of the Olympian gods, the Olympic Games have developed into the world's preeminent sports competition. Despite the fanfare of the modern Games, even world-class athletes can't resist lining up along the ancient starting line for a sprint down the stadium whose length was reportedly measured by the Greek hero Heracles.

The ancient sanctuary sits in a valley shaded by the gentle slopes of Kronion Hill, dedicated to Cronus, god of time and father of Zeus. The sacred grove, Altis, was renowned throughout the Greek world but gained special importance in 776 BC when the Olympic Games were instituted by King Iphitus of Pisa as tribute to the gods. The contests, founded to encourage friendly competition among rival cities, spread to the entire Greek world. At their peak, the contests lasted five days and comprised several events, including chariot races. Victors were worshipped as heroes, and their cities erected statues and treasuries for offerings in their names at Olympia. Buildings span the 8th century BC through Roman times, when bathhouses and aqueducts were added.

At the height of the tourist season, the best way to avoid the crowds is to spend the night in Olympia and arrive before the tour buses from Athens get here. Follow the pedestal-lined stoa down to the Temple of Hera, one of the oldest temples in Greece. Continue past the treasuries and a series of pedestals to enter the ancient stadium through the vaulted krypte stoa. Emerging you can almost hear the roar of the crowd and imagine the throngs seated on the stadium's banks to observe the races.

Year-round, Olympia is an excellent springboard for exploring the western Peloponnese and lesser-known inland sights like the Temple of Apollo at Bassae. Or you can head farther north to Kyllini, a famous spa with several modern resorts. From here, you can take the ferry over to Zakynthos and the renowned Laganas Beach, home to clubbers and loggerhead turtles alike.

Best Attractions

Archaeological Museum Praxiteles's famed statue of Hermes, friezes from the Temple of Zeus, and other sculptures are on display in this newly renovated museum. 262-402-2517

Archaeological Site of Olympia Highlights include the Stadium, Temple of Zeus, and Temple of Hera. 262-402-2517

Museum of the Olympic Games Features exhibits on both the ancient and modern Olympics. 262-402-2544

184

Peloponnese Famous for its long stretches of sandy beach, lapped by the deep blue Ionian. Some of the prettiest beaches are along the Gulf of Kyparissia that curls between Pyrgos, north of Olympia, and Kyparissia to the south.

Best Hotels

Aldemar Olympian Village It's a 30-minute drive away from Olympia, but attractive as a resort destination since it's one of the premier spas and thalassotherapy centers in Greece. Skafidia, Pyrgos, 262-105-4640, aldemarhotels.com

Amalia A popular class-A hotel with large conference facilities and pool. Olympia, 262-402-2190, amaliahotels.com

Europa Best Western A good basic hotel, with private tennis courts and views of ancient Olympia. Olympia, 262-402-2650

Grecotel Olympia Riviera A brand-new five-star resort on a private beachfront, with mix of bungalows and hotel accommodations. Kyllini, 210-725-0817

Praxiteles Small pension-style hotel known for its restaurant, Taverna tou Praxitele. Olympia, 262-402-2592

Best Restaurants

Don't expect anything more exciting than standard tourist-oriented menus at the restaurants and tavernas around Olympia. In the village, try Zeus Restaurant, Bacchus, Kladeos, or Taverna tou Praxitele. There is one notable restaurant: En Plo.

En Plo Enjoy home-style food while dining in the beachside village of Katakalo. Katakolo, 262-104-1300

Best Nightlife

Olympia offers basic tourist amenities—a handful of cafes, hotels, tavernas, banks, ATM machines, and souvenir shops—but nothing in terms of entertainment. You'll have to return to Patras or continue on to Kalamata; both seaside towns have a vibrant clubbing scene, especially in summer.

Getting There: In addition to organized tours from Athens, you reach Olympia on your own using public transportation. There are several buses daily between Athens (KTEL Athinon, 100 Leoforos Kifissou, 210-513-4110) and Pyrgos, then switch to local service (KTEL Pyrgou, 262-102-2592). There's also regular train service from Athens' Larissa train station to Olympia (210-513-4110), which takes five hours. If you're driving, the quickest way is via the Athens Patras highway along the northern Peloponnese coast, then continue south to Pyrgos and from there to Ancient Olympia (about 3.5 hrs.). If you're not pressed for time, chart an inland route through the Peloponnese mountains, switching to the Athens-Tripoli highway at Corinth, then following the signs through the Mantineia peaks (about 4.5 hrs.).

LEAVING

Thessaloniki

Hot Tip: A year-round destination, but cinephiles will enjoy cutting-edge film from around the world—and great post-screening parties—in November when the film festival takes over the city.

The Lowdown: Many Greeks consider their northern "Second City" greater than Athens in everything but pollution and traffic. Certainly Thessaloniki's location at a literal crossroads between East and West has made it one of the most sophisticated and cosmopolitan centers of the region since even before the days of its one-time ruler, Alexander the Great. It has been home to centuries of great civilizations—Macedonian, Hellenic, Roman, Byzantine, Jewish, Ottoman, and modern Greek—all of whom have left their mark in this city by the sea. Thessaloniki is home to Turkish hammams, Roman baths, and Greece's oldest and most beautiful Byzantine churches. But perhaps the best effect of all this multiculturalism is the food, which even snobby Athenians may tell you is the best in the country. And while all Greeks love lively nightlife, Thessaloniki is renowned not only for a chic, international scene that goes until dawn, but also for its live music venues, which for years have been quietly nurturing some of the best new jazz and progressive music acts in Europe.

Thessaloniki's tree-lined avenues and alleys offer an abundance of charming architecture and top-notch old-style cafes and ouzeries. Start by taking a taxi to the Ano Poli (upper city) at the top of the hill, still surrounded by ancient stone fortifications. Stop at any one of the wonderful cafes for a thick, sweet Greek coffee, or an ouzo accompanied by spicy Thessalonian mezedes. Wander down through the cobbled streets toward the city center, stopping at any tiny frescoed churches that catch your eye while aiming toward the magnificent basilica of Aghios Dimitrios. From there it's a few blocks to the seaside promenade, where you can see the city's landmark 15th-century White Tower. At the north end of the promenade are two of the city's best museums—the Archaeological Museum and Museum of Byzantine Culture. To make the most of Thessaloniki's nightlife, learn two words, Ladadika and Mylos. The first is the city's former warehouse district, now transformed into a trendy maze of ever-changing clubs and restaurants, the second is an old mill, now converted into a complex of music clubs.

Best Attractions

Archaeological Museum Don't miss the opulent Hellenistic goldwork from the realm of Alexander the Great. Plateia Hanth, opposite the exhibition grounds, 231-083-0538

Museum of Byzantine Culture Possibly the world's most comprehensive collection of art and artifacts from the 1,000-year span of the Byzantine Empire. Leofororos Stratou 2, 231-086-8570

Best Hotels

Andromeda Every room in this restored 1920s mansion near the city center has been decorated by a different high-end designer. Kominon 5, 231-037-3700 andromedahotels.gr

Capsis Bristol A favorite with business travelers, this restored Ottoman building in the middle of the trendy Ladadika neighborhood has sleek rooms and a rooftop pool garden. Oplopiou 2 at Katsoni, 231-050-6500, capsishotel.gr

Electra Palace This landmark hotel, set on lively Aristotelous Square at the center of town is a comfortable and stylish place to stay, thanks to a brand-new renovation. Plateia Aristotelous 9, 231-023-2221, electrahotels.com

Les Lazaristes Located in a converted tobacco warehouse and now a five-star luxury hotel, newcomer Les Lazaristes is just slightly off-center, in an artsy part of town next to the city's major cultural center. Kolokotroni 16, Stavroupoli, 231-064-7400, domotel.gr

Best Restaurants

Aigli Turkish-tinged haute cuisine in a beautifully restored hammam. Kassandrou at Aghiou Nikolaou, 231-027-0061

Aristotelous Throngs have come for years to the marble-topped tables of this beloved ouzerie. Aristotelous 8, 231-023-0762

Susami Pretty young things in designer ensembles, champagne cocktails, and stylish Levantine cuisine all come together fetchingly at this bar-restaurant. Kerasoundos 2, 231-042-4120

To Peran To Peran showcases the best of Politiki Kouzina, the home-style Greek cooking originating from Constantinople for which Thessaloniki is famous. The restaurant serves a variety of pilafs and souzoukakia (spicy, sauce-laden meatballs), yogurt-drenched kebabs, and other Eastern flavors like raki (fiery grape liqueur). Cheap and chic. (Politiki kouzina) 22 Iktinou, 231-025-2977

Best Nightlife

The Bar Head here after dinner (around 2am) for drinks with views over the sea and the White Tower. Nikiforou Foka 3, 231-024-3219

Mylos Maybe the best place in all of Greece to hear jazz and progressive pop; it's also crammed with trendy art galleries and excellent ouzeries. Andreadou Georgiou 25, 231-051-6945

Omilos The bubbling energy of a white-hot see-and-be-seen scene, tempered with the beauty and tranquility of a space open directly to the sea and stars. Alexander the Great 12, 231-088-8200

Getting There: Olympic Airways (210-966-6666) has several daily flights from Athens to Thessaloniki. Flights are about one hour. There are also four to six daily trains from Athens to Thessaloniki; the trip is about six hours and leaves from Larissa Station. Tickets can be reserved in advance directly from the station (210-323-6747); the best bet for comfort is to take a first-class overnight sleeper train, which arrives in Thessaloniki at 7am.

Wineries of Attica

Hot Tip: Pitch in during the fall grape harvest, or trygos, for a real winery experience.

The Lowdown: Wine has been an integral part of the Greek experience since the days of Dionysus, but not until the last decade have Greek vintners started taking real advantage of the ideal growing conditions that are the god's legacy. Flick through the pages of any glossy food magazine and you'll inevitably find a paean to the crumbly, sun-warmed soils, old-growth vines, and unique varietals that are now, with a new serious approach to cultivation, making a splash with palates in the know. Happily, some of the best wine country in Greece is in Attica, the peninsula surrounding Athens. There are about 30 vineyards within an hour's drive from the city; eight of these are open to the public. A day trip to two or three wineries can give you a taste of some of the best Greek vintages, along with true Greek hospitality and a view of the same landscape where Theseus slew monsters and Solon composed poetry. Unfortunately, the Attica landscape and wine industry got a serious blow when Athens' new airport, a handful of new Olympic venues, and a highway were carved through its heart, so not all the driving is as picturesque as it once was. The vineyards themselves, however, remain memorable, as do the wines, which also make perfect souvenirs—if you can keep from quaffing them before you get home.

There are three major, easily navigable wine roads running through Attica, each with a cluster of good wineries that give tastings and tours. The Attica Wine Growers' Association provides visitors with a map of wine roads with all wineries marked. You can pick up the map, along with brochures about winery-touring, from their booth at the airport, or have them mail or fax information to your hotel. Alexandros Megaponos, head of the association, can also provide customized itineraries, including recommendations for restaurants and sightseeing along the way. Here are a couple of suggestions to get you started. Taking the National Road north out of Athens leads you to the wineries of Giorgos Kokotos, which produces a highly regarded Semeli on a wooded hilltop with a stunning panorama, and Harlaftis-Athanasiadi, which produces a good variety of both reds and whites on the pistachio-tree-clad slopes of Mt. Pendeli. Heading south toward the airport on the new Attiki Odos (beltway) leads you through some unfortunately developed countryside to the preserved estates of Fragou Asiminia, Ktima Vasileiou, and Alexandros Megaponos. For an idyllic afternoon of wine-drinking and sightseeing, take the coastal Sounion road to the popular Strofilia winery at Anavysos, then continue on to the Temple of Poseidon.

Best Attractions

Alexandros Megaponos Witty, friendly Megaponos cut his teeth working as a vintner at no less than Chateau Margaux before returning home to cultivate exquisite Savatiano wines and provide a welcome fount of knowledge on Greek vintages—and Greek life—to lucky visitors. 1km. south on the road from Pikermi to Spata, Pikermi, 210-603-8038

Attica Wine Growers' Association Eleftherios Venizelos International Airport, 210-353-1315

Fragou Asiminia The two-century-old stone chateau and the sight of workers still trampling grapes the old-fashioned way makes this one of the prettiest wineries in Greece, as long as you can ignore the sight of planes flying in over the new nearby airport. The light, fruity Savatianos and Chardonnays are a delight. Spirou Prifti and Kostas Palamana 21, Spata, 210-663-2087

Giorgos Kokotos The Semeli wines (named for Dionysus' mother) at this scenic spot at the foothills of Mt. Pendeli have been raved about by the snootiest of British, American, and French wine writers. Semeli 1, Stamata, 210-364-3582

Harlaftis-Athanasiadi The star of this rolling six-acre vineyard on the slopes of Mt. Pendeli is the heady, mouth-filling, vanilla-scented Chateau Harlaftis. Stamata Attikis, Stamata, 210-621-9374

Katogi Strofilia This friendly old standby makes easily drinkable Greek varietals from Savatiano to Xynomavro. Mikra Asaia, Anavysos, 229-104-1650

Ktima Vasileiou This 100-year-old winery started producing humble retsina but has now become famous for its sophisticated Savatiano fume, aged in charred wood barrels. 26th km on the Lavrio-Koropi Road, Koropi, 210-662-6870

Getting There: Plan your route by looking at map of the wine roads of Attica; you may want to supplement this with a Road Editions map of Attica, available at bookstores. You can also call Alexandros Megaponos for recommendations. Call the wineries a day before you plan to visit; they can give you specific directions from the main roads to the vineyards.

LEAVING

Hydra

Hot Tip: Avoid transatlantic jetlag by spending your first weekend here: Dinner's at 11 pm and the clubs don't get hopping until after midnight so your body clock won't need to adjust much. May to October is high season.

The Lowdown: Hydra was one of first Greek islands to be "discovered," hitting the big screen in 1957 with the film *Boy on a Dolphin* starring Sophia Loren. Canadian poet-songwriter Leonard Cohen bought a house on the island in 1960, retreating for months on end to a secret world of music and escapism. It was here he met Norwegian Marianne Jensen, of "So Long Marianne" fame, and wrote "Bird on the Wire" upon seeing (with horror) Hydra's first telephone wires being installed. Along with Cohen came a select group of glamorous, hard-partying, cosmopolitan artists and jetsetters, including Joan Collins, David Bowie, and Bryan Ferry, all of whom were captivated by the island's untouched rugged beauty, aristocratic stone mansions, and lack of publicity and policemen.

Today the scene is rather more low-key; the party animals began moving on to Mykonos and Santorini during the 1980s, and arriving in their place were Greek ship-owners and businessmen, who keep peaceful summer villas here. The year-round population is a mere 2,000.

Local hearsay has it that the islanders owe their early wealth to treasure captured by pirates, which was hidden in deep wells and later used to fund the Greek War of Independence. Hydra became a prosperous shipping power during the 18th and 19th centuries (the population peaked at 28,000, with 186 ships), and local sea captains built the elegant archontika (stone mansions) that compose the old town today. However, with the advent of the steamship, Hydra fell into relative obscurity, locals either working as sponge divers or emigrating to the US.

Built into steep rocky hills overlooking three sides of a natural harbor that is filled with wooden fishing boats and flashy yachts, Hydra Town is the island's chief settlement and port. Beautifully kept, it remains totally authentic, with a labyrinth of steep cobbled streets cutting their way through a dense conglomeration of white terracotta-roofed houses and a picture-postcard portside lined with chic bars, art galleries, and jewelry stores. Hydriots have imposed strict conservation laws and resisted all attempts at commercialization; still today there are no cars (donkeys being the sole mode of transport) and no concrete buildings. The majority of visitors are day-trippers who depart before sunset, but nonetheless you should reserve in advance if you plan to stay in one of Hydra's small but swank hotels.

Best Attractions

Lazaros Kountouriotis Historical Museum An 18th-century mansion built by a local ship owner. 10-min. walk uphill at the west end of the harbor, 229-805-2421

Monastery of Profitis Ilias and Convent of Agia Efpraxia Lace up your boots and trek uphill above town through olive groves and pine woods, to visit this monastery and nearby convent, offering great hilltop views. 50-min. hike above town

Vlichos Bay Arrive at this pretty hamlet with several tavernas, a restored 19th-century bridge, and a pebble beach. Return by taxi boat. Follow the coastal promenade west of town for 40 min.

Best Hotels

Hotel Bratsera Hydra's most exclusive hotel is a restored 1860 sponge factory with an open-air pool and 23 rooms furnished with antiques. Tombazi, Hydra Town, 229-805-3971, bratserahotel.com

Hotel Miranda An early 19th-century sea captain's mansion, with painted ceilings and antique furniture. Breakfast is served in a courtyard fragrant with lemon trees and jasmine. Maiouli, Hydra Town, 229-805-2230, mirandahotel.gr

Hotel Orloff A late 18th-century mansion built for a Russian count. The nine guest rooms are decorated in blues and whites, with dark wooden furniture. Rafalia 9, Hydra Town, 229-805-2564, orloff.gr

Best Restaurants

Kodylenia's Taverna A whitewashed building with a terrace overlooking a tiny bay. Upscale taverna and continental fare with good presentation in a casual beach-side atmosphere. Kamini Bay, 20-min. walk west of Hydra Town, 229-805-3520

Moita Creative Mediterranean cuisine in a pretty courtyard. Off Maiouli, Hydra Town, 229-805-2020

Taverna Xeri Elia (O Douskos) Hydra's oldest eatery opened 200 years ago. Tables on a peaceful piazza in the shade of two magnifcent pine trees. Live Greek music after 8pm. 5-min. walk inland from harbor, 229-805-2886

Best Nightlife

Amalour Ethnic décor, youthful hip clientele, cocktails, and Latin American music. One block inland from the harbor

Hydronetta Potent cocktails, great music, and stunning sunsets overlooking the sea. 10-min. walk west of town, on the coastal path to Kamini

Pirate Since 1976, countless celebrities have taken a waterside table at this chic late-night bar. On the seafront at the west end of the harbor

Getting There: Hydra lies 35 nautical miles south of Athens' port, Piraeus. There is no airport on Hydra, but the island can be reached by ferry (1-2 daily, journey time 3 hrs., 210-411-7341) or hydrofoil (4-6 daily, journey time 1.5 hrs., 210-419-9200, dolphins.gr) from Piraeus.

LEAVING

Mykonos

Hot Tip: Early spring to late autumn, this is the place to be, although the truly cool only nip over for the weekend. High season is May to October.

The Lowdown: "Good boys go to heaven, bad boys go to Mykonos," says the T-shirt. Wild and rugged, this small island has a thriving cosmopolitan nightlife with some of the country's hottest clubs, and great sandy beaches, which is why it's a summer mecca for the international gay community and one of the most visited (and most crowded and expensive) of all the Greek islands.

It was first "discovered" by the Onassis family, who moored their yachts here during the early 1960s. Gay tourism developed during the 1980s after the first gay visitors found the islanders remarkably tolerant, and the word soon spread.

The capital, Mykonos Town, is made up of a labyrinth of narrow winding streets lined with two-story whitewashed cubic houses with flat roofs and blue wooden shutters and balconies. Lush exotic plants add splashes of color, while small cafes, tavernas, art galleries, and jewelry shops lend a cultured, bohemian dimension to the scene. Compact and magical, it's a great place to get lost, both literally and metaphorically.

Its hallmark is the much-photographed skyline of five thatched windmills rising up on a low hill behind the old town. It's also famed for its stunning sunsets and gossip-magazine assortment of celebrities who are known to wander its lovely paved streets.

Most visitors stay in Mykonos Town, which offers a number of tastefully designed hotels complete with spas and pools. The prettiest and most fashionable area is Little Venice (Alefkandra), and it's here on Matogiani that you'll find the main concentration of late-night bars, restaurants, galleries, and boutiques.

Mykonos is one island where you can get that all-over tan. Nudism is acceptable on many of its golden sand beaches, most of which can be reached by taxi boat from Mykonos Town. Both naturists and textilers are welcome at Paradiso and Super Paradiso beaches (note the latter is mainly gay) and Elia (the best place for water sports).

On the cultural front, take a boat trip to the small, uninhabited island of Delos with its ancient holy site, said to be the birthplace of Apollo and Artemis.

Best Attractions

Delos Archaeological Site Can be reached by water taxi or a half-day boat trip. Six nautical miles from Mykonos Town, 228-902-2259

Elia Beach A broad stretch of beach, probably the best on the island. Accessible by taxi-boat from Mykonos Town

Watermania A water park close to Elia Beach. 228-907-1685 / 228-907-1129

Best Hotels

Belvedere Hotel A five-star establishment, much-loved by American and European designers and musicians, with a faithful gay clientele. A traditional white-washed building with a series of terraces centering on an open-air pool and a luxury spa. School of Fine Arts District, Mykonos Town, 228-902-5122, belvederehotel.com

Mykonos Grand In peaceful Aghios Ioannis, the cool Mykonos Grand is everything one expects from a first-rate Mykonos hotel: clean lines, simple elegance, beautiful people, a private beach, a candlelit "infinity pool," and style to spare. Ayios Yiannis, Mykonos, 228-902-5555, mykonosgrand.gr

Santa Marina Hotel A 3km (2mi) coastal walk from Mykonos Town, at Ornos Bay. A 90-room resort set on 20 acres of landscaped grounds, complete with private beach, health club, outdoor pool, tennis court, and heliport. Ornos Bay, 228-902-3411, santamarinahotel.com

Best Restaurants

Archeon Gefsis Revives ancient Greek cuisine in an atmospheric setting. In a side street just off Matogiani, 228-907-9256

El Greco Chic eatery with a longstanding reputation. Plateia Tria Pigadia, Matogiani, 228-902-2074

Matsuhisa Mykonos Opened in summer 2003 by celebrity chef Nobuyuki Matsuhisa, founder of Nobu in New York and London. Belvedere Hotel, School of Fine Arts District, 228-902-5122

Sea Satin Sophisticated fusion cuisine and tables by the water's edge. On the seafront close to Mitropolis (Cathedral), 228-902-4676

Best Nightlife

Astra A late-night bar, with mixed clientele, popular with glamorous Athenians. Enophon Dinameon St., Matogiani, 228-902-4767

Cavo Paradiso After-hours dancing and open-air concerts. Paradise Beach, 228-902-6124

Pierro's A classic, long-standing gay bar, with the Icarus transvestite show upstairs. Agias Kiriakis Sq., Matogiani, 228-902-2177

Getting There: Mykonos lies 95 nautical miles from Athens' port, Piraeus. It can be reached by plane (5-6 flights daily, journey time 30 min.) or by ferry (2 daily, journey time 5.5 hrs.) or hydrofoil (3 daily, journey time 4 hrs.) from Piraeus. Mykonos airport (JMK), 228-902-3404 is 4km from Mykonos Town.

LEAVING

160 miles SE

Rhodes

Hot Tip: The island's a favorite port of call for cruise ships, and when they dock, you'll want to pass on Rhodes Town or Lindos and head for the surfer beach at Prassonisi. High season is May to October.

The Lowdown: Rhodes is one of the great islands of the Mediterranean. The size of a small country, it has long golden beaches, a lush inland, and picturesque towns filled with medieval castles, fortresses, and minarets. It's also a party island, packed with luxury resorts and nightlife, from dancing to ethnic music in a restored 13th-century mansion to beer-fueled pub crawls.

Rhodes gained prominence in ancient times, when its location on trade routes made it one of the Mediterranean's most advanced societies. During the Crusades, the Knights of St. John came, building a European-style medieval city. In the 16th century, Rhodes fell to the Ottomans, who made their own additions in the form of delicate mosques and harems. Today Rhodes Town remains the largest inhabited medieval town in Europe. It's more than just photogenic, though—the island has more bars and nightclubs per capita than New York or Paris. Outside the Old Town walls sprawls the modern glitz of the New Town, home to huge resorts, throbbing discos, and Rhodes' only casino. Beyond the town, Rhodes' west coast is lined with beaches. An essential stop is the town of Lindos, where dazzling white Cycladic-style houses are clustered above the sea and the spectacular remains of a 4th-century BC acropolis. Inland are sleepy villages and stunning scenery—green trees carpeting mountains that plunge into the sea, and a handful of fairy-tale castles. This is also Rhodes' wine country, and two of its wineries—CAIR and Emery—give tastings.

For pure atmosphere, nothing beats staying in a restored Old Town medieval mansion, but for decadent luxury, the New Town beach resorts are some of the best in Greece. No matter where you stay, you'll want a day exploring the Old Town. Start at the Palace of the Grand Masters, then tour along the medieval walls. At night, head to Miltiadou street for stylish partying until the wee hours.

The easiest way to explore the rest of the island is by renting a car. Go along the west coast, making sure to stop at Lindos, which also makes a good base for exploring Rhodes' scenic south side. Meander through the inland on your way back, stopping to tour a winery. Triton Holidays, based in Rhodes Town, also organizes full-day boat, bus, and hiking excursions around the island.

Best Attractions

Acropolis of Lindos This magnificent 4th-century BC temple has gorgeous architecture, exquisite sculptures, and a sweeping sea view. Lindos, 224-403-1258

Emery wineries This charming vineyard produces several good wines, and the occasional excellent one. Embonas, 224-602-9111

Palace of the Grand Masters Set at the highest point in the Old Town, the palace has useful displays on island history and lovely mosaics, and is the best place to begin a walking tour of the medieval city walls. Ippoton, Rhodes Old Town, 224-102-3359

Best Hotels

Marco Polo Mansion Antique Eastern canopied beds, Turkish rugs, unusual antiques, and an exquisite breakfast courtyard in an Ottoman mansion hidden in the Old Town labyrinth. Aghiou Fanouriou 40-42, Rhodes Old Town, 224-102-5562, marcopolomansion.web.com

Melenos Hotel Each of the 12 rooms in this stone villa has hand-carved Ottoman beds, antique furnishings from throughout the near East, and private pebble-paved terraces overlooking the sea. At the edge of Lindos, on the path to the Acropolis, 224-403-1332, melenoslindos.com

Miramare Wonderland Ochre and indigo bungalows with verandas looking straight out to the sea. Ixia, 224-109-6251, bluegr.com

Best Restaurants

Alexis Sokratous Don't bother with a menu at the Old Town's most famous seafood institution—just ask for suggestions from the day's catch, which range from smoked eel to sea urchins. 18, Rhodes Old Town, 224-102-9347

Mavrikos Aristotle Onassis, Nelson Rockefeller, and Pink Floyd guitarist David Gilmour (who lives down the street) have all raved about the perfect simplicity of the fresh-caught fish, bursting-with-flavor sauces, and airy old-fashioned courtyard here. Main Square, Lindos, 224-403-1232

Best Nightlife

Hammam The live folk and rembetika sets start at midnight at this antique-chandelier-lit club set, naturally, in an old hammam (Turkish bath). Aeschylou 26, Rhodes Old Town, 224-103-3242

Selini Try the shots of aromatic masticha liquor (made only in Greece), while lounging in this pebble-paved courtyard decorated with frescoes of the moon. Evripidou 48, Rhodes Old Town, 224-475-7450

Theatro Miltiadou This medieval stone edifice comes alive in the evenings with live music, and a sophisticated crowd spilling out to the pebble-paved street. 2, Rhodes Old Town, 224-107-6973

Getting There: There are over 10 flights a day from Athens to Rhodes, on Olympic Airways (210-966-6666) and Aegean Airlines (210-998-8300). Flights are about 45 min. Rhodes Town is about a 20-min. taxi ride from the airport.

LEAVING

Santorini (Thira)

Hot Tip: Hit the beaches early so you'll have plenty of time to pick the perfect bar perch on the caldera's edge to sip cocktails during the spectacular sunsets. High season is May to October.

The Lowdown: This must be one of the most dramatically beautiful islands in the world, with its two whitewashed towns of Thira and Ia perched atop spectacular reddish-brown cliffs that plummet a thousand feet down into deep blue waters that fill a caldera. The landscape was formed by a volcanic eruption that blew out the island's center some 3,500 years ago.

Former home to the sophisticated ancient Minoan civilization and summer playground of the rich and famous today, this mysterious island is unique for its black sand beaches and fertile, volcanic soil that produces plump green grapes, used to make a highly esteemed sweet white wine.

Santorini's capital town is hilltop Thira, commanding a spectacular location directly above the caldera. Hit by an earthquake in 1956, it was hastily rebuilt and is now the center of commercial tourism, filled with bars, restaurants, and late-night clubs. The big cruise ships stop here, with passengers arriving at Skala port by boat, then taking either the cable-car or the winding path of 580 steps (with the option of a mule ride) up to town.

From Thira, an 12km (8mi) mountain path leads along the cliff edge to Ia, a smaller and rather more exclusive destination, also overlooking the caldera. The walk takes three hours over rough terrain. Noted for its beautiful white buildings with blue domes, Ia is the Aegean's most photographed settlement. Nightlife centers on the marble paved pedestrian lane of Nikolaos Nomikou, lined with bars, tavernas, jewelry shops, and art and crafts stores. There's a small but informative maritime museum, though the highlight for most people is watching the magnificent sunsets over the sea.

Visit Akrotiri on the south of the island to see the remains of a once-splendid Minoan city. Other pleasures include a submarine tour of the caldera and wine tasting at the Boutari winery at Megalopolis. Santorini's most popular beaches are Perissa and Kamari, while Red Beach is more tranquil.

Best Attractions

Boutari Winery Tours of the modern winery, including a multimedia exhibit. Megalohori, 228-608-1011

Naval Museum Good collection of seafaring history. Ia, 228-607-1156

Submarine Tours Up to 30 passengers are submerged approximately 30m (98ft) below the surface to get deep-sea views of the caldera. Trips last about 2 hrs. Minibus picks up in Thira and Ia, 228-602-8900, 228-602-3660

Best Hotels

Katikies Blissful views of the caldera, an infinity pool floating right into the sea, private "caves" carved into the cliff face, and great dining all capture the island's romance. Oia, 228-607-1401, katikies.com

Perivolas Seventeen luxury studios and suites, each with a terrace overlooking the caldera, plus a pool that flows over the edge of the cliff into the Aegean horizon. Ia, 228-607-1308, perivolas.gr

Tsitouras Collection Five houses on offer, each its own mini-museum with artifacts from art collector Dimitris Tsitouras. A totally unique hotel experience, from the personal butlers available to the rare Picasso ceramic and other objets d'art. Firostefani, 228-602-3747 or 22760, tsitouras.com

Villa Vedema Thirty-six individually furnished villas and apartments, with a pool and wine-tasting sessions. Megalohori, 228-608-1796, vedema.gr

Best Restaurants

Canava Roussos At this age-old winery, wine tastings can be sampled the leisurely way Greeks favor: accompanied by mezedes (hors d'oeuvres). The best offerings can be had on their flower-filled terrace with a sea view. Top it off with a mavrodaphne dessert wine. Mesa Gonia, 228-603-1278

Domata Traditional dishes with a contemporary twist, using local produce. The setting is a refurbished tomato canning factory, hence the name. Near Monolithos beach, 228-603-2069

1800 A sophisticated bar-restaurant; excellent Mediterranean cuisine in a romantic setting. Main Street, Ia, 228-607-1485

La Maltese A spacious veranda offers stunning views over the caldera and Pan-Mediterranean cuisine. Imerovigli, 228-602-8080

Selene Sit out on the terrace or in the vaulted-ceiling dining room; revamped traditional dishes. In narrow street close to Hotel Atlantis, Ia, 228-602-2249

Best Nightlife

Enigma This nightclub opened in 1979, but is still definitely "in." Three spaces with bars and great music well into the early hours. 5-mile walk from main square, Thira, 228-902-2466

Franco's Bar Chaise longues, classical music, and champagne cocktails. On cliffside path, Thira, 228-602-4428

Santorini Jazz Festival Attracts international musicians and is held at the open-air cinema on Kamari Beach, complete with a bar serving cocktails. Kamari Beach, 5 miles southeast of Thira, 228-603-3452

Getting There: Santorini lies 127 nautical miles from Athens' port, Piraeus. It can be reached by plane (5-6 flights daily, journey time 55 min.), or by ferry (3 daily, journey time 9 hrs.) or hydrofoil (1 daily, 4 hrs.) from Piraeus. Santorini airport (JTR, 228-603-1538) is 7km from Thira, the island's capital.

LEAVING

Skiathos

Hot Tip: Club fashions here are fickle, so hook up with holidaying Greeks to find out where the best beach parties are. High season runs from May to October.

The Lowdown: Before the dawn of commercial tourism in the 1970s, Skiathos was a sleepy place—a peaceful, pine-covered island with a modest economy based on fishing and farming. Today, it owes its fortune to its long stretches of fine golden sands. Holiday brochures put the count at around 70 "idyllic paradise" beaches, several of which are rated among the best in Greece. In peak season (July and August) the island's population of less than 5,000 swells to more than 50,000.

The action centers on Skiathos Town, the island's main settlement, which was built in 1830 when locals abandoned the clifftop fortified retreat of Kastro (where they had sheltered for centuries from bands of marauding pirates and Turks) and moved down to the more accessible south coast. Tranquil through winter but pulsating with energy in summer, this cosmopolitan resort is packed with small-scale hotels, waterside restaurants and tavernas, chic boutiques, and souvenir shops. A vibrant nightlife is part of the package, with cafes, bars, and clubs lining much of the harborside, where locals and visitors alike initiate each evening with a civilized volta (promenade)—and those who make it through the entire night put on shades to drink espresso as the sun rises over the Aegean. (The main concentration of nightclubs lies east of the harbor, overlooking the sea.) The town's medieval Bourtzi fortress, overlooking the harbor, hosts the annual Aegean Festival (late June to early October), featuring theater, music, and dance under the stars. West of town, a practically unbroken line of hotels, villas, and private rooms strings along the south coast, with the best hotels sited in sheltered coves with their own beaches.

The most talked about beaches are Koukounaries, a crescent-shaped stretch of fine sand backed by pine woods (it can be reached by bus), and Lalaria, on the island's northern tip, said to be one of the most beautiful beaches in Greece (reachable by taxi-boat). The water is crystal-clear aquamarine blue, thanks to the reflective marble seabed. Others to check out are Vromolimnos, on the southwest coast, popular for bathing, windsurfing, and waterskiing by day, and all-night waterside parties by night; Banana Beach, on the southwest tip, with excellent water sports facilities and the opportunity to bare all (nudism tolerated); and the tiny island of Tsougrias, south of Skiathos Town (served by taxi-boat) for Robinson Crusoe-style beaches.

Best Attractions

Day Sailing The harbor is filled with sailing vessels available for charter at reasonable prices. Chartering Captain Zagkos' "New Start" is a good way to find great beach tavernas. From Skiathos Town harbor

Kastro Built as a fortified village in the 14th century, the Kastro perches on a dramatic rocky outcrop, high above the sea. On the north coast, 1.5 hrs. by boat, or 2.5 hrs. walk from town

Best Hotels

Aegean Suites Hotel A member of Small Luxury Hotels of the World, this hotel has 20 suites, a pool, and a first-class restaurant, and overlooks the beach. It's walking distance from downtown Skiathos. Megali Ammos, 1.5km (1mi) southwest of town, 242-702-4066 / 242-702-4069, slh.com

Atrium Hotel Skiathos' swankiest hotel, perched on a pine-clad slope above the sea. 76 rooms, stunning pool, fitness center, massage, sauna, plus a glorious stretch of sandy beach. Agia Paraskevi Beach, 8km (5 mi) southwest of town, 242-704-9345, atriumhotel.gr

Kassandra Bay Hotel A modern resort offering various accommodations (including family units, two pools, a fitness center, and a beach with watersports facilities). Vassilias Beach, 3km (2 mi) southwest of town, 242-702-4201, kassandrabay.com

Best Restaurants

Asprolithos Taverna fare served with a contemporary twist; a favorite with locals. Skiathos Town, 242-702-1016 / 242-702-3110

Karnagio The best fresh fish in a romantic garden setting—expensive, but worth it. Skiathos Town on seafront next to Hotel Alkyon, 242-702-2868

Skuna Tables are set up on a wooden platform built over the sea; tasty traditional dishes. Skiathos Town on seafront overlooking port, 242-702-2185

Best Nightlife

BBC Pulses with pop and techno 'til dawn. On the seafront, east of the harbor

Kalhua Another fun and happening club—mainstream hits and a happy crowd. On the seafront, east of the harbor

Remezzo The craziest club in town; a bar and dancing downstairs, a Mexican restaurant up top. On the seafront, east of the harbor

Getting There: Skiathos lies 41 nautical miles from Volos and 58 nautical miles from Agios Konstandinos (which is 103 miles, or a 3-hr. bus ride, from Athens). It can be reached by plane (1 daily through summer, journey time 50 min.) from Athens, or by ferry (3-4 daily, journey time 3 hrs.) or hydrofoil (4-5 daily, journey time 2 hrs.) from Volos, or by ferry (2-3 daily, journey time 2.5 hrs.) or hydrofoil (1 daily, journey time 1.5 hrs.) from Agios Konstandinos. Skiathos airport (JSI, 242-702-2945 and 242-702-2376) is 3km from Skiathos.

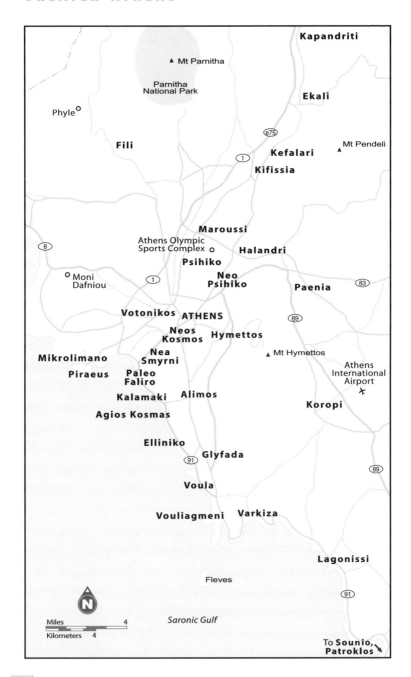

Kapandriti

▲ Mt Parnitha

Parnitha
National Park

Ekali

Phyle○

e75

Fili

Mt Pendeli ▲

Kefalari

1

Kifissia

Maroussi

Athens Olympic
Sports Complex ○

Halandri

8

Psihiko

Neo
Psihiko

○ Moni
Dafniou

1

Paenia

83

Votonikos ATHENS

89

Neos
Kosmos

Hymettos

Mikrolimano

Nea
Smyrni

▲ Mt Hymettos

Athens
International
Airport
✈

Piraeus

Paleo
Faliro

Kalamaki

Alimos

Koropi

Agios Kosmas

Elliniko

91

Glyfada

Voula

89

Vouliagmeni

Varkiza

Lagonissi

Fleves

91

N

Miles   4
Kilometers   4

Saronic Gulf

To Sounio,
Patroklos ↘

ATHENS
BLACK BOOK

You're solo in the city–where's a singles-friendly place to eat? Is there a good lunch spot near the museum? Will the bar be too loud for easy conversation? Get the answers fast in the *Black Book*, a condensed version of every listing in our guide that puts all the essential information at your fingertips.

A quick glance down the page and you'll find the type of food, nightlife, or attractions you are looking for, the phone numbers, and which pages to turn to for more detailed information. How did you ever survive without this?

BLACK BOOK

Athens Black Book By Neighborhood

Code: H-Hotels; R-Restaurants; N-Nightlife; A-Attractions
Blue page numbers denote listings in 99 Best, black denotes listings in Experience section.

BLACK BOOK

Athens Black Book By Neighborhood (cont.)

Notes

Athens Black Book

Hotels

NAME TYPE (ROOMS)	ADDRESS WEBSITE	AREA PRICE	PHONE	EXPERIENCE 99 BEST	PAGE PAGE
Astir Palace Resort Modern (508)	Apollonos 40 astir-palace.com	VL €€€	210-890-2000	By-the-Water Rooms with a View	129 39
Athenaeum InterContinental Modern (543)	Syngrou 89-93 intercontinental.com	VA €€€€	210-920-6000	Hip & Cool	81
The Athenian Callirhoe Trendy (84)	Kallirois 32 & Petmeza tac.gr	MA €€€€	210-921-5353	Hip & Cool	81
Athens Acropol Trendy (167)	Pireos 1 grecotel.com	OM €€	210-528-2100	Downtown	107
Athens Hilton Modern (527)	Vassilissis Sofias 46 athens.hilton.com	IL €€€€	210-728-1000	Hip & Cool	81
Athens Park Hotel Timeless (152)	Alexandras 10 athensparkhotel.gr	EX €€€€	210-889-4500	Downtown	107
Central Hotel Trendy (84)	Apollonos 18 centralhotel.gr	PL €	210-323-4357	Downtown	107
Divani Apollon Palace & Spa Modern (286)	Aghiou Nikolaou 10 divaniapollon.gr	VL €€€€	210-891-1100	By-the-Water	129
Divani Palace Acropolis Modern (250)	Parthenonos 19–25 divaniacropolis.gr	MA €€	210-928-0100	Classic Rooms with a View	57 39
Electra Palace Timeless (150)	Nikomidou 18 electrahotels.gr	PL €€	210-337-0000	Classic	57
Eridanus Luxury Art Hotel Timeless (38)	Pireos 78 eridanus.gr	VA €€	210-520-5360	Downtown	108
The Fresh Hotel Trendy (133)	Sofokleous 26 & Klisthenous 2 thefreshhotel.gr	OM €€	210-524-8511	Downtown	108
Grand Resort Lagonissi Modern (318)	15km (9 miles) SW of Vouliagmeni lagonissiresort.gr	VA €€€€	229-107-6000	By-the-Water	130
Hera Hotel Timeless (38)	Falirou 9 herahotel.gr	MA €€	210-923-6682	Classic	57

Neighborhood (Area) Key

AK = Agios Kosmas	**KO** = Kolonaki	**MO** = Monastiraki
AM = Ambelokipi	**KK** = Koukaki	**RO** = Rouf
CM = Central Market	**OM** = Omonia	**SO** = Sounio
EX = Exarchia	**PA** = Pangrati	**SN** = Syntagma
GA = Gazi	**PI** = Piraeus	**SY** = Syntagma Square
GL = Glyfada	**PL** = Plaka	**TH** = Thisio
IL = Ilisia	**PS** = Psirri	**VA** = Various Neighborhoods
KF = Kefalari	**MA** = Makrigianni	**VK** = Varkiza
KI = Kifissia	**ME** = Metaxourgio	**VL** = Vouliagmeni

Note: Use the prefix 30 when placing an international call to Greece.

NAME TYPE (ROOMS)	ADDRESS WEBSITE	AREA PRICE	PHONE	EXPERIENCE 99 BEST	PAGE PAGE
Herodion Timeless (90)	Rovertou Galli 4 herodion.gr	MA €	210-923-6832	Classic	58
Hotel Grande Bretagne Timeless (321)	Syntagma Square grandebretagne.gr	SY €€€€	210-333-0000	Classic Hotel Rooms	58 30
King George II Palace Timeless (102)	Vasileous Georgiou A'3 grecotel.com	SY €€€	210-322-2210	Downtown	108
The Margi Timeless (90)	Litous 11 themargi.gr	VA €€€	210-896-2061	By-the-Water	130
NJV Athens Plaza Trendy (159)	Vasileos Georgiou A' 2 grecotel.com	SY €€€€	210-335-2400	Hip & Cool	82
Ochre & Brown Trendy (11)	Leokoriou 7 ochreandbrown.gr	PS €€	210-331-2950	Classic Hotel Rooms	82 30
Omonia Grand Trendy (115)	Pireos 2 grecotel.com	OM €€	210-528-2100	Downtown	109
Periscope Trendy (22)	Haritos 22 periscope.gr	KO €€	210-623-6320	Hip & Cool	82
Residence Georgio Modern (136)	Oktovriou& Halkokondili 14 residencegeorgio.com	OM €€	210-332-0100	Downtown	109
The St. George Lycabettus Trendy (154)	Kleomenous 2 sglycabettus.gr	KO €€	210-729-0711	Hip & Cool Rooms with a View	82 39
Semiramis Hotel Trendy (51)	Harilaou Trikoupi 48 semiramishathens.com	KI €€€€	210-628-4400	Hip & Cool Hotel Rooms	83 30

Notes

Restaurants

NAME / TYPE	ADDRESS / WEBSITE	AREA / PRICE	PHONE / SINGLES/NOISE	EXPERIENCE / 99 BEST	PAGE / PAGE
Achinos / Seafood	Akti Themistokleous 51	PI / €€	210-452-6944 / ΥF =	By-the-Water	124, 131
Aegli* / International	Zappeion, National Gardens / aeglizappiou.gr	SY / €€€	210-336-9363 / ΥF =	Hip & Cool	78, 84
Aiolis / Meze	Aiolou 23 & Agias Irinis	MO / €	210-331-2839 / ΥF =	Hip & Cool / Cafes	78, 84 / 23
Akrotiri Lounge / Mediterranean (G)	Vasileos Georgiou 11 / akrotirilounge.gr/enhtml	AK / €€€€	210-985-9147 / ΥF	Hip & Cool	84
Alexandria / Middle Eastern	Metsovou 13 & Rethymnou 7	EX / €€	210-821-0004 / - =	Downtown	103, 110
Archeon Gefsis / Contemporary (G)	Kodratou 22	ME / €€	210-523-9661 / - =	Classic / Classic Dining	53, 59 / 25
Aristera-Dexia / Contemporary (G)	Pireos 140 & Andronikou 3 / aristera-dexia.gr	RO / €€€	210-342-2606 / - =	Downtown / Nouveau Greek	102, 110 / 34
Athinaikon / Meze	Themistokleous 2	EX / €€	210-383-8485 / - =	Classic / Ouzeries	53, 59 / 35
Balthazar* / Mediterranean	Tsoha 27 & Soutsou / balthazar.gr	AM / €€€€	210-644-1215 / ΥF ≡	Hip & Cool / Trendy Tables	84 / 48
Bedlam / Contemporary	Zappeion, National Gardens	SY / €€€	210-336-9340 / ΥF	Hip & Cool	85
Big Deals* / International (G)	Harilaou Trikoupi 50	KI / €€€€	210-623-0860 / ΥB =	Hip & Cool	78, 85
Boschetto / Italian	Evangelismos Park	KO / €€€€	210-721-0893 / - =	Hip & Cool	77, 85
Bowling Center Café / Cafe	Profitis Ilias	PI / €	210-412-0271 / - =	By-the-Water	124, 131
Byzantino / Traditional	Kidathineon 18	PL / €€	210-322-7368 / - =	Classic	52, 59
Cafe Avyssinia / Meze	Kinetou 7	MO / €	210-321-7047 / - =	Downtown	104, 110
Café Freddo / Cafe	Plateia Alexandras 14	VA / €	210-422-6637 / - =	By-the-Water	123, 131
Central* / International	Plateia Kolonaki 14	KO / €€€	210-724-5938 / ΥF =	Hip & Cool / Bar-Restaurants	76, 85 / 18

Restaurant and Nightlife Symbols

Restaurants	Nightlife	Restaurant + Nightlife
Singles Friendly (eat and/or meet)	Price Warning	Prime time noise levels
⬛ = Communal table	C = Cover or ticket charge	— = Quiet
Υ = Bar scene	Food served at bar or club	= = A buzz, but still conversational
B = Limited bar menu	B = Limited bar menu	≡ = Loud
F = Full menu served at bar	F = Full menu served at bar	
(G) = Gourmet Destination		

Note regarding page numbers: Italic = itinerary listing; Roman = description in Experience section.

NAME TYPE	ADDRESS WEBSITE	AREA PRICE	PHONE SINGLES/NOISE	EXPERIENCE 99 BEST	PAGE PAGE
Cookou Food Traditional	Themistokleous 66	EX €	210-383-1955 - ≡	Downtown	103, 110
Da Capo* Cafe	Tsakalof 1	KO €	210-360-2497 - ≡	Hip & Cool	76, 85
Daphne's Modern (G)	Lisikratous 4	PL €€€	210-322-7971 - ≡	Classic Classic Dining	54, 59 25
Diasimos Seafood	Akti Themistokleous 306	PI €€	210-451-4887 F ≡	By-the-Water	124, 131
Diporto Taverna	Sokratous 9	CM €	210-321-1463 - ≡	Downtown	101, 111
Dourabeis Seafood	Akti Dilaveri 29	PI €€€	210-412-2092 - ≡	By-the-Water	124, 131
Eden Vegetarian	Lissiou 12 edenvegetarian.gr	PL €€	210-324-8858 - ≡	Classic	59
Edodi Contemporary (G)	Veikou 80	VA €€	210-921-3013 - ⊟	Classic Romantic Dining	52, 60 38
El Pecado International	Tournavitou 11 & Sarri	PS €€	210-324-4049 - ≡	Downtown	104, 111
Envy Belle Helene* International	Constantinou Paliologou 1	VA €€	210-800-1111 ΧΒ ≡	Hip & Cool	77, 86
Estiatorio 24 Traditional	Syngrou 44	MA €	210-922-1159 - ≡	Hip & Cool Late-Late-Night	76, 86 31
Filistron Meze	Apostolou Pavlou 23	TH €€	210-346-7554 ΧΒ ≡	Classic Tables with a View	54, 60 46
48* Contemporary (G)	Armatolon & Klefton 48 48therestaurant.com	AM €€€€	210-641-1082 ΧΒ ≡	Hip & Cool Trendy Tables	77, 86 48
Frame* International	Deinokratous 1 sgl-frame.gr	KO €€€€	210-721-4368 ΧΒ ≡	Hip & Cool	86
Freud Oriental Sushi (G)	Xenokratous 21	KO €€€	210-729-9595 - ⊟	Hip & Cool Sushi	76, 86 45
Gefsis Me Onomasia Pro. Contemporary (G)	Kifissias 317	KI €€€€	210-800-1402 - ≡	Hip & Cool	78, 87
Giantes Modern	Valtetsiou 44	EX €€	210-330-1369 - ≡	Downtown	103, 111
Hytra Contemporary (G)	Winter: Navarchou Apostoli 7 Summer: Grand Resort Lagonissi	PS FA €€€	210-331-6767 229-107-6000 - ≡	Downtown Trendy Tables	104, 111 48
Ideal Modern	Panepistimiou 46	OM €€	210-330-3000 - ≡	Classic	53, 60
Ilias Bakery	Karaiskaki 23	PS €	210-321-6797 - ≡	Downtown	104, 111
Interni International	Ermou 152 inernirestaurant.gr	TH €€€	210-346-8900 ΧΒ ≡	Downtown Bar-Restaurants	112 18
Island Mediterranean (G)	Limanakia Vouliagmenis	VK €€€	210-965-3563 ΧΒ ≡	By-the-Water	132

Restaurants (cont.)

NAME TYPE	ADDRESS WEBSITE	AREA PRICE	PHONE SINGLES/NOISE	EXPERIENCE 99 BEST	PAGE PAGE
Ithaki Mediterranean (G)	Apollonos 28 ithakirestaurant-bar.gr	VL €€€€	210-896-3747 B ≡	By-the-Water	132
Jimmy and the Fish Seafood	Akti Koumoundourou 46 jimmyandthefish.gr	PI €€€	210-412-4417 - ≡	By-the-Water Seafood	124, 132 40
Karavitis Taverna	Arktinou 33 & Pavsaniou 4	PA €	210-721-5155 - ≡	Classic Tavernas	53, 60 47
Kavouras Souvlaki	Themistokleous 64	EX €	210-383-7981 - ≡	Downtown Late-Late-Night	103, 112 31
Kiku Sushi	Dimokritou 12	KO €€€€	210-364-7033 - ☐	Hip & Cool Sushi	75, 87 45
Kitchen Bar Cafe	Posidonos 3	VA €€	210-981-2004 - ≡	By-the-Water	125, 132
Kostoyiannis Modern	Zaimi 37	EX €	210-822-0624 - ≡	Downtown	103, 112
Lykovrisi* Cafe	Plateia Kolonaki	KO €	210-361-6712 - ≡	Hip & Cool	76, 87
Mamacas Contemporary	Persefonis 41	GA €€	210-346-4984 - ≡	Downtown	112
Margaro Seafood	Hatzikyriakou 126	PI €	210-451-4226 - ≡	By-the-Water	124, 132
Maritsa's Modern	Voukourestiou 47	KO €€	210-363-0132 - ≡	Classic	54, 60
Messiah* International	Karneadou 25-29	KO €€	210-729-4290 B ≡	Hip & Cool	78, 87
Milos Restaurant Contemporary (G)	Vassilissis Sofias 46 milos.ca/en/athens/index.html	IL €€€	210-724-4400 - ≡	Hip & Cool Nouveau Greek	77, 87 34
Milton's International	Adrianou 91	PL €€	210-324-9129 F ≡	Hip & Cool	78, 88
O Kostas Souvlaki	Adrianou 116	PL €	210-322-8502 - ≡	Classic Souvlaki	61 43
O Platanos Souvlaki	Diogenous 4	PL €€	210-322-0666 - ≡	Classic Tavernas	51, 61 47
Oceanis International	Apollonos 1	VL €€	210-896-1133 - ≡	By-the-Water	125, 133
Ochre & Brown Restaurant Mediterranean	Liokoriou 7 ochreandbrown.gr	PS €€	210-331-2950 F ≡	Classic	88
Oineas Contemporary	Aisopou 9 oineas.gr	PS €€	210-321-5614 - ≡	Downtown	104, 112
Orea Ellas Meze	Mitropoleos 59 & Pandrossou 36	PL €	210-321-3842 - ≡	Classic Ouzeries	51, 61 35
Orizondes* Contemporary	Mt. Lycabettus	KO €€€	210-721-0701 YB ≡	Hip & Cool Tables with a View	76, 88 46
Ouzadiko Meze	Karneadou 25-29	KO €€	210-729-5484 - ≡	Hip & Cool Ouzeries	75, 88 35
Papandreou's Taverna Taverna	Aristogeitonos 1	CM €	210-321-4970 - ≡	Downtown Late-Late-Night	104, 112 31

NAME TYPE	ADDRESS WEBSITE	AREA PRICE	PHONE SINGLES/NOISE	EXPERIENCE 99 BEST	PAGE PAGE
Patroklos Taverna Taverna	Patroklos	VA €	229-103-7326 -	By-the-Water	133
Philippou* Traditional	Xenokratous 19	KO €	210-721-6390 -	Classic Tavernas	54, 61 47
Pil-Poul French (G)	Apostolou Pavlou 51 pilpoul.gr	TH €€€€	210-342-3665 -	Hip & Cool Romantic Dining	77, 88 38
Plous Podilato Seafood (G)	Akti Koumoundourou 42	PI €€€	210-413-7910 -	By-the-Water Seafood	124, 133 40
Prytanion International	Milioni 7 prytaneion.gr	KO €€	210-364-3353 -	Hip & Cool	75, 89
Red* Mediterranean (G)	Kastorias 34–36 athinais.com.gr	VA €€€	210-348-0000 ΣΒ	Hip & Cool Nouveau Greek	76, 89 34
Rozalia Traditional	Valtetsiou 58	EX €	210-330-2933 -	Classic	61
Sea Satin Contemporary	Fokilidou 1 Stratigou Sarafi 5	KO AL €€	210-361-9646 210-981-4319 -	Hip & Cool	89
Septem Mediterranean	Vasileos Georgiou balux-septem.com	GL €€€	210-894-1620 ΣF	Hip & Cool Bar-Restaurants	78, 89 18
Spondi International (G)	Pirronos 5 spondi.gr	PA €€€	210-756-4021 -	Classic	54, 61
Square Sushi Sushi	Diligianni 56 65 Deinokratous squaresushi.gr	KI KO €€	210-808-1512 210-725-5236 -	Hip & Cool Sushi	77, 89 45
St'Astra Mediterranean (G)	Alexandras 10 parkhotel.gr/htmlsite/stastra	EX €€€	210-889-4500 ΣΒ	Hip & Cool	78, 90
Stavlos* International	Irakleidon 10 stavlos.gr	TH €€	210-345-2502 ΣΒ	Downtown Cafes	104, 113 23
Strofi Traditional	Rovertou Galli 25	MA €€	210-921-4130 -	Classic	52, 62
Symposium Modern (G)	Erechtheiou 46	MA €€€	210-922-5321 -	Classic	52, 62
Syrtaki Traditional	2km north of the Temple of Poseidon syrtaki.gr	SO €€	229-203-9125 -	By-the-Water	133
Ta Agrafa Souvlaki	Valtesiou 50-52 & Benaki	EX €	210-380-3144 -	Downtown Souvlaki	113 43
Thalatta Mediterranean	Koustantinoupoleos 84	GA €€€	210-346-4204 -	Downtown	102, 113
Thanassis Souvlaki	Mitropoleos 69	MO €	210-324-4705 -	Classic Souvlaki	53, 62 43
To Kafeneio Meze	Loukianou 26	KO €€	210-722-9056 -	Classic	54, 62
To Parko* International	Eleftherias Park toparko.gr	AM €€	210-722-3784 F	Classic	53, 62
Tou Psarra Traditional	Erechtheos 16 & Erotokritou 12 psaras-taverna.gr	PL €€	210-321-8733 -	Classic Romantic Dining	63 38

Restaurants (cont.)

NAME TYPE	ADDRESS WEBSITE	AREA PRICE	PHONE SINGLES/NOISE	EXPERIENCE 99 BEST	PAGE PAGE
Vardis French (G)	Deligianni 66 hotelpentelikon.gr/english/vardis	KI €€€€	210-623-0650 - ≡	Hip & Cool	90
Varoulko Seafood	(winter) Deligeorgi 14 (summer) 80 Pireos St. varoulko.gr b2	PI KE €€€€	210-411-2043 210-522-8400 - ≡	By-the-Water Seafood	125, 133 40
Varsos Cafe	Kassaveti 5	KI €	210-801-2472 - ≡	Hip & Cool	77, 90
Vive Mar Seafood	Karamanli 18 vivemar.gr	VL €€€	210-899-2453 - ≡	By-the-Water Tables with a View	125, 134 46
Vlassis Traditional	Paster 8, Plateia Mavili	AM €€	210-646-3060 - ≡	Classic Classic Dining	53, 63 25
Zeidoron Meze	Taki 10-12 zidoron.gr	PS €€	210-321-5368 - ≡	Downtown	104, 113

Nightlife

NAME TYPE	ADDRESS WEBSITE	AREA COVER	PHONE FOOD/NOISE	EXPERIENCE 99 BEST	PAGE PAGE
Aegli Café Bar/Lounge	Zappeion, National Gardens aeglizappiou.gr/BistroCafe.html	SY -	210-336-9363 F ▬	Classic	54, 64
Aegli Village Cool Cinema	Zappeion, National Gardens aeglizappiou.gr/Cinema.html	SY C	210-336-9327 B ▬	Classic Summer Cinemas	53, 64 44
Akrotiri Lounge Lounge/Nightclub	Vasileos Georgiou 11 akrotirilouge.gr/en.htm	AK C	210-985-9147 B ≡	Hip & Cool Dance Clubs by Sea	91 27
An Live Music	Solomou 13-15	EX C	210-330-5056 - ≡	Downtown	103, 114
Athinaion Politeia Bar/Lounge/Nightclub	Akamantos 1 & Ag Pavlou athinaionpoliteia.gr	TH -	210-341-3795 F ≡	Classic	54, 64
Balthazar* Bar/Restaurant	Tsoha 27 & Soutsou	AM C	210-644-1215 B ≡	Hip & Cool	76, 91
Balux Beach/Nightclub	Vasileos Georgiou baluxseptem.com	GL C	210-894-1620 B ▬	Hip & Cool	91
Bebek Nightclub/Restaurant	Posidonos 3	VA C	210-981-3950 F ≡	Hip & Cool	78, 91
Bedlam Nightclub	Zappeion, National Gardens	SY C	210-336-9340 ≡	Hip & Cool Glamorous Clubs	78, 91 29
Bee Bar/Cafe	Miaouli 6	PS C	210-321-2624 - ≡	Downtown	104, 114
Bios Bar/Nightclub	Pireos 84	ME -	210-342-5335 - ≡	Downtown	102, 114
Cine Paris Cinema	Kidathineon 22	PL C	210-322-2071 - ▬	Classic	53, 64
Cine Psirri Cinema	Sarri 40-44	PS C	210-321-2476 - ▬	Downtown Summer Cinemas	104, 114 44

NAME TYPE	ADDRESS WEBSITE	AREA COVER	PHONE FOOD/NOISE	EXPERIENCE 99 BEST	PAGE PAGE
Club 22 Nightclub	Vouliagmenis 22 club22.gr	VA C	210-924-9814 - ≡	Downtown	*102*, 114
Danza Nightclub	Aristophanous 11 & Katsikoyianni	PS C	210-331-7105 - ≡	Downtown Dance Clubs	115 26
Diogenis Studio Bouzoukia	Syngrou 259	VA C	210-942-5754 - ≡	Hip & Cool Bouzoukia Winter	*76*, 92 21
Don Quixote's Bar/Cafe	Vasileos Pavlou 68	PI -	210-413-7016 - ≡	By-the-Water Candlelit Bars	*124*, 135 24
Dora Stratou Dance Theatre Dance	Arakinthou & Voutie grdance.org	TH C	210-921-4650 - -	Classic Shows Under Stars	*54*, 64 42
Dragoste Lounge/Nightclub	Patriarchou Loakim 37	KO C	210-722-1558 F ≡	Hip & Cool Glamorous Clubs	*78*, 92 29
En Delphis Bar	Delphon 5 endelphis.gr	KO C	210-360-8269 - ≡	Hip & Cool	*78*, 92
Eyeland Bar/Nightclub	Ikarion 24	GA C	694-615-0196 - ≡	Hip & Cool Gay & Lesbian Bars	*76*, 92 28
Floral Liberal Bar/Cafe	Themistokleous 80	EX C	210-330-0938 B ≡	Downtown	*103*, 115
Frame Bar/Restaurant	Deinokratous 1 sgl-frame.gr	KO C	210-721-4368 F ≡	Hip & Cool	*77*, 93
Fresh Hotel's Air Lounge* Bar/Restaurant	Sofokleous 26 & Klisthenous 2	OM C	210-524-8511 F ≡	Downtown	*101*, 115
Galaxy* Bar/Lounge	Vassilissis Sofias 46 athens.hilton.com	IL -	210-728-1000 B ≡	Hip & Cool	*77*, 93
Gazaki Bar	Triptolemou 31	GA C	210-346-0901 - ≡	Downtown	*102*, 115
Half Note Live Music	Trivonianou 17 halfnote.gr	PA C	210-921-3310 - ≡	Downtown Live Music Venues	*103*, 116 32
Home Lounge/Home Club Bar/Restaurant	Lounge: Voutadon 34 Club: Posidonos 5	GA GA -	210-346-0347 210-894-4138 B ≡	Downtown	116
Inoteka Wine Bar	Plateia Abyssinia 3 inoteka.com/home2.html	MO -	210-324-6446 - ≡	Downtown	*104*, 116
Interni Bar/Restaurant	Ermou 152	TH C	210-346-8900 F ≡	Downtown	116
Island Bar/Restaurant	Limanakia Vouliagmenis	VK C	210-965-3563 B ≡	By-the-Water Dance Clubs by Sea	135 27
Istioploikos Bar/Cafe	Yacht Club of Greece istioploikos.gr/home.html	PI -	210-413-4084 - ≡	By-the-Water	*124*, 135
Kidathineon Bar/Cafe	Farmaki 1 & Plateia Filomousou	PL C	210-323-4281 F ≡	Classic Cafes	65 23
Lamda Bar/Nightclub	Lembessi 15 lamdaclub.gr	MA C	210-922-4202 - ≡	Downtown Gay & Lesbian Bars	*102*, 116 28
Liberty Bar/Nightclub	behind Posidonos 22	VA C	210-982-1200 - ≡	Hip & Cool	*78*, 93

Nightlife (cont.)

NAME TYPE	ADDRESS WEBSITE	AREA COVER	PHONE FOOD/NOISE	EXPERIENCE 99 BEST	PAGE PAGE
Love Cafe Bar/Cafe	Akti Koumoundourou 58	PI -	210-417-7778 F =	By-the-Water	124, 135
Mao Nightclub	Ayion Anaryiron & Agatharhou 3	PS C	210-331-7639 - ≡	Downtown Dance Clubs	102, 117 26
Megaro Mousikis Concerts/Opera	Vassilissis Sofias megaron.gr	AM C	210-728-2333 - ≡	Classic Live Music Venues	53, 65 32
Melina Bar	Lissiou 22 & Aerides	PL -	210-324-6501 - ⌐	Classic Candlelit Bars	52, 65 24
Mikra Asia Bar/Lounge	Konstantinopoleous 70	RO C	210-346-3851 ≡	Downtown	102, 117
Mnisikleous Remebetika	Mnisikleous and Lyceiou mnisikleous.gr	PL C	210-322-5558 F ≡	Classic Rembetika Clubs	52, 65 37
Mommy Bar/Lounge	Delphon 4 mommy.gr	KO C	210-361-9682 F =	Hip & Cool See-and-Be-Seen	78, 93 41
Mt. Lycabettus Theater Concerts	Mt. Lycabettus culture.gr	KO C	210-928-2900 - =	Hip & Cool Shows Under Stars	76, 93 42
Neon Bar/Cafe	Akti Dilaveri 5	PI -	210-347-5655 F =	By-the-Water	124, 135
Nipiagogio Bar/Cafe	Elasidon & Kleanthous 8	GA -	210-345-8534 - =	Downtown	102, 117
Ochre & Brown Bar/Restaurant	Liokoriou 7 ochreandbrown.gr	PS C	210-331-2950 ΥB =	Classic	94
Odeon of Herodes Atticus Theater/Concerts/Dance	Dionyssiou Areopagitou hellenicfestival.gr	PL C	210-323-2771 - -	Classic Shows Under Stars	52, 65 42
Passa (Summer) Nightclub	Karamanli 14	VL C	210-895-9645 F ≡	By-the-Water Dance Clubs by Sea	125, 136 27
Passa (Winter) Bar/Nightclub	Leventi 4	KO C	210-721-1310 B ≡	Hip & Cool See-and-Be-Seen	78, 94 41
Peacock Lounge Bar/Restaurant	(Hera Hotel) Falirou 9 herahotel.gr	MA -	210-923-6682 F ⌐	Classic Candlelit Bars	52, 65 24
Playback Bar/Nightclub	Aristophanous 11	PS C	210-331-7105 F =	Downtown Gay & Lesbian Bars	104, 117 28
Posidonio Bouzoukia	Posidonos 18	VA C	210-894-1033 - ≡	By-the-Water Bouzoukia Summer	124, 136 20
Privilege Nightclub	Winter: Changes seasonally Summer: Changes seasonally privilege-athens.com	GA VA C	210-801-8304 F ≡	Hip & Cool By-the-Water Glamorous Clubs	78, 94 136 29
Rex Bouzoukia	Panepistimiou 48	OM C	210-381-4592 - ≡	Classic Bouzoukia Winter	54, 66 21
Riviera Bar/Cafe	Valtetsiou 46	EX C	210-383-7716 B ⌐	Downtown	103, 117
Romeo (Summer) Bouzoukia	Ellinikou 1	GL C	210-894-5345 - ≡	By-the-Water Bouzoukia Summer	124, 136 20
Romeo (Winter) Bouzoukia	Panepistimiou 48	OM C	210-381-4592 - ≡	Classic Bouzoukia Winter	53, 66 21

| NAME | ADDRESS | AREA | PHONE | EXPERIENCE | PAGE |
TYPE	WEBSITE	COVER	FOOD/NOISE	99 BEST	PAGE
Soul	Evripidou 65	PS	210-331-0907	Downtown	*104*, 118
Bar/Nightclub		-	Ⓑ ═	See-and-Be-Seen	41
Stavros tou Notou	Frantzi and Tharipou 37	VA	210-922-6975	Downtown	118
Nightclub		Ⓒ	- ≡	Live Music Venues	32
Stoa Ton Athanaton	Sophokleous 19	CM	210-321-4362	Downtown	*103*, 118
Rembetika		Ⓒ	Ⓕ ≡	Rembetika Clubs	37
Tapas Bar	Triptolemou 44	GA	210-347-1844	Hip & Cool	*76*, 94
Bar/Restaurant		Ⓒ	Ⓑ ═		
Taximi	Harilau Trikoupi & Isavron 29	EX	210-363-9919	Downtown	*103*, 118
Rembetika		Ⓒ	Ⓕ ≡	Rembetika Clubs	37
Terina	Kapnikareas 35	PL	210-321-5015	Classic	*53*, 66
Bar/Cafe	terina.gr	-	Ⓕ ≡		
Thalassa	Posidonos 58	VA	210-898-2979	By-the-Water	*124*, 136
Bouzoukia		Ⓒ	Ⓑ ≡	Bouzoukia Summer	20
Thirio	Lepeniotou 1	PS	210-321-7836	Downtown	*104*, 118
Bar/Lounge		Ⓒ	Ⓑ ═		
Thission	Apostolou Pavlou 7	TH	210-342-0864	Classic	*53*, 66
Cinema		Ⓒ	Ⓑ —	Summer Cinemas	44
To Tristato	Diadalou 34 & Aggelou Geronda	PL	210-324-4472	Classic	67
Bar/Cafe		-	Ⓕ ═		
Veakio Theatre	Profitis Ilias	PI	210-419-4520	By-the-Water	*124*, 137
Theater		Ⓒ	═		
Venue	Winter: Agias Eleousis 3	PS/VA	210-331-7801	Downtown	118
	Summer: Athens Sounio Coastal Hwy.		210-897-1163	By-the-Water	137
Nightclub		Ⓒ	Ⓑ ≡	Dance Clubs	26
Voyage	Kriezotou 11	KO	210-361-5996	Hip & Cool	94
Bar/Restaurant		Ⓒ	Ⓕ ≡		
Zygos	Kidathineon 22	PL	210-324-1610	Classic	67
Live Music		Ⓒ	- ≡		

Notes

BLACK BOOK

Attractions

NAME TYPE	ADDRESS WEBSITE	AREA PRICE	PHONE	EXPERIENCE 99 BEST	PAGE PAGE
Acropolis Archaelogical Site	 culture.gr	PL €	210-321-0219	Classic Archeological Sites	51, 68 16
Acropolis Museum Museum	on the Acropolis culture.gr	PL €	210-323-6665	Classic 	51, 68
Aegean Dive Center Dive School	Zamanou 53 & Pandhoras adc.gr	GL €€€€	210-894-5409	By-the-Water 	125, 138
Afternoon Shop	Deinokratous 1 sglycabettus.gr	KO -	210-722-5380	Hip & Cool 	95
Agora Museum Museum	Adrianou 24 culture.gr	TH -	210-321-0185	Classic 	51, 68
Ananea Spa Spa	103 Thiseos lux-hotels.com/gr/lifegallery/spa	VA €€	210-626-0456	Hip & Cool 	77, 95
Ancient Agora Archaeological Site	Adrianou 24 culture.gr	TH -	210-321-0185	Classic Archeological Sites	51, 69 16
Apollon Divani Thal. Spa Spa	Aghiou Nikolaou 10 & Iliou divanis.gr/hotels/view	VL €€€	210-891-1100	By-the-Water 	125, 138
Archaeological Museum of Piraeus Museum	Harilaou Trikoupi 32 culture.gr	PI €	210-452-1598	By-the-Water 	123, 138
Archaeological Promenade Walk	Dionissiou Areopagitou 	TH -		Classic 	54, 69
Artower Art Gallery	Athinas & Armodiou 10 artower.gr	OM -	210-324-6100	Downtown 	101, 119
Asteria Seaside Beach Beach	Balux Club balux-septem.com	GL €	210-894-5676	Hip & Cool Beaches	78, 95 19
Astir Palace Resort Beaches Beach	Apollonos 40 astir-palace.com	VL €€€€	210-890-2000	By-the-Water 	124, 138
Astrolavos Art Gallery/Shop	Irodotou 11 astrolavos.gr	KO €€	210-722-1200	Hip & Cool 	76, 95
Athens Polytechnic Historical Site	Patission & Stournari ntua.gr	EX -		Downtown 	103, 119
Athinais Multipurpose Center Entertainment Complex	Kastorias 34-36 	VA €	210-348-0000	Hip & Cool Art Spaces	96 17
Benaki Museum Museum	Koumbari 1 & Vassilissis Sofias benaki.gr/index-en/htm	KO €	210-367-1000	Hip & Cool Museums	75, 96 33
Benaki Museum, Islamic Art Museum	Ayion Assomaton & Dipilou benaki.gr/collections/islamic.en/	PS €	210-325-1311	Downtown 	102, 119
Bettina Shop	Pindarou 40 & Anagnostopoulou 29 	KO -	210-339-2094	Hip & Cool 	76, 96
Byzantine Museum Museum	Vassilissis Sofias 22 culture.gr	KO €	210-723-1570	Classic Byzantine Sights	54, 69 22
Cellier Shop	Kriezotou 1 & Papdiamanti 10 	KO -	210-361-0040	Hip & Cool 	76, 96
Center of Hellenic Tradition Shop	Mitropoleous 59 & Pandroussou 36 	PL 	210-321-3023	Downtown 	70

NAME TYPE	ADDRESS WEBSITE	AREA PRICE	PHONE	EXPERIENCE 99 BEST	PAGE PAGE
Central Market Market	Sofokleous & Evripidou	CM €		Downtown	*101*, 119
Church of St. John Church	Evripidou 72	PL -		Downtown	*101*, 120
DESTE Fdtn., Cont. Art Art Space	Omirou 8 deste.gr	VA €	210-672-9460	Hip & Cool Art Spaces	*77*, 96 17
Fanourakis Shop	Patriarchou Ioakim 23 gofas.gr/fan.htm	KO -	210-721-1762	Hip & Cool	*77*, 97
Frissiras Museum Museum	Monis Asteriou 3 & Plaka 7 frissirasmuseum.com/en/collection	PL €	210-323-4678	Hip & Cool	*78*, 97
Ghiolman Yachts Boat Rental	Filellinon 4 ghiolman.com	SY €€€€	210-323-0330	By-the-Water	139
Glyfada Golf Club Golf	Panopis 15 & Kypros athensgolfclub.com	GL €€€€	210-894-6820	By-the-Water	*125*, 139
Goulandris Msm., Cyc. Art Museum	Neofytou Douka 4 & Irodotou cycladic-m.gr	KO €	210-722-8321	Hip & Cool Museums	*76*, 97 33
Goulandris Msm., Nat. History Museum	Levidou 13 goulandris-nhm.gr	KI €	210-801-5870	Hip & Cool	*77*, 97
Grand Beach Lagonissi Beach	Athens-Sounio Rd. lagonissiresort.gr	VA €€	229-107-6000	By-the-Water Beaches	*125*, 139 19
Hellenic Maritime Museum Museum	Akti Themistokleous greece.org/poseidon/work/museums	PI €	210-451-6264	By-the-Water	*123*, 139
Hotel Grande Bretagne Spa Spa	Syntagma Square	SY €€€	210-333-0000	Hip & Cool	*54*, 70
Ikotehnia Shop	Filellinon 14	SY -	210-325-0240	Classic	*53*, 70
Kalogirou Shop	Patriarchou Ioakim 4; Panagitsas 5	KI/KO -	210-335-6401	Hip & Cool	*77*, 98
Kapnikarea Church	Ermou & Kapnikareas culture.gr	MO -		Classic Byzantine Sights	*53*, 70 22
Kem Shop	Patriarchou Ioakim 2 kemgroup.gr	KO -	210-721-9230	Hip & Cool	*76*, 98
Keramikos Archaeological Site	Ermou 148	VA €	210-346-3552	Downtown	120
Kessariani Archaeological Site	6 miles (8km) east of city center	VA -	210-723-6619	Classic Byzantine Sights	*54*, 70 22
Lalaounis Shop	Panepistimiou 6	SY -	210-362-4354	Classic	70
Mastic Spa Shop	Irakleitoul & Solonos masticspa.com	KO -	210-360-3413	Hip & Cool	98
Mastiha Shop Shop	Panepistimiou 6 mastihashop.com	SY -	210-363-2750	Classic	*53*, 71
Megali Mitropoli Church	Plateia Mitropoleos	PL -	210-322-1308	Classic	*52*, 71

Attractions (cont.)

NAME TYPE	ADDRESS WEBSITE	AREA PRICE	PHONE SINGLES/NOISE	EXPERIENCE 99 BEST	PAGE PAGE
Melina Mercouri Cul. Ctr. Art Space	Iraklidon 66	TH -	210-345-2150	Downtown	*104*, 120
Monastiraki Flea Market Market	Plateia Abyssinias & Ifestou	MO -		Downtown	*103*, 120
Mt. Lycabettus Park	Aristippou & Ploutarchou	KO -	210-722-7092	Hip & Cool	*76*, 98
Museum of Greek Folk Art Museum	Kidathineon 17 culture.gr	PL €	210-321-3018	Classic	*52*, 71
Museum of Greek Pop. Inst. Museum	Diogenous 1-3 culture.gr	PL -	210-325-0198	Classic	*52*, 71
National Arch. Museum Museum	Patission 44 culture.gr	EX €	210-821-7717	Classic Museums	*53*, 71 33
National Gardens Park	East of Vassilissis Amalias	SY -		Classic	*53*, 72
Old Athens Shop	Kanari 17	KO -	210-361-4762	Hip & Cool	*76*, 98
Pame Volta Bike Rental	Hajihristou 20 pamevolta.gr	PL €	210-922-1578	Classic	*52*, 72
Panathenaic Stadium Historical Site	Vasileos Konstantinou culture.gr	PA -	210-752-6386	Classic	*54*, 72
Parliament Historical Site	Syntagma Square culture.gr	SY -		Classic	72
Patroklos Beach	35km (22mi) SE of Vouliagmeni	VL €	229-103-7326	By-the-Water Beaches	140 19
The Poet Shop	Aghias Theklas 2	PL -	210-321-9247	Hip & Cool	72
Preview Shop	Patriarchou Ioakim 19; Panagitsas 6	KO KI -	210-722-4731 210-801-1120	Hip & Cool	*77*, 99
Roman Agora Archaeological Site	Aiolou & Diogenous culture.gr	PL -	210-324-5220	Classic Archeological Sites	*52*, 73 16
Sport Academy & Spa Gym/Spa	Vassilissis Sofias 46 hilton.com	IL €€€	210-725-7070	Downtown	*104*, 120
Technopolis Art Space	Pireos 100	GA -	210-346-7322	Downtown Art Spaces	*102*, 121 17
Temple of Olympian Zeus Archaeological Site	Vassililssis Olgas 1 & Amalias culture.gr	PL -	210-922-6330	Classic	*53*, 73
Temple of Poseidon Archaeological Site	70km (44 miles) SE of Athens culture.gr	SO €	229-202-2817	By-the-Water	140
Vouliagmeni Lake Hot Spring		VL €	210-896-2239	By-the-Water	*125*, 140
Zolotas Jewelers Shop	Panepistimiou 10 zolotasjewelers.gr	SY -	210-360-1272	Classic	*53*, 73
Zoumboulakis Art Gallery/Shop	Plateia Kolonakis; Kriezotou 7 (Shop)	KO -	210-363-4454	Hip & Cool	*76*, 99

Athens Unique Shopping Index

NAME	PHONE (210)	AREA	PRODUCTS	PAGE
Achilleas Accessories	323-9970	GL	Women's clothes	128
Afternoon	722-5380	KO	Avant-garde women's clothes	80, 95
Anavasi	321-8104	EX	Maps	106
Aristokratikon	322-0546	SY	Chocolates	56
Bahar	321-7225	PS	Spice market; teas	106
The Bead Shop	322-1004	PL	Handcrafted beads	56
Bettina	339-2094	KO	Women's clothes	80, 96
Carla G	968-1462	KI	Clothes from young Greek designers	80
Cellier	361-0040	KO	Greek wine	80, 96
Center Hellenic Tradition	321-3023	PL	Handmade Crafts	56, 70
Christakis	361-3030	SY	Suitmaker, custom shirts	56
Christoforos Kotentos	325-5434	PS	Women's designer clothing	106
Closet	331-1286	PS	Trendy women's clothing	106
Deux Hommes	361-4155	KO	Women's designer clothes	80
Diplous Pelekys	322-3783	SY	Souvenirs	56
Fanourakis	721-1762	KO	Designer jewelry	97
First	898-2423	GL	Women's clothes	128
Fresh Line	413-7038	PI	Locally made cosmetics, bath products	128
Greek Women's Inst.	325-0524	PL	Needlework, pillowcases, tapestries	56
Ice Cube	483-8230	PI	Outlet for top Greek women's designer	128
Ikotehnia	325-0240	SY	Traditional handicrafts	56, 70
Kalogirou	335-6404	KI/KO	Designer shoes	98
Kem	721-9230	KO	Leather goods, purses, wallets	80, 98
Lalaounis	362-4354	SY	Designer jewelry	56, 70
Mastic Spa	360-3413	KO	Products made with mastic	80, 98
Mastiha Shop	363-2750	SY	Products and food made with mastic	56, 71
Ochi	321-3298	PS	Men's and women's clothing	106
Old Athens	361-4762	KO	Vintage clothes and accessories	80, 98
Parthenis	413-2325	PL	Unisex casual clothing	128
The Poet	321-9247	PL	Handcrafted shoes and sandals	56, 72
Preview	722-4731	KI/KO	Designer shoes	80, 99
Psaltiri	330-4198	EX	Custom made musical instruments	106
Soho Soho	623-4707	KI	Hip clothes and shoes	80
Soho Soho Private	961-6688	GL	Women's designer clothes	128
Tsaknis	322-0716	EX	Roasted nuts and food	106
Tsitouras Collection	362-2326	EX	Decorative objects	106
Vardas	483-1802	PI	Outlet for designer clothes/accessories	128
Zolotas Jewelers	360-1272	SY	Designer jewelry	56, 73
Zoumboulakis	363-4454	KI	Silk screens, artwork	80

For Neighborhood (Area) Key, see p. 206.

BLACK BOOK

Athens 99 Best—The Short List

RESTAURANTS	PHONE (210)	AREA	BEST ...	PAGE
Aiolis	331-2839	MO	Cafes	23, 84
Archeon Gefsis	523-9661	ME	Classic Dining	25, 59
Aristera-Dexia	342-2606	RO	Nouveau Greek Dining	34, 110
Athinaikon	383-8485	EX	Ouzeries	35, 59
Balthazar	644-1215	AM	Trendy Tables	48, 84
Central	724-5938	KO	Bar Restaurants	18, 85
Daphne's	322-7971	PL	Classic Dining	25, 59
Edodi	921-3013	VA	Romantic Dining	38, 60
Estiatorio 24	922-1159	MA	Late-Late-Night Eats	31, 86
Filistron	346-7554	TH	Tables with a View	46, 60
48	641-1082	AM	Trendy Tables	48, 86
Freud Oriental	729-9595	KO	Sushi Restaurants	45, 86
Hytra	331-6767	PS	Trendy Tables	48, 111
Interni	346-8900	TH	Bar Restaurants	18, 112
Jimmy and the Fish	412-4417	PI	Seafood Restaurants	40, 132
Karavitis	721-5155	PA	Tavernas	47, 60
Kavouras	383-7981	EX	Late-Late-Night Eats	31, 112
Kiku	364-7033	KO	Sushi Restaurants	45, 87
Milos Restaurant	724-4400	IL	Nouveau Greek Dining	34, 87
O Kostas	322-8502	PL	Souvlaki	43, 61
O Platanos	322-0666	PL	Tavernas	47, 61
Orea Ellas	321-3842	PL	Ouzeries	35, 61
Orizondes	721-0701	KO	Tables with a View	46, 88
Ouzadiko	729-5484	KO	Ouzeries	35, 88
Papandreou's Taverna	321-4970	CM	Late-Late-Night Eats	31, 112
Philippou	721-6390	KO	Tavernas	47, 61
Pil-Poul	342-3665	TH	Romantic Dining	38, 88
Plous Podilato	413-7910	PI	Seafood Restaurants	40, 133
Red	348-0000	VA	Nouveau Greek Dining	34, 89
Septem	894-1620	GL	Bar Restaurants	18, 89
Square Sushi	808-1512	KI	Sushi Restaurants	45, 89
Stavlos	345-2502	TH	Cafes	23, 113
Ta Agrafa	380-3144	EX	Souvlaki	43, 113
Thanassis	324-4705	MO	Souvlaki	43, 62
Tou Psarra	321-8733	PL	Romantic Dining	38, 63
Varoulko	411-2043	PI	Seafood Restaurants	40, 133
Vive Mar	899-2453	VL	Tables with a View	46, 134
Vlassis	646-3060	AM	Classic Dining	25, 63
NIGHTLIFE				
Aegli Village Cool	336-9327	SY	Summer Cinemas	44, 64
Akrotiri Lounge	985-9147	AK	Dance Clubs by the Sea	27, 91
Bedlam	336-9340	SY	Glamorous Clubs	29, 91
Cine Psirri	321-2476	PS	Summer Cinemas	44, 114
Danza	331-7105	PS	Dance Clubs	26, 115
Diogenis Studio	942-5754	VA	Bouzoukia in Winter	21, 92

For Neighborhood (Area) Key, see p. 206.

NIGHTLIFE (CONT.)	PHONE (210)	AREA	BEST ...	PAGE
Don Quixote's	413-7016	PI	Candlelit Bars	24, 135
Dora Stratou Dance Thtre.	921-4650	TH	Shows Under the Stars	42, 64
Dragoste	722-1558	KO	Glamorous Clubs	29, 92
Eyeland	(694) 615-0196	GA	Gay and Lesbian Bars	28, 92
Half Note	921-3310	PA	Live Music Venues	32, 116
Island	965-3563	VK	Dance Clubs by the Sea	27,135
Kidathineon	323-4281	PL	Cafes	23, 65
Lamda	922-4202	MA	Gay and Lesbian Bars	28, 116
Mao	331-7639	PS	Dance Clubs	26,117
Megaro Mousikis	728-2333	AM	Live Music Venues	32, 65
Melina	324-6501	PL	Candlelit Bars	24, 65
Mnisikleous	322-5558	PL	Rembetika Clubs	37, 65
Mommy	361-9682	KO	See-and-Be-Seen Bars	41, 93
Mt. Lycabettus Theater	928-2900	KO	Shows Under the Stars	42, 93
Odeon of Herodes Atticus	323-2771	PL	Shows Under the Stars	42, 65
Passa (Summer)	895-9645	VL	Dance Clubs by the Sea	27, 136
Passa (Winter)	721-1310	KO	See-and-Be-Seen Bars	41, 94
Peacock Lounge	923-6682	MA	Candlelit Bars	24, 65
Playback	331-7105	PS	Gay and Lesbian Bars	28, 117
Posidonio	894-1033	VA	Bouzoukia in Summer	20, 136
Privilege	801-8304	GA	Glamorous Clubs	29, 94
Rex	381-4592	OM	Bouzoukia in Winter	21, 66
Romeo (Summer)	894-5345	GL	Bouzoukia in Summer	20, 136
Romeo (Winter)	894-5345	GL	Bouzoukia in Winter	21, 66
Soul	331-0907	PS	See-and-Be-Seen Bars	41, 118
Stavros tou Notou	922-6975	NK	Live Music Venues	32
Stoa Ton Athanaton	321-4362	CM	Rembetika Clubs	37, 118
Taximi	363-9919	EX	Rembetika Clubs	37, 118
Thalassa	898-2979	VA	Bouzoukia in Summer	20, 136
Thission	342-0864	TH	Summer Cinemas	44, 66
Venue	331-7801	PS	Dance Clubs	26, 118

SIGHTS AND ATTRACTIONS				
Acropolis	321-0219	PL	Archaeological Sites	16, 68
Ancient Agora	321-0185	TH	Archaeological Sites	16, 69
Asteria Seaside Beach	894-5676	GL	Beaches	19, 95
Athinais Multi. Ctr.	348-0000	VA	Art Spaces	17, 96
Benaki Museum	367-1000	KO	Museums	33, 96
Byzantine Museum	723-1570	KO	Byzantine Sights	22, 69
DESTE Foundation	672-9460	VA	Art Spaces	17, 96
Goulandris Museum	722-8321	KO	Museums	33, 97
Grand Beach Lagonissi	107-6000	VA	Beaches	19, 139
Kapnikarea		MO	Byzantine Sights	22, 70
Kessariani	723-6619	KE	Byzantine Sights	22
National Arch. Museum	821-7717	EX	Museums	33, 71
Patroklos	(229) 103-7326	VL	Beaches	19, 140
Roman Agora	324-5220	PL	Archaeological Sites	16, 73
Technopolis	346-7322	GA	Art Spaces	17, 121

BLACK BOOK

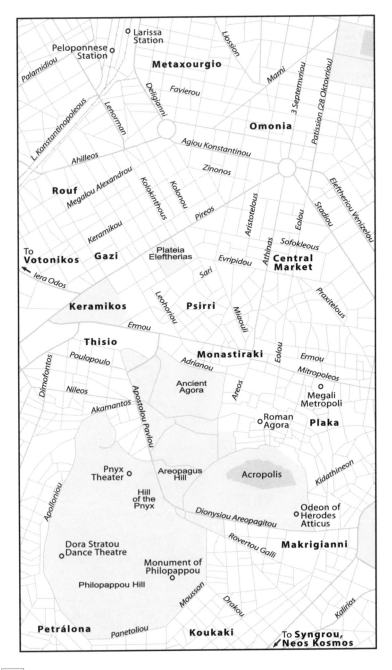

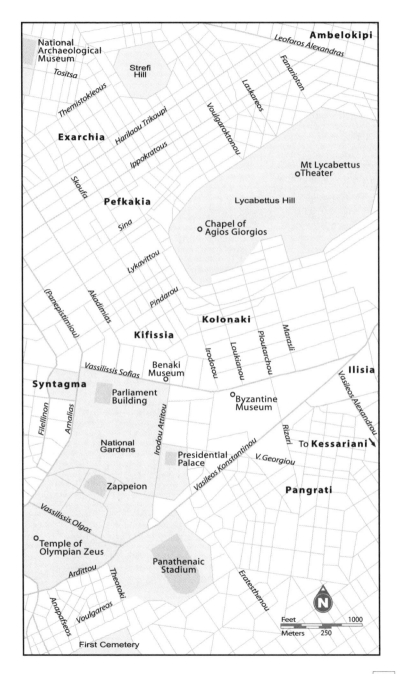

National Archaeological Museum

Ambelokipi

Leoforos Alexandras

Fanariotan

Tositsa

Strefi Hill

Themistokleous

Laskareos

Exarchia

Harilaou Trikoupi

Voulgarokonou

Ippokratous

Mt Lycabettus
o Theater

Lycabettus Hill

Pefkakia

Skoufa

Sina

Chapel of
o Agios Giorgios

Lykavittou

(Panepistimiou)

Akadimias

Pindarou

Kolonaki

Marasli

Ploutarchou

Kifissia

Irodotou

Loukianou

Ilisia

Vassilissis Sofias

Benaki Museum
o

Syntagma

Parliament Building

Byzantine
o Museum

Vasileos Alexandrou

Filellinon

Amalias

National Gardens

Irodou Attikou

Presidential Palace

Vasileos Konstantinou

V. Georgiou

Rizari

To Kessariani

Zappeion

Pangrati

Vassilissis Olgas

Temple of
o Olympian Zeus

Panathenaic Stadium

Ardittou

Theotoki

Eratesthenou

Anapafseos

Voulgareos

N

Feet   1000
Meters   250

First Cemetery

Odeon of Herodes Atticus—just one of the things that puts Athens on the list of the world's most exciting cities (see pages 42, 52, and 65).